Classic Albums

THE BEATLES

Production by GEORGE MARTIN
Orchestrations by GEORGE MARTIN

R. Nort

Sor

Classic Albums

The vinyl that made a generation

Alan J. Whiticker

NEW HOLLAND

First published in 2018 by New Holland Publishers
London • Sydney • Auckland

131–151 Great Titchfield Street, London WIW 5BB, United Kingdom
1/66 Gibbes Street, Chatswood, NSW 2067, Australia
5/39 Woodside Ave, Northcote, Auckland 0627, New Zealand

newhollandpublishers.com

ISBN 9781921024382
Group Managing Director: Fiona Schultz
Publisher: Alan Whiticker
Project Editor: Rebecca Sutherland
Designer: Andrew Davies
Photography: John Van Put
Production Director: James Mills-Hicks
Printer: Toppan Leefung Printing Limited

10 9 8 7 6 5 4 3 2 1

Keep up with New Holland Publishers on Facebook
facebook.com/NewHollandPublishers

DEDICATION

For Bob and Ray Oats, who were always so generous in lending their classic record albums to their 12-year-old cousin.

Contents

Introduction   9

1. *The Beatles* 'The White Album' / The Beatles (1968)   21

2. *Tommy* / The Who (1969)   41

3. *Led Zeppelin III* / Led Zeppelin (1970)   61

4. *All Things Must Pass* / George Harrison (1970)   81

5. *L.A. Woman* / Doors (1971)   101

6. *Ram* / Paul and Linda McCartney (1971)   121

7. *Sticky Fingers* / The Rolling Stones (1971)   141

8. *Imagine* / John Lennon (1971)   161

9. *American Pie* / Don McLean (1971)   181

10. *Harvest* / Neil Young (1972)   201

11. *School's Out* / Alice Cooper (1972)   221

12. *Goodbye Yellow Brick Road* / Elton John (1973)   241

Honourable mentions   257

Pisces, Aquarius, Capricorn & Jones Ltd. / The Monkees (1967)
Cosmo's Factory / Creedence Clearwater Revival (1970)
Teaser and the Firecat / Cat Stevens (1971)
The Yes Album / Yes (1971)
Hunky Dory / David Bowie (1971)
Nilsson Schmilsson / Harry Nilsson (1971)
Sail Away / Randy Newman (1972)
Tubular Bells / Mike Oldfield (1973)
Wish You Were Here / Pink Floyd (1975)
Desire / Bob Dylan (1976)

References   277

The early 1970s was a time when a piece of black vinyl inside a 12 inch by 12 inch cardboard sleeve could change the world. Or so it seemed to a teenager like me. It was the heyday of many of the 'classic' rock stars we revere today: the Beatles, the Stones, the Who, Led Zep and the Doors; everyone from Neil Young to Elton John, from Alice Cooper to Don McLean, with a myriad of artists in between.

If you're reading this book, you may also have seen the Cameron Crowe film *Almost Famous,* about a young writer in the early 1970s who ingratiates his way into the good graces of *Rolling Stone* magazine and ends up traveling with a rock and roll band to get the all-important music interview. In the movie the young man, a fictional portrayal of Crowe himself (Crowe started his writing career posting stories for *Rolling Stone* at the tender age of 16), has his world opened for him after his rebellious older sister gifts him her late 1960s/early 1970s record collection on her way out of the family home. The boy discovers the Rolling Stones, Led Zeppelin, Neil Young, Cream, Joni Mitchell, Jimi Hendrix and Bob Dylan records under the bed of his sister's bedroom, and when he plays 'Sparks' from the Who's rock opera *Tommy*, his sees his entire future laid out for him.

When I saw the film in theatres early in 2001, that one scene brought a smile to my face because I had a similar experience as a young boy in the early 1970s. I found my own future in rows of neatly stacked records in my cousin Bob's bedroom, ripe to be discovered by the teenaged me.

My cousin Bob had the best job ever. In 1969, having had enough of the confines of his public-school education and having reached the school-leaving age of 15, he said goodbye to his schooldays and got a job at the local electrical appliance store … which happened to have its own well-stocked music department. While learning his trade selling furniture, fridges, washing machines and even 'stereo' phonograms (remember them?), Bob would park himself in the music section and take advantage of the latest music releases that came his way.

Bob was privy to advance copies, rare imports and promotional posters of the world's greatest bands, but he only invested his hard-earned cash in albums, not singles. The mathematics supported this: a $33^{1}/_{3}$ rpm album cost about $5, and for that price you would get 10–14 songs – about 40 minutes of music, sometimes even more. A 45rpm single cost a little over a buck, and for that you got a major hit of the day and often a throwaway on the B-side, which would have only a fraction of the album's runtime. So the best investment was in buying the whole album, according to Bob.

My cousin was a serious music connoisseur!

Bob bought himself a small, free-standing stereo record player that looked like a wooden school desk with a flip up lid, and he parked it in a corner of the small bedroom he shared with his brother Ray. Bob decorated the room with posters and promotional material – I remember he took the pages of the rare *Let It Be* promotional booklet and plastered them over an entire wall – and stocked his collection with the best vinyl of the era. It was a treasure trove of material for a young music fan such as me.

When Ray entered the workforce in 1970, he too started on his record collection and together Bob and Ray became walking encyclopedias of pop culture and rock music. They were the mentors of my music education, along with my other cousins Mal (who owned, among others, a copy of Richard Harris' 'McArthur Park'), Mike (a Crosby, Stills, Nash & Young fan who also was an early devotee of prog-rock), Ken (an acerbic critic, even as a teenager) and Greg, who I recall was a big fan of surf music and Status Quo.

During the school holidays while Bob and Ray were at work, I would drop by and spend hours in their room listening to their albums. Every now and then, they would let me take a couple of discs home so I could play them over and over again, poring over the lyric sheets and marveling at the album art packaging. The only album I didn't borrow was *Goodbye Yellow Brick Road*, because when Ray got up in the morning he liked to put this album on to put him in a positive frame of mind for work.

That was the power of the music.

It was the era of stereo and mono, not that my untrained ear could tell much of a difference (it depended on the quality of the machine you played the records on); when artists had just 40 minutes of vinyl to tell their stories, carefully selecting the order of songs and which songs would open either side of the record. Hidden messages, sound effects, backward loops and false starts … they were all there in the grooves of the vinyl. All you had to do was listen and use your imagination.

It was also the golden era of record packaging, with many bands viewing their album art as an important extension of the music.

Bands incorporated various features that changed the standard cardboard package and made their album look special to their fans – adding extra panels, dye cuts and embossing, or using unique configurations such as round album covers, 3D box sets or various foldout parts. Artists such as Andy Warhol, Peter Blake, Richard Hamilton, Tom Wilkes, Drew Struzan, Ian Beck, Storm Thorgerson and Roger Dean became synonymous with album art and their work is as highly regarded today as any piece hanging in an art gallery. In fact, much of the original album art in this book today hangs in art galleries, museums or Hard Rock Cafes around the world.

The classic albums in this book cover the years 1968 to 1973, which for many people of my generation was the classic era of rock-pop. All of my teenage years were spent in the 1970s; we were the post hippy, post 'flower-power' generation, pining for the Beatles but prepared to explore new musical worlds – singer-songwriters, prog-rockers, blues devotees, heavy metal. The albums in this book reflect that era, although it is a personal – and highly nostalgic – selection rather than a comprehensive survey of artists recording at the time.

The albums in this book reflect my reality as a white, middle class suburban kid in the early 1970s. Black, soul or funk music wasn't part of an experience I could relate to (as Ben Folds sings, 'Y'all don't know what it's like / Being male, middle-class and white …') and I was never a big fan of 'blues' music, although several groups featured in this book (the Stones, the Doors and Led Zeppelin) were originally 'white blues' outfits. And while I liked some female artists of the era, especially Melanie (Safka) and Joni Mitchell, with limited funds at my disposal their albums never enticed me to invest in them.

Safe choices? Perhaps, but they provided me with a firm foundation to explore other music in the years ahead. And this is the point; buying an album was like investing in the band. These players became heroes, mentors and, yes, friends.

The starting point in any music collection should be the Beatles. As an album listener and future album buyer, 'The White Album' was my starting point, although I retrospectively collected all their records from the 1960s. This led to me buying solo Beatles records in the 1970s – especially *All Things Must Pass* (George Harrison), *Ram* (Paul McCartney) and *Imagine* (John Lennon) – which helped prolong the Beatles myth for several more years. I also bought and enjoyed Ringo Starr's *Ringo* in 1973, but it didn't have the impact on me the other albums had.

Other records in this collection have tenuous links to each other in theme, personnel and production, from the Rolling Stones' *Sticky Fingers* and Neil Young's *Harvest*, to Alice Cooper's *School's Out* and Elton John's *Goodbye Yellow Brick Road*.

At the end of 1973, I got my first job at the age of 15, mopping floors in the local fish and chip shop three nights a week while continuing with my high school studies. The job paid $12 a week, about the price of a double LP at the time. Every fortnight I would buy myself an album, starting with the records that had long been favorites through the generosity of my cousins, Bob and Ray.

It was time to stand on my own two feet, so to speak, and for the remainder of the decade I gathered an eclectic collection of vinyl. The weekly magazine *The Story of Pop* was also released at that time and, in this pre-internet era, it filled in a lot of gaps in the history and pop culture of many of the artists I had been listening too. The magazine's balance of wonderful artwork and cutting-edge articles was very influential because rock and roll was still in its infancy – dating from when Bill Haley & His Comets released 'Rock Around the Clock' in 1955, it was not even two decades old. Over the years I added biographies, histories and album art collections to my personal library. I read widely, and listened carefully.

The invention of the CD in the mid-1980s brought an end to golden era of vinyl. Records had become increasingly expensive, from $5 an album to about $25 an album by the end of the 1980s, and then there was always the problem of scratching a track or gouging and warping the record. CD technology allowed the listener to play the entire record in one sitting, without having to get up and flip the record over (a first world problem, I know) but we also lost something along the way. The digital sound washed out many of the idiosyncrasies of vinyl records and a lot of the charm of certain songs was lost in early CD mixes. Just as importantly, the impact of album cover art was reduced from 12 inches square to just a little over 5 x 5 inches, locked away in a cheap plastic jewel case.

Even Rolling Stone Keith Richards lamented the loss of a pop culture art form. Original record albums were precious, tactile pieces of art that you handled with care, not disposable objects you threw in your car and played on a CD player. Soon, the music itself would be disposable; shared on the internet, streamed on technological devices and shattered into millions of digital files. The record album was no more.

Each album and artist has their own story, a context in pop culture history that is both fascinating and illuminating. In *Classic Albums: The vinyl that made a generation* I want to go behind the scenes and explore how each album was recorded, the decisions that resulted in the album art being made and the cultural impact each record has had over time. Apart from what I personally think about each album, contemporaneous and more recent reviews are also included.

YouTube and iTunes have also been helpful in the process of piecing together what these landmark albums achieved, as have the many documentaries, biographies and histories that have been created about them over the years.

I trust you'll enjoy the journey revisiting these classic albums of the era. Some of them may even be your favorites and in your collection too. If you are discovering these albums for the first time, I trust you'll be encouraged enough to go out and listen to them in full; perhaps even to buy them on vinyl now that record albums are making a welcome comeback.

This is the vinyl that made a generation.

Alan Whiticker, 2018

Back in the U.S.S.R.   Dear Prudence   Glass Onion
Ob-La-Di, Ob-La-Da   Wild Honey Pie
The Continuing Story of Bungalow Bill
While My Guitar Gently Weeps   Happiness is a Warm Gun
Martha My Dear   I'm so tired   Blackbird   Piggies
Rocky Raccoon   Don't Pass Me By
Why don't we do it in the road?   I Will   Julia
Birthday   Yer Blues   Mother Nature's Son
Everybody's Got Something to Hide Except Me and My Monkey
Sexy Sadie   Helter Skelter   Long, Long, Long
Revolution 1   Honey Pie   Savoy Truffle   Cry Baby Cry
Revolution 9   Good Night

CHAPTER 1

The Beatles ('The White Album')
The Beatles 1968

'Feel so suicidal, even hate my rock and roll ...'

Growing up in the 1960s I, along with millions of other people, had the great luxury of hearing Beatles songs as they were being released. Just as the coming of the new millennium drew a red line between those of us born in the 20th Century and new Millennials, I believe music fans are divided into two broad groups – those who were old enough to marvel at Beatles music when they heard it the first time on the radio, and those who can be described as second and even third generation Beatles fans, born after the band stopped recording in 1970.

The Beatles, circa 1968, were no longer the cute 'mops tops' who had conquered the world in matching suits just four years before. Nor were they the psychedelic avatars who had adorned the front cover of the *Sgt. Pepper's* album, surrounded by pop art cutouts. They were, however, still ground-breaking, benignly antiauthoritarian and, at the height of the Summer of Protest that rocked the world, subversively influential.

In May 1968, John Lennon, having separated from his wife Cynthia and taken up with avant-garde Japanese artist/musician

Yoko Ono, was developing his interest in an increasing number of political causes … and growing his hair. Paul McCartney had broken off his engagement to actress Jane Asher and formed a relationship with American photographer Linda Eastman, the mother of a young girl. George Harrison immersed himself in Indian music and, having dragged the lads and assorted wives and friends to India to study under the guidance of Maharishi Mahesh Yogi, he was now working on his solo album, *Wonderwall Music*. And Ringo was, well, busy being Ringo. He made his solo film debut that year in *Candy*, a sex farce based on the Terry Southern novel, and would star alongside Peter Sellers in *The Magic Christian* the following year.

Given that the world was changing in the late 1960s, the big question was, what would the Beatles do next? The release of any song, a new album or a film from them was a world event.

Not that the Beatles were resting on their laurels after the success of *Sgt. Pepper's Lonely Hearts Club Band* in the summer of '67. The Beatles started the New Year holding down the top two positions on the Top 40 charts with the double A-side single 'Hello, Goodbye' / 'I Am the Walrus' and the *Magical Mystery Tour* EP. They then released two multi-million selling singles – 'Lady Madonna' / 'The Inner Light' in March and the phenomenally successful 'Hey Jude' / 'Revolution' in August, which also happened to be their first release on their new label, Apple. In typical Beatles fashion, none of these songs would appear on their self-titled album at the end of the year. The Beatles had always believed in giving their fans value for money.

'The White Album', as the new LP would be widely known, was certainly that. It was the band's first double album, with 30 new songs in all: 12 each from John and Paul, four compositions from

George Harrison and even Ringo Starr's first-penned effort ... and the perplexing 'Revolution 9'.

Most of the songs that ended up on *The Beatles* were demoed at George Harrison's home 'Kinfauns' in Esher, Surrey, at an informal get-together by the band that May. Having returned from Rishikesh, India, where many of these songs were written (much to the chagrin of George, who thought they were in India to mediate), it was only fitting that Harrison host the unveiling of the songs for the new album. Twenty-seven songs were played at George's deluxe bungalow and were recorded on an Ampex reel-to-reel tape deck (various tracks ended up on bootleg offerings for years to come). John Lennon, in a burst of enthusiasm, composed more than half of them. The Beatles, their wives (John was still with Cynthia at this time) and aides Mal Evans and Neil Aspinall in tow, sound upbeat and united. But it wouldn't last.

Many of the songs were already fully formed and required little or no production from their acoustic origins. John's 'Cry Baby Cry', for example, is almost exactly like the finished track on the album; melancholy, almost ghostly. So too 'The Continuing Story of Bungalow Bill', 'I'm So Tired', 'Dear Prudence' and 'Julia'. Other tracks, such as 'Back in the U.S.S.R.', 'Sexy Sadie' and 'Yer Blues' would require the full band treatment in the studio to fully flesh out the songs. Paul's 'Blackbird' is stark and beautiful in its simplicity; the respective charms of 'Rocky Raccoon' and 'Mother Nature's Son' are already there too – but not so 'Ob-la-di Ob-la-da', which would need some major workshopping before being recorded.

Not every song was a winner. George's acoustic version of 'While My Guitar Gently Weeps' is wonderfully simple but his demo of 'Sour Milk Sea' would be given to Jackie Lomax and the merely passable 'Not Guilty' would be rejected (after more than 100 takes) and shelved for almost a decade. Several half-realized songs were saved for *Abbey Road* ('Mean Mr. Mustard' and 'Polythene Pam') while others ended up on solo records (Paul's 'Junk' surfaced on *McCartney* in 1970 and John's melodic 'Child of Nature' would later appear on his second solo album *Imagine* as 'Jealous Guy'). The meritless 'What's the New Mary Jane?' was recorded by John but quickly rejected.

Recording began at Abbey Road on 30 May under the direction of George Martin and Geoff Emerick, and would not conclude until mid-October, just in time for a Christmas 1968 release. Music historians would later state that The White Album is the sound of a band shattering into four distinct pieces – Paul with his backing band, George with his backing band etc., as Lennon would famously remark. Martin and Emerick would characterize the sessions as the most volatile and divisive in the band's history. So disappointed in the band's behavior was Martin that he took off on holiday and left most of the work to his assistant, Chris Thomas, with Emerick working closely with engineers Ken Scott and Richard Lush.

When I play the album, however, all I can hear is the band's brilliance and inventiveness; a vast array of songs, musical styles, stories, word pictures and mental images. As the plain white cover attests, 'The White Album' is a blank canvas that fans can project their hopes, dreams, joys and fears onto. *The Beatles* album demonstrated that the Beatles, 'the band we've known for all these years', could be anything we wanted them to be.

The opening song, 'Back in the U.S.S.R.', bookended with sound effects of a plane landing, is the perfect album opener and, perhaps, a symbol of the band's overall experience of making it. An affectionate take on Chuck Berry's 'Back in the USA' and friendly rivals, the Beach Boys' 'California Girls' (including faux Beach Boys harmony), the song was first referenced in Hunter Davies' celebrated biography of the band released that year (Paul's brother Mike suggests that he give the song to the Beach Boys to record ... in 1968, the Wilson brothers could have done with the hit!). Beach Boy Mike Love was also in India with the Beatles earlier that year, so it's not hard to believe the inspiration for the song may have been sitting across from McCartney at the dinner table at the Maharishi's ashram.

The real drama, however, occurred in the recording of the song, with Paul's insistence that Ringo play a certain way leading the drummer to momentarily quit the band. Paul actually plays drums on the album track (he's obviously very good) but the boys soon made up and Ringo returned to the fold after a short holiday. 'Back in the U.S.S.R.' quickly became a Beatles classic and has been performed by countless bands – often while actually on tour in Russia – including McCartney himself, Elton John, Billy Joel and even the Beach Boys.

John wrote 'Dear Prudence' in India for the sister of actress Mia Farrow, who had joined the Beatles for some 'time out' after the breakup of her marriage to Frank Sinatra. Prudence Farrow had taken to staying in her room, stating that she preferred to stay in and meditate rather than socialize with the famous gathering, thus Lennon's plaintive, childlike approach ('Dear Prudence, won't you come out to play?'). The song features Lennon's newly mastered guitar technique, taught to him by fellow meditative devotee, the pop star Donovan.

'Glass Onion' is a clever tease from Lennon and a treat for all those budding Beatle-ologists (including the author) who relished dissecting the latest recordings. John was having some fun when he sang, 'The walrus was Paul ...' – everyone knows that 'the walrus' was John in the 'I Am the Walrus' film clip (Paul was the hippo!) – and namechecks various Beatles songs ('Strawberry Fields Forever', 'I Am the Walrus', 'Lady Madonna', 'Fool on the Hill', 'Fixing A Hole'). It's a wonderful meta-song for Beatle fans.

'Ob-La-Di, Ob-La-Da' is one of the more frustrating songs in the Beatles canon – you either love it or you hate it. A pastiche of emerging reggae influences on UK pop at the time (McCartney's reference to 'Desmond' in the song is for Desmond Dekker, who had a hit with the indecipherable 'Israelites' that year), the band seems to be having fun but the reality was quite different. John and George disliked the song immensely, with its corny title a play on the popular English expletive, 'Oh bloody!' It was only through McCartney's perseverance (and 27 tapings) that they finally got the track recorded. Lennon allegedly galvanized the recording when he called out, 'This is it! Come on!' and then launched into the frenetic piano opening.

George later references the song on the album track 'Savoy Truffle' ('We all know "Ob-la-di-bla-da" (sic) / But can you show me where you are?') in a thinly veiled swipe at his bandmate. John famously dissed the song as 'Paul's granny music', but the end result was a little piece of Beatles magic, with a touch of humor at the end that links back to 'Yellow Submarine', 'Altogether Now' and the band's other novelty songs. Arguably the most commercial song on the album, it was a No.1 UK hit for Scottish band Marmalade in January 1969 and ultimately found its way onto *The Beatles 1967–1970* compilation. The song was eventually released as a single in the by then Beatles-starved UK in 1976.

One of the things that frustrated the group during the five months of recording was the preference for members to record songs individually. McCartney, especially, would go off and record little pieces of music by himself, much to Lennon's chagrin; perhaps not wishing to engage with the others because relationships were so fraught. This was the first time John had brought new muse Yoko Ono into the band's inner sanctum, and it is widely documented that her constant presence in the studio was counterproductive. 'Wild Honey Pie' is the least successful of these solo pieces; a musical riff on McCartney's song 'Honey Pie' (although it has little in common with that song other than the title), it is easily the most disposable track on the album.

'The Continuing Story of Bungalow Bill' is a quirky singalong that could only have come from the mind of John Lennon. The song is based on Lennon's interactions with a young American named Richard A. Cooke III, who was on a tiger hunt in India. Lacking the corny sentimentality that undermines many of McCartney's 'story songs', 'Bungalow Bill' is sung in a wonderful faux Spanish style (I love Lennon's call out, 'all the children sing!'). It also features the debut, on record, of Yoko Ono, who takes the part of the 'mommy' ('Not when he looked so fierce …'). Unfortunately, the vocal cuts off at the end so that 'fierce' sounds like 'fear' – a less than auspicious debut for Ms. Ono.

'While My Guitar Gently Weeps' was viewed as George's crowning moment on the album, though I tend to agree with those critics who regard it as a 'near classic' that doesn't quite get where it wants to go (George's mournful nasal wailing at the end of the song does not help). Harrison brought his friend Eric Clapton to the recording session to lift the mood among his bandmates, noting that they would all be 'on their best behavior' in front of such an accomplished musician (Clapton was at a loose end at the time, having broken up with his band, Cream). The finished track struggles under the weight of over-production and I prefer the acoustic version, which features prominently in both the *Beatles Anthology* and *Living in the Material World* documentaries.

Lennon's 'Happiness is a Warm Gun' is not only one of my favorite songs on the album but it's in my Top 10 Beatles tracks of all time. It contains a series of brilliantly worded non-sequiturs punctuated with a searing bridge ('I need a fix…'), topped off with a cool, doo-wop chorus. Lennon, whose vocal agility has rarely been better as he belts through five different musical movements in the one song, was inspired by an ad in a gun magazine he saw in New York that summer: 'Happiness is a Warm Gun' (a play on the popular cartoon strip *Peanuts*, where Charlie Brown holds Snoopy under the banner 'Happiness is a Warm Puppy'). With Lennon, of course, there is also the added sexual innuendo ('When I feel my finger on your trigger …') that makes the song a mini-masterpiece of imagery.

Side Two of the album lacks the punch of the first, with too many throw-away songs. Opening with McCartney's breezy 'Martha My Dear', a ballad which namechecks his Old English Sheepdog, Martha, the song can more deeply be viewed as a an ode to former fiancé, the actress Jane Asher. McCartney plays most of the instruments, with George Martin's brass and string arrangement filling out the sound.

'I'm so Tired', brilliantly realized by Lennon and played with confidence and aplomb by the band, links back thematically to 'I'm Only Sleeping' from the *Revolver* album. On the line, 'And curse Sir Walter Raleigh, he was such a stupid git …', Lennon pronounces 'git' as 'get' in a broad Northern accent so that it rhymes with cigarette (Raleigh being the 17th Century explorer who introduced tobacco to England). On a deeper level, it's also a window into Lennon's then battle with insomnia, a by-product of his growing heroin addiction. 'You know I'd give you everything I got for a little peace of mind …' indeed.

The song 'Blackbird' has taken on a life of its own in recent years. Seen at the time as a typical McCartney ballad (again, no other Beatle plays on the track, with the only accompaniment to McCartney's exquisite guitar work being the tapping of his foot and added bird sound effects), it wasn't until much later that the song was interpreted as championing the US civil rights movement. 'You have only been waiting for this moment to arise…' may be the gentlest call to arms in pop music, but the context here is essential. Remember that Civil Rights leader Martin Luther King Jr had been assassinated on 4 April that year and the line 'Take these broken wings and learn to fly …' takes on a new poignancy.

Here is where Side Two goes off track a little. George Harrison's second offering, 'Piggies', is a caustic take on the anti-materialistic themes he first tackled with the song 'Taxman' two years before. The song has some nice harpsichord from Chris Thomas and is redeemed (almost) by a touch of Beatles humor at the end of the song, with a tape loop of pigs grunting. As a parody, the song misses the mark though.

'Rocky Raccoon' is another McCartney pastiche (of old western movies this time), based on a stream of consciousness he first played on guitar on the roof of the house the band shared in India. Clever in parts, McCartney's American accent becomes tiresome towards the end (future wife Linda Eastman can be heard on the closing verse) and the song limps to a predictable conclusion.

Similarly, 'Don't Pass Me By' could easily be dismissed if it were not for the fact that it was Ringo's first solo composition on a Beatles record. The song has some nice violin, but also features the most deliberately tortured lyric on a Beatles song ('I'm sorry that I doubted you, I was so unfair / You were in a car crash, and you lost your hair ...'). Ringo would do better a year later with 'Octopus's Garden'.

'Why Don't We Do It in the Road?' is, again, mostly Paul (Ringo overdubbed drums and handclaps), but it's a shame McCartney's great vocal is wasted on such an unrealized song and lyric. Inspired, allegedly, by the sight of two monkeys fornicating in the middle of a road whilst the group was in India, the use of a Moog synthesizer is certainly innovative but not enough to save the song.

The next offering, the beautiful 'I Will', also by McCartney, would not have been out of place on the *Revolver* album. It is an economical 1:46 minutes but Lennon saves Side Two with arguably the most personal and beautifully realized song of his career.

'Julia' is an ode to John's mother, tragically killed in a car accident in 1958, just as the teenager was becoming reacquainted with her. That he also connects her memory to his new life with Yoko ('Ocean Child calls me ...', Yoko being 'ocean child' in English) shows how quickly Ono had filled that void for him. Featuring one of the more complicated guitar finger patterns (again taught to Lennon by Donovan in India), there is a great outtake on *Anthology III* where Lennon almost makes it to the end of the song before 'fluffing' the playing ('Almost made it!' Lennon laughs).

Side Three opens with the rollicking 'Birthday', and is my favorite of the double album. Nothing too deep and meaningful here ('They say it's your birthday / It's my birthday too, yeah ...') the song was pretty much made up in the studio ('Twelve bars in A, and we'll change to D, and I'm gonna do a few beats in C,' McCartney explains to the others). And the band have rarely sounded better playing it.

'Yer Blues' is Lennon's take on the British blues scene at the time, but even though the Beatles are clearly toying with the genre, they actually do it better than most blues bands. Lennon and Harrison trade brilliant guitar licks before a clunky edit brings the song to an abrupt end.

'Mother Nature's Son' is a McCartney ballad that easily surpasses the obligatory John Denver cover in the 1970s; 'Everybody's Got Something to Hide Except Me and My Monkey' is an underrated rocker that sounds as if it came straight out of the 'Birthday' sessions; 'Sexy Sadie' is a thinly veiled attack of the Maharishi (Lennon changed the title of the song at the last moment, but imagine, if you will, 'Maharishi, what have you done ...' and you get the gist); and finally, George's 'Long, Long, Long' is one of his most atmospheric ballads.

'Helter Skelter' may be the most controversial song on the album, but not at the time of the album's release (that would be 'Revolution 9', which left most critics scratching their heads). In the context of the album, 'Helter Skelter' is another McCartney rocker, loosely inspired by the Who's Pete Townshend's guitar performances, with a lyric using a 'helter skelter' park slide as a metaphor for sex, drugs or perhaps both. The track starts with a one-note guitar riff and ends with Ringo's primal scream, 'I've got blisters on my fingers!', but the title would take on a darker meaning when used by a drug-crazed group of LA drifters as a blueprint for murder.

In the mid-1960s, Charles Manson was a former convict who had spent half his life in jail. Having ingratiated himself into LA's hippie community and gathered around him a 'family' of lost girls, drug-addled thieves and psychopaths, he too was a budding musician and had befriended Dennis Wilson of the Beach Boys. High on LSD, Manson told his followers that 'Helter Skelter' was coming; a war between blacks and whites which he and his family would be the sole survivors of, and the rulers of whoever was left. The Beatles had told him as much on The White Album, he said, with secret messages in 'Blackbird' and 'Piggies' filling in the gaps.

Incredibly, Manson was able to convince his 'family' to murder in his name. In June 1969, a part-time drug dealer named Gary Hinman was their first victim, the perpetrators smearing the words 'Political Piggy' on the wall in blood. On 8 August, he sent a group of young women led by Charles 'Tex' Watson to Cielo Drive in the Hollywood Hills, telling them to kill everyone they found there. Five people were murdered, including actress Sharon Tate and celebrity hairdresser Jay Sebring. This time the word 'Pig' was smeared in blood on the front door. The following night, Leno and Rosemary LaBianca were stabbed to death in another part of LA. The words 'Rise', 'Death to Pigs' and 'Healter [sic] Skelter' were also written in blood.

It was prosecuting attorney Vincent Bugliosi who pieced together the Beatles references from the three crimes scenes after interviewing members of the 'Manson Family' to ascertain the motives behind the murders. It was a shocking case that had inadvertently drawn the Beatles into Manson's circle of madness and the two worlds would be inexorably linked for decades to come. On 1988's *Rattle and Hum*, U2 lead singer Bono shouts, 'This is a song Charles Manson stole from the Beatles, well we're stealing it back', before launching into a live version of the song. To paraphrase another McCartney classic, 'Helter Skelter' was back where it once belonged.

Side Four opens with the original recording of 'Revolution', a slower version rendered somewhat superfluous by the release of the incendiary B-side to 'Hey Jude' the previous June. As on the album, 'Revolution 1' lacks the punch of the latter version, even on a purely ironic level – a call to revolution in a gentle pop ballad? – and George Martin made the right call when he encouraged the band to record a much quicker version with a more aggressive vocal.

There is nothing ironic about 'Honey Pie', McCartney's ode to 1920s music hall. This song is so authentically recorded that I thought it was a cover when I first heard it. Of particular note is the sung introduction, a feature of traditional pop songs that McCartney would repeat on the single 'My Valentine' four decades later on his 2012 album *Kisses on the Bottom*.

'Savoy Truffle' is brought to life by Harrison's sardonic wit, a James Bond-like theme on the chorus ('You'll have to have them all pulled out after the Savoy Truffle …') and George Martin's brass arrangement. The song was written in Eric Clapton's garden – the same garden where Harrison would later compose 'Here Comes the Sun' – as the friends shared a box of chocolates. As George later remarked, the song 'almost wrote itself'. It shows.

'Cry Baby Cry' is another of my all-time favorite Beatles songs; an otherworldly ballad from Lennon with wonderful lyrics evocative of Lewis Carroll-like children's games. Harrison's minimalistic guitar lick is a killer while McCartney's 'Can you take me back' coda – part of another, unrealized song – caps off a poignant, three-minute incursion into another world. Reminiscent of 'A Day in Life' and 'I'm Only Sleeping' in structure, the song is one of Lennon's best although he later said he never really rated it.

Which brings us to 'Revolution 9'. Do the 50 years that have passed give any more clarity to the sound collage put together by

Lennon and Ono, with a little help from George Harrison? Lennon was fixated by the number 9 (he was born on 9 October) and was so excited by the finished product that he wanted to release it as a single backed with 'Revolution' (calmer heads prevailed and 'Hey Jude' won the day). Like many other willing fans, I played the track over and over, trying to see into it what Lennon saw, without much success I must say. An oddity.

The last song on the album, 'Good Night', written by Lennon for Ringo, benefits from George Martin's lush orchestral arrangement and Ringo's sentimental vocal. That most punters thought that it was a McCartney song speaks volumes for Lennon's ability to write simple, direct music when he wanted too – it's just that he didn't want to. And he was heading into a whole different territory with Yoko Ono.

By November 1968, the long wait for fans was over. *The Beatles* set a record, with advance orders topping the two million mark. The cover of 'The White Album' was the polar opposite of the intricate detail and planning that had made *Sgt. Pepper's* such a pop culture icon; an 'anti-image' statement from the world's most recognizable pop group. But then, the Beatles were already so iconic that they didn't need their picture on the front of an album to sell it. Even the name of the album – *The Beatles* (no verb attached), brilliant in its simplicity – was enough.

And that was the suggestion by artist Richard Hamilton, who realized the concept – keep it simple! A colleague of Robert Fraser and a pioneer of the Pop Art movement, Hamilton had been the art director for *Sgt. Pepper's* and suggested to McCartney that the new cover be as stark a contrast to their previous album as possible. No doubt John Lennon and Yoko liked the decision too, having taken to wearing only white and utilizing a blank white canvas for the 'You are Here' art exhibition at Robert Fraser's gallery. But largely, the concept was Hamilton's.

At one stage, the album was going to be called *A Doll's House*, the same title as the famous Henrik Ibsen play. A scathing commentary on the middle class of the Victorian era, why the Beatles would want to call an album this is beyond me but remember, this was the same band who conscripted controversial playwrite John Osborne to pen a follow up to the film *Help!* The original cover was to feature a wonderfully evocative painting of the band by the artist 'Patrick', the name used by Scottish painter/writer John Byrne, which was later chosen as the cover of the 1980 album, *The Beatles Ballads*. When the British band Family released their album *Music from A Doll's House* in July 1968, the Beatles went in a different direction with Hamilton's concept.

Tastefully packaged in a white, gatefold album with only the embossed name *The Beatles* on the front cover (later editions did away with the embossing and just printed the name *The Beatles*). The addition of a production number was an ironic touch by Hamilton; a 'limited edition' numbered in the millions! The album, however, was printed at more than a dozen production plants around the world, each using their own number sequences for their home territory and making the sequencing irrelevant (except for the first 100 copies, which quickly became collector's items). Original pressings of the double album also had black paper inner sleeves and opened from the top.

On the inside of the album gatefold, the names of the 30 songs are on the left, opposite four formal portraits of the band – charismatic as always, but no longer young. Taken by photographer John Kelly during the summer of 1968, the portraits capture the

Beatles in transition, in between moustaches from the *Sgt. Pepper's* era and the long-haired look of the *Let it Be / Abbey Road* sessions. Of the four, it is Lennon who has changed most, from the full-faced spectacles-less youth of 1963 to a painfully thin, straggly haired man of just five years later.

The album's many 'extras' were keenly embraced by fans, but then the Beatles were always generous with their packaging. Also included were individual, 5 x 7-inch color portraits and a 23 x 34-inch collage of images with the words to every song printed on the back. The collage was made up of private images provided by the band, separated in part by white spaces added by Hamilton to let the pictures 'breathe a little'. Lennon's doodle of himself and Ono in the nude was removed from some later reprints, but a semi-nude photo of a young Paul McCartney (with a strategically placed post hiding the vital bits) somehow got through the censors.

Reviews of the album were overwhelming positive, even allowing for the fact that it was a Beatles album. 'The extra-ordinary quality of the 30 new songs is one of simple happiness,' English journalist Tony Palmer wrote. 'The lyrics overflow with a sparkling radiance and sense of fun that it is impossible to resist.' *Rolling Stone* founder Jann Wenner gushed, 'Whatever else it is or isn't, it is the best album they have ever released, and only the Beatles are capable of making a better one. You are either hip to it, or you ain't.'

There were dissenters too. The album lacked cohesion, some said; there are too many novelty songs and the double album would have been better served as a single album – a view shared by George Martin. But which songs do you leave out? Even the lesser efforts are still Beatles songs. And with all great albums, it's the minor tracks and throwaways that sometimes 'make' the album. The sum total of

The White Album, like the very Beatles themselves, is much greater than the individual parts.

Instead of sitting back and basking in the album's success, the Beatles made the fatal error of rushing back into the studios in January 1969 – in the cold, sterile surrounds of Twickenham Studios no less – and filmed the rehearsal of a new batch of songs for a documentary film, to be called *Get Back*. But relations within the band soon fell to an all-time low; Yoko's omnipresence, John's indifference, George's resentment, Ringo's passive resignation and Paul's badgering to pull the group together were all laid bare before the cameras, and the sessions were quickly abandoned shortly after the band's final, rooftop concert at their Apple headquarters.

The Beatles regrouped to release *Abbey Road* in September 1969, before the Get Back sessions were repackaged for the *Let It Be* album the following year. McCartney in particular was dismayed with Phil Spector's heavy-handed production (God knows what George Martin thought about it), especially the lush orchestration on 'Let It Be' and the addition of female choral voices on 'The Long and Winding Road'. Decades later, McCartney would strip all the production off the album and release *Let it Be: Naked*, but in 1970 it was a less than worthy end for the greatest band in the world.

And that's what makes the double LP The White Album so magnificent. It shows the Beatles at their very best: innovative, inventive and sometimes indulgent. It remains a showcase of the talents of the four main players, and fifty years after its release it stands the test of time. The White Album remains my favorite Beatles album, and would probably be my choice for a 'desert island record' (even on CD or MP3). It contains more classic songs in a bare 90 minutes than most bands can hope to record in a lifetime.

The White Album / The Beatles (November 1968)   93:35

All songs written by Lennon–McCartney, except where noted.*

SIDE ONE		SINGER	LENGTH
1.	Back in the U.S.S.R.	McCartney	2:43
2.	Dear Prudence	Lennon	3:56
3.	Glass Onion	Lennon	2:17
4.	Ob-La-Di, Ob-La-Da	McCartney	3:08
5.	Wild Honey Pie	McCartney	0:52
6.	The Continuing Story of Bungalow Bill	Lennon	3:14
7.	While My Guitar Gently Weeps (Harrison*)	Harrison	4:45
8.	Happiness Is a Warm Gun	Lennon	2:43
SIDE TWO			
9.	Martha My Dear	McCartney	2:28
10.	I'm So Tired	Lennon	2:03
11.	Blackbird	McCartney	2:18
12.	Piggies (Harrison*)	Harrison	2:04
13.	Rocky Raccoon	McCartney	3:33
14.	Don't Pass Me By (Starr*)	Starr	3:51
15.	Why Don't We Do It in the Road?	McCartney	1:41
16.	I Will	McCartney	1:46
17.	Julia	Lennon	2:54
SIDE THREE			
18.	Birthday	McCartney	2:42
19.	Yer Blues	Lennon	4:01
20.	Mother Nature's Son	McCartney	2:48
21.	Everybody's Got Something to Hide Except Me and My Monkey	Lennon	2:24
22.	Sexy Sadie	Lennon	3:15
23.	Helter Skelter	McCartney	4:29
24.	Long, Long, Long (Harrison*)	Harrison	3:04
SIDE FOUR			
25.	Revolution 1	Lennon	4:15
26.	Honey Pie	McCartney	2:41
27.	Savoy Truffle (Harrison*)	Harrison	2:54
28.	Cry Baby Cry	Lennon	3:02
29.	Revolution 9	Lennon	8:22
30.	Good Night	Starr	3:13

Please note: 'SINGER' indicates the song-writer of each track.

CHAPTER 2

Tommy

The Who 1969

'Ten years old with thoughts as bold / As thought can be …'

W hen I first heard the single 'Pinball Wizard', I got what Townshend was trying to say straight away. In 1969, to paraphrase *Tommy* creator Pete Townshend, I became 'aware'; aware that my actions had consequences, that what I said and did impacted on other people. I also changed schools that year and became very aware of what it was like to be different, an outsider. The premise of a deaf, dumb and blind kid becoming a star – 'the new messiah' – when he gains international fame as a pinball champion had nothing mystical about it as far as I was concerned. I had polio as a child, I went to Catholic school. Tommy's story resonated with me – I could buy it. And so could millions of others.

In early 1968, the Who were at the crossroads of their music career. They had failed to make a dent in the charts with their concept album *The Who Sell Out* (1967), and then watched their 'ace in the hole' single 'I Can See For Miles' stall in the UK charts at No.10. Now the band returned home from a disastrous tour of Australia and New Zealand, with the Small Faces, and literally collapsed. The Who could have been finished then and there, without ever reaching their full potential. The mod movement had run its course, and when the band tried to sever ties with their American producer, Shel Talmy, the matter ended up in court. The Who were unfocused, ill-disciplined; like petulant school boys, erratic and self-destructive. Where would they go now?

Guitarist and chief songwriter Pete Townshend promptly had a nervous breakdown and took himself off to bed for six weeks to contemplate the band's future. Working in his home studio in Twickenham, Townshend demoed the songs that would become central to the release of *Tommy* the following year. That Townshend, at the age of 23, could conceive, write and execute rock and roll's first rock opera, or at least the genre's best example of a concept album, speaks volumes for both his talent and vision. The resulting double album, *Tommy*, both *made* the band as rock superstars and, for a while, threatened to eclipse the remainder of the Who's career.

The story of a messiah whose followers turn against and ultimately destroy him was not unique; it's a story as old as the ages. But, despite parallels with the Old and New Testaments, *Tommy* is not a 'preachy' album – there is more realism within the album's four sides than spiritualism – exploring abuse, betrayal, anger, violence. It's a rock and roll record, not a devotional one. *Tommy* would be such as a success (though not quite 'bigger than Jesus') that it would take on numerous incarnations over the years – an 'All-Star' concert and album, a ballet (!), a controversial 1975 movie and a Tony-award winning Broadway show.

Having found a copy of *Tommy*, I needed a quick education on just who the Who were as a band. I was able to access a copies of their previous albums, *A Quick One* (1966) and *The Who Sell Out* (1967) and was immediately hooked; here was another blues-inspired, rock and roll band pushing the limitations of rock and pop. The leap in quality between those two albums is extraordinary. *A Quick One* is basically a collection of pop songs, and very well-played pop songs at that ('Run, Run, Run' is a standout, with its early guitar flourishes from Townshend; 'Boris the Spider' gives an insight into the macabre mind of bassist John Entwistle; 'Heat Wave' is an interesting cover of the Motown hit; and 'So Sad About Us' is a nice period piece, again by Townshend).

The title track, 'A Quick One', gives a hint of what was to come – a 'mini-opera' if you will, about Ivor the engine driver getting a 'quickie' whilst away on the job. It's pretty juvenile stuff, but it's clear the Who were desperately trying to find their place in the pop world.

The Who Sell Out is one of my favorite albums, but the production is heavy-handed and the mix just has too much extraneous noise on it. But individually, the songs work – 'Mary Anne With the Shaky Hand', 'Odorono', 'Tattoo', 'I Can See For Miles', 'Can't Reach You' and the beautiful 'Sunrise'– each hit their mark (and Entwistle's 'Silas Stingy' shows a band who knew how to have fun and be inventive with their vocals). Again, the final track is a precursor to *Tommy* – 'Rael' is a 5:44 minute mini-opera with several musical themes that would be recycled in *Tommy*. The Who were building to something serious, but the success of their next record would surprise even them.

The inspiration for *Tommy* grew out of Pete Townshend's devotion to Meher Baba. Born Merwan Sheriar Irani in Pune, India, Meher Baba was seen by his followers as the earthly avatar of God. He died in 1969, having taken a vow of silence that he had maintained for 44 years. His most popular teaching, 'Don't worry, be happy', would find its own pop culture resonance in Bobby McFerrin's 1988 hit song of the same name.

Early success had left Townshend somewhat hollowed out and, like many of his music contemporaries (the Beatles went to India in search of 'the answer' in 1968), he was looking for inner peace as well as some sort of meaning behind all the madness. Townshend was introduced to the teachings of Meher Baba by artist Michael McInnerney, who would later be assigned art duties for the new album, and Small Faces keyboardist Ronnie Lane, with whom he would collaborate on a joint album, 1977's *Rough Mix*.

As early as 1967, Townshend was reported in the music press as being determined to write a 'rock opera', which was originally to be called 'Amazing Journey'. Kit Lambert, who co-managed the band with Chris Stamp – the brother of actor Terrence Stamp – was himself the son of composer Constant Lambert and had long encouraged Townshend to write something more demanding than a three-minute pop song. In 1968, the project was regularly referred to as 'Deaf, Dumb and Blind Boy', with Townshend providing tidbits of the narrative to a somewhat skeptical press, many whom described the concept as 'sick'.

Townshend's choice of the male name that would give the rock opera its eventual title is interesting … *Tommy*. Why not Terry or Wally or Jimmy? (He would use Jimmy in his next rock opera, 1973's *Quadrophenia*). 'Tommy' is the popular term used to describe British soldiers in World War I, which is the original setting of the story. Townshend too was a 'war baby', having been born in May 1945, just days after the end of World War II in Europe. Setting his story in World War I may have given Townshend some space and perspective, but even an amateur psychologist can see sources in the narrative from Townshend's own upbringing.

Pete Townshend's parents were World War II-era dancehall

musicians – father Cliff was a saxophonist, and mother Betty was a singer. As a child, Townshend was left in the care of his abusive maternal grandmother, who suffered from mental issues. His parents reclaimed him at the age of five, but their marriage was in trouble and his mother conducted a number of affairs while her husband was away working. As a child, Pete was witness to these infidelities and these two themes – betrayal and abuse – found their way into the *Tommy* story.

But more than just a biographical narrative, *Tommy* also parallels Townshend's spiritual awakening, with many of the songs being 'open prayers' to Meher Baba. Being 'deaf, dumb and blind' is a metaphor for man's inability to understand the spiritual world, just as becoming a 'pinball wizard' was a symbol for achieving, in Townshend's mind at least, the equally inconsequential status of pop stardom.

Firstly, a quick synopsis: Tommy is born to Mrs Walker after her husband is reported missing while fighting in World War I. In 1921, Mr Walker returns home and finds his wife in the arms of a lover, whom he murders. The shock at witnessing such violence renders young Tommy 'deaf, dumb and blind' – it's also a response to the berating by his parents ('You didn't see it, you didn't hear it …'). Tommy lives in his own inner world, impervious to miracle cures (The Hawker), drugs (Acid Queen), physical abuse (Cousin Kevin) and even molestation (Uncle Ernie). As a young man, Tommy achieves fame as a pinball playing sensation, able to respond to the vibration of his 'crazy flipper fingers'. A doctor makes the breakthrough that Tommy's problems are psychosomatic and, after gazing at his own reflection in a mirror, the boy 'crashes through' and recovers his senses. Tommy is seen as a new messiah and starts a religious movement, but his followers ultimately reject him and destroy his message.

Or something like that!

The Who started recording the album in London's IBC Studios in September 1968, a process that was meant to last eight weeks and perhaps be ready for the lucrative Christmas market. The Who had recently returned from a highly successful tour of the US and, having married girlfriend Karen Astley the previous May, songwriter Pete Townshend was in high spirits. Somehow, he also found time to produce the Thunderclap Newman hit 'Something in the Air' during the *Tommy* sessions, which proved to be a highly creative period for him. All four members of the band would remember the sessions, that would ultimately take more than eight months to complete, as the happiest to date. They spent a lot of time discussing the evolution of the story, often adjourning to a nearby pub to clarify or complicate matters.

Kit Lambert, who was given producer credit on the finished album, acted as both 'encourager' and 'provocateur' in the studio. Lambert wrote Townshend's narrative down as a film treatment he called 'Tommy, 1914–1984' to keep the band on course, as well as monitoring studio time and generally keeping the band on task. Lambert hoped to make a movie out of his script, but his particular vision would remain unrealized in the years after the album's release and success. It also led to a major falling out with Townshend that was not resolved before Lambert's death in 1981, at the age of 45.

Originally conceived as a single album, the project quickly expanded to include an overture (and an 'Underture'!) at Lambert's urging. Having arrived at the studio with a number of key tracks already demoed at home, Townshend composed new material to plug the narrative gaps, but wisely resisted the temptation to tell the 'whole' story. Townshend, like many of his generation, was heavily influenced by the release of the Stanley Kubrick film *2001: A Space Odyssey* that year, which avoided the same trap. The audience filled in the gaps with their own narrative, and *Tommy*'s legion of fans would be the same.

Not so much a rock opera as a 'rock cantata' (technically there are no spoken parts or 'libretto' in *Tommy*), the resulting album has an operatic structure, with an overture, distinct characters and a narrative (such as it was). It does not, however, have an orchestral arrangement, with all instruments played by the four members of the band (including Entwistle on French horn and trumpet). It was essential that *Tommy* was able to be performed on stage by the band, and thus the production of the album is sparse, with very few sound effects (perhaps a smashing mirror or two) or overdubs.

The five-minute 'Overture' at the beginning of the album was an afterthought, by Lambert, that showcases the musical themes encountered across the four sides of vinyl. The rock opera aspirations of *Tommy* become very real in this one song and offer the listener a point of reference for what unfolds on record. The first voice you hear on *Tommy* is Pete Townshend's, singing 'It's a boy Mrs Walker, it's a boy…' heralded by Entwistle's four-note phrase on French horn. The refrain was originally used for a song called 'Glow Girl', which Townshend wrote on tour in the US in 1968.

'1921' cements the story in a time and place, just after the end of World War I. The tune has a particularly gentle turn of phrase ('I have no reason to be over-optimistic …') before the track suddenly changes direction. 'What about the boy? He saw it all …' What exactly the boy saw is left to the listener's imagination, but Townshend inserts an air of menace in the overlapping threats ('You didn't see it, you didn't hear it …'). The song was called 'You Didn't Hear It' on US pressings of the album, just in case fans couldn't follow.

'Amazing Journey' is full of chord changes leftover from the 'Rael' mini-opera and set against a synthesized Moog beat. The boy Tommy might be mute, but Keith Moon tells the story with his drum fills. The track also samples backward loops pioneered by the Beatles – Townshend was experimenting with tape loops at the time. 'Sparks' is slightly indulgent; Townshend may have needed more story here but hey, it was the '60s. The use of synthesizer is effective and it has some nice chord changes at the end. Originally titled 'Dream Sequence', the song got its title from a 1962 collection of Meher Baba sayings called *Sparks of the Truth.*

'The Hawker', written by Sonny Boy Williamson, is the only cover song on the album. Moss Alison had recorded it as a jazz version, which Townshend liked, and he was really keen to include it because it fit his narrative so well. The song features a great vocal from Daltrey, especially on 'She brings eyesight to the blind …'

'Christmas' is a totally underrated and well-crafted song that serves the narrative well. With great production values from Townshend, who recorded the song as a sparse, piano-based demo, the background vocals bring the song alive with a wonderfully ironic chorus ('And Tommy doesn't know what day it is / He doesn't know who Jesus was or what praying is / How can he be saved?'). The slightly off key background vocal intimates that something is amiss and Townshend explores the different ways he can sing, 'Tommy can you hear me …' as well as introducing the 'See me, feel me, touch me' refrain for the first time.

Two of the songs on the album are written by John Entwistle: 'Fiddle About' and 'Cousin Kevin'. Townshend later reflected, 'I didn't want to do them. I didn't think I could be cruel enough. They're ruthlessly brilliant songs because they are just as cruel as people can be. I wanted to show that the boy was being dealt with very cruelly and it was because he was being dismissed as a freak.'

'Cousin Kevin' uses an effective descending chord pattern, almost 'chopsticks'-like in its simplicity. Entwistle was the master of dark humor, even though this song shows a sadistic side. It has some brutal lyrics ('Do you know how to play hide and seek? / To find me would take you a week …'); others not so much ('What would you do if I shut you outside to stand in the rain / And catch cold so you died? I'm the school bully …'), before returning to the docile, childlike beginning.

On 'The Acid Queen', Daltrey is finally unleashed: 'I'm the Gypsy / The acid queen … I'll tear your soul apart …' he sings. The song is about 'not just drugs,' Townshend later explained, but the 'whole thing' with his grandmother. Not everything is revealed in the song … is the Acid Queen the Hawker's wife? Is Cousin Kevin the son of Uncle Ernie?

Side Two finishes with 'Underture', which is superfluous to the narrative but features some great bass lines from Entwistle, timpani drums from Moon and discordant acoustic guitar from Townshend. It's far too long at 10 minutes, but it is supposed to represent 'a trip' after Tommy's run in with the Acid Queen.

The third side of the album explodes with the vibrant, 'Do You Think It's Alright?'. Although the song is only 24 seconds long, suddenly things are starting to happen. Townshend loved the Beach Boys' harmonies and he makes the most of the opportunity here.

'Fiddle About', the second Entwistle song, is not unlike 'Silas Stingy' on *The Who Sell Out* (especially the refrain, 'Fiddle, fiddle, fiddle …'). It's very comical, until you realize the song is about sexual abuse. Although it's sung by Entwistle on the record, the role was taken over by Keith Moon on stage and in the subsequent film.

The success of *Tommy* is directly related to Townshend's conception and the band's execution of the hit 'Pinball Wizard'. Released as a single before the album was even finished, this song has become one of the Who's most enduring rock anthems. The spectacular acoustic opening is built around descending jazz chords centering around B major. The song has great dynamics – Townshend's guitar, Moon's inventive drum fills, Entwistle's thumping bass and Daltrey's vocal (answered by Townshend, 'what makes him so good?') around a rhythmic lyric ('He's got crazy flipper fingers, never seen him fall / That deaf, dumb and blind kid sure plays a mean pinball …').

That Tommy should become a pinball champion was the suggestion of English music critic Nik Cohn. After Townshend played him an outline of his 'opera', Cohn found the concept a little too 'intense', so Townshend asked, somewhat factiously, would he like it better if it had pinball in it? Cohn, a noted fan of the pinball arts, responded 'Of course I would!' Townshend thought the concept contrived, but it was important that Tommy had 'some colorful event and excitement,' Townshend said, so that he could attract a following. The finished song, with its singalong chorus and power chord changes, represents arguably the Who's finest moment in pop music.

'There's a Doctor' sounds like it belongs in a Gilbert and Sullivan operetta (think *HMAS Pinafore*) and though it lasts just 24 seconds, it sets up Tommy's cure. For me, 'Go to the Mirror!' is the best song on the album. The 'see me, feel me, touch me, heal me …' refrain is sung three times before it is finally answered with 'Listening to you I get the music / Gazing at you I get the heat …' Moon answers the command 'Go to the mirror boy …' with a blast of drums, proving *Tommy* is as much Moon's album as it is Townshend's or Daltrey's.

The reprise of 'Tommy Can You Hear Me?' is very much in the style of Crosby, Stills, Nash & Young, and features a great bass line from Entwistle. 'Smash the Mirror' is a funky time capsule (Daltrey throws in a cool 'alright' at the end of the first line) and it features some great guitar work from Townshend.

'Sensation' could easily have been a single. The song has its origins in 'Can't Reach You' from *The Who Sell Out* and features Entwistle again on French horn. The overall sound of the song is Beach Boys-like and is quickly followed by the 'Miracle Cure' call of 'extra, extra, read all about it!' Things are moving fast in the *Tommy* narrative.

'Sally Simpson' is a story within the story – a totally encapsulated, McCartney-like vignette. As written, Tommy experiences pop stardom and a young girl (Sally Simpson) is injured when the crowd of followers rushes the stage. The song was inspired by the fate of a young fan who leapt the stage at a Doors concert in Queens, New York when the Who supported them in 1968. Townshend was shocked by the vicious way the bouncers dealt with the girl and was inspired to write this cautionary tale on piano.

'I'm Free' has one of the Who's most recognizable guitar riffs at the beginning of the song, but it too was composed on piano. Again, Moon's drumming is a standout and Townshend adds some nice bluegrass guitar at the end. The use of an acoustic guitar 'wall of sound' was inspired by the Stones' 'Street Fighting Man', which had been released that year. Townshend overdubs himself playing acoustic guitar multiple times to achieve the effect.

The hymn-like 'Welcome' is a gentle ballad that sounds like it could have been sung by a church choir. 'Come to this house / Be one of us …' But the mob is never too far away ('There's more at the door …') and when Tommy commercializes his message ('A colorful palace / Spare no expense now …') he is doomed as a messiah.

The suggestion that Tommy build a holiday camp for his followers rather than a church came from Keith Moon. It was another pop culture touch that made the story more accessible to a wider audience; many post-War Brits had spent their summers at seaside holiday camps. (In 1973, Moon would appear in the film *That'll be The Day*, with David Essex and Ringo Starr, which is set in a British holiday camp in the 1950s.) Although the song is credited to Moon, it was actually written by Townshend on organ (he also sings it in a whacky, falsetto voice on the record). Having asked Moon to write the tune, it seems Townshend knocked it off quickly in the studio and was happy to attribute it to his drummer because, he said, 'it sounded like something Moon would write.'

The album's final track 'We're Not Gonna Take It' brings the narrative to a violent end. Tommy becomes didactic ('Put in your ear plugs / Put on your eye shades / You know where to put the cork…') and his followers reject him ('We forsake you, gonna rape you / Let's forget you better still …'). It's a surprise twist from Townshend; rather than venerating Tommy, the mob destroy him. The reprise of 'See Me, Feel Me' is a lovely touch here – Townshend says that he had tears in his eyes when he wrote that piece of music – before the album concludes with the inspired chorus, 'Listening to you / I get the music, gazing at you I get the heat, following you I climb the mountains / I get excitement at your feet.'

The band were still in the recording studio in March 1969 before Lambert called a halt, rushing the album out in May. The mix is subdued, unlike some of the band's incendiary performances on stage ('Have the Who gone soft?' asked one reviewer). The other members of the band wanted to go back into the studio and do overdubs, but Townshend was determined to have the voices 'up front' of the music in order to tell his story.

Tommy was finally released on 17 May 1969 in the US, and 23 May in the UK, because of delays with the album cover. A lot of thought had gone into the cover concept, which was designed by Mike McInnerney and photographed by Barrie Meller. An 'art deco photomontage' over a double gatefold that opened out again to display a three-panel triptych, the artwork was a brilliant piece of 'Op Art' which gave the illusion of movement through the use of pattern and color.

Rather than portray what Tommy did or didn't look like, McInnerney uses a series of images on the inner panels to display 'a world without conventional senses.' As McInnerney told journalist Mike Goldstein in 2007, 'The outer cover has its globe (Earth/Self) hanging in an endless infinite space that can never be touched – only imagined. The inside cover has its wall and wall lights, a symbol of domestic space – the room we all live in. The light from these lamps, however, does not fix things as in our sighted world – it shifts and changes for Tommy.'

The Who debuted the album for members of the media by playing it live at London's Ronnie Scott Club in June, deafening those present, confusing some and amazing others. Reviews of *Tommy* were mixed. *Disc and Music Echo* called it 'A masterpiece ... The Who, as a magnificent group, project the story brilliantly in music.' *NME* labeled it, 'Who's Sick Opera ... pretentious is too strong a word, maybe over-ambitious is the right term, but sick certainly does apply.' *Melody Maker* named it 'Album of the Year', ahead of the Beatles' *Abbey Road*. The album went on to sell 20 million copies around the world, reaching No.4 in the US and No.2 in the UK, but staying in the charts for the next year on the back of the band's constant touring.

Before *Tommy*, singer Roger Daltrey never really knew where he stood with the band. With Townshend as chief songwriter (and sometime singer), Daltrey's career was really in Townshend's hands. But with *Tommy*, he was able to fashion a rock god persona – with long curly hair and buckskin suit with tassels on each arm – around the album's inspirational songs. This new persona found their voice at Woodstock in August 1969.

The Who stole the show at Woodstock, even surpassing the performance of their Track stablemate, Jimmy Hendrix. Kicking anti-Vietnam protester Abby Hoffman off stage as they launched into *Tommy*, the band sang 'See Me, Feel Me' as the first rays of dawn hit the stage ... nature's great theater. The Who repeated the dose at the Isle of Wight the following month, and the release of the Oscar-winning film, *Woodstock*, the following year cemented the legend. The Who, at last, had a vehicle to promote their greatness as a live band.

Over the ensuing years, *Tommy* was performed on stage, in stadiums across America, in opera houses – in 1970 the Who were the first and only rock band to play the famed New York's Metropolitan Opera House. In 1972, it spawned a fully-orchestrated 'All-Star' stage spectacular that also became a million-copy seller when it was released on album. Rocker Rod Stewart was tagged to play 'Tommy' for that show, but after heavy lobbying from Townshend, who took on the much-needed role of narrator, Roger Daltrey assumed the lead role that he had made his own (Stewart was bumped to the role of 'Pinball Wizard'). The concerts were a huge success, but the resulting album has little of the charm and musicianship of the original *Tommy*, despite the equally ornate packaging.

The Who displayed their newfound confidence by following the best ever concept album with arguably the best ever live album, *Live at Leeds* in 1970. But even then, *Tommy* had started to eclipse the band – they dropped songs from the album from their setlist before reluctantly inserting a truncated version, five or six songs at the most, back into their set, where it would remain. When Townshend tried to articulate his vision for the Who's next concept album, tentatively entitled *Lifehouse* in 1971, not even he could understand it. *Tommy* set the mold. The resulting album salvaged from that concept, *Who's Next*, is arguably the band's best record. Not even 1973's *Quadrophenia* – the story of young mods – could replicate the success of *Tommy*, primarily because there were no hits on that album and the band couldn't play it on stage. It did, however, spawn a superior movie, released in 1979.

Alas, the same cannot be said for the movie *Tommy*, which was finally released in 1975. The idea of a *Tommy* movie had gone through various drafts before controversial film director Ken Russell (*The Music Lovers, The Devils*) became involved. The film is very much Russell's vision, shifting the context to post-World War II ('1921' becomes '1951') and changing Tommy's father to the victim, rather than the murderer, in the mother's adulterous relationship.

There are also some great visuals in the film – the Pinball Wizard (Elton John) sequence, the introduction of the Acid Queen (Tina Turner), the 'Cousin Kevin' (Paul Nichols) attacks and especially after Tommy (played by Daltrey) has recovered his senses – but there was controversy too. Russell uses real handicapped people in the sequence 'Miracle Cure', where Tommy (Daltrey) is led by his mother (Anne Margaret) to the altar of a faith healer, with a plaster cast of Marilyn Monroe as their goddess!

Pete Townshend added several news songs to the narrative but he lamented that the resulting soundtrack had too many actors who had 'no business singing on it' – namely Anne Margaret (who is barely passable as a singer), Oliver Reed (dreadful) and Jack Nicholson (who talks his way through his one song as 'The Doctor'). The film soundtrack overuses synthesizer, which was very much in vogue in the mid-1970s, but at least Townshend got an Oscar nomination out of it all (for Music Score, Original or Adaptation), as did Anne Margaret for Best Actress. Unlike the record, the film *Tommy* has not aged well.

The Who broke up in 1983, having limped on for several years after the death of drummer Keith Moon in 1978, aged just 31. *Who Are You*, released in 1978, can be considered the last 'real' Who album, with former Small Faces/Faces drummer Kenny Jones taking over on the band's last two studio albums (*Face Dances*, in 1981, and *It's Hard* the following year). The band were shattered by the deaths of 11 fans in a stadium seating crush at a Cincinnati concert in December 1979, but they never really recovered from the death of Keith Moon. Even Roger Daltrey lamented that, as likeable as Kenny Jones was, he was 'the wrong drummer' for the Who. Jones played with the band at the Live Aid concert in 1985, but wasn't invited back for subsequent tours.

Reforming in the late 1980s and 1990s, the band was dealt the blow of losing bassist John Entwistle, who died on tour in the US in 2002, aged 57. By that time Pete Townshend had enjoyed the success of *Tommy* on the Broadway stage (five Tony awards, including one for Townshend's score), but the lasting legacy of the Who as a touring band proved infinitely stronger. Townshend and Daltrey soldiered on into the new millennium without their underrated rhythm section, the band augmented by Zak Starkey (the son of Ringo Starr) on drums, Simon Townshend (Pete's younger brother) on guitars, John 'Rabbit' Bundrick on keyboards and Pino Palladino on bass.

Tommy is never far away from the Who on stage. A Who concert without its *Tommy* set would be incomplete: it's in the band's DNA. As Roger Daltrey says, 'We treat it with the respect that you'd treat a Mozart opera.' Rightfully so.

Tommy / **The Who** (May 1969)   75:12

All songs written by Pete Townshend, unless otherwise noted*

SIDE ONE		LENGTH
1	Overture	3:50
2	It's a Boy	2:07
3	1921	3:14
4	Amazing Journey	3:25
5	Sparks	3:45
6	The Hawker (Sonny Boy Williamson*)	2:15

SIDE TWO		
7	Christmas	5:30
8	Cousin Kevin (John Entwistle*)	4:03
9	The Acid Queen	3:31
10	Underture	9:55

SIDE THREE		
11	Do You Think It's Alright?	0:24
12	Fiddle About (John Entwistle*)	1:26
13	Pinball Wizard	3:50
14	There's a Doctor	0:25
15	Go to the Mirror!	3:50
16	Tommy Can You Hear Me?	1:35
17	Smash the Mirror	1:20
18	Sensation	2:32

SIDE FOUR		
19	Miracle Cure	0:10
20	Sally Simpson	4:10
21	I'm Free	2:40
22	Welcome	4:30
23	Tommy's Holiday Camp (Keith Moon*)	0:57
24	We're Not Gonna Take It	6:45

CHAPTER 3

Led Zeppelin III

Led Zeppelin 1970

'Will drive our ships to new lands ...'

In 1972, the older brother of a school friend of mine had a party at his house while his parents were out of town. The following morning, I called in to their house on my Saturday rounds of the neighbourhood while they were furiously cleaning up before his folks got home. Lots of records were strewn around the living room among the empty beer bottles – that's what happened in the early '70s, kids had record parties – and in helping to clean up we found one record, without its cover, under a sofa.

As we surveyed the vinyl, my friend and I laughed at the thought of some poor guy getting home with his record stash, missing one album. 'Man, he'll be pissed,' my friend remarked as he read the record label: *Led Zeppelin III.* The label was divided into two sections, green and red, with the Atlantic logo and label at the top. The name of the first track, 'Immigrant Song', was written above the white bar that cut through the hole in the center. We put it on the turntable and lowered the needle.

The song runs for a bare 2:26 but listening to that tune absolutely changed my life. At the moment Robert Plant unleashed his voice with the unmistakable 'Ah-ah-ah-ahhhhh' over the driving beat and opening guitar riff, I was transported to the front of that Viking ship with the band ... and then, all too quickly, it was over. The look on our faces said it all. What the fuck was that?

Led Zeppelin in 1970 were the heaviest music group around, and this was at a time when 'heaviosity' included bands with real clout: Black Sabbath, Deep Purple, Moby Grape, Ten Years After, Fleetwood Mac ... well, not really Fleetwood Mac. But 'Led Zep' broke free of the 'British blues' tag with the release of their third album, the imaginatively titled *Led Zeppelin III*, at the end of 1970. They also defined what 'heavy metal' was for a new generation. For me, they were a long way from the Beatles, but not so far that I couldn't relate to them.

Formed in 1968 by famed session musician Jimmy Page who, left with the name of noted blues outfit the Yardbirds but without any players, recruited fellow session man John Paul Jones on bass, and ex-Band of Joy bandmates, drummer John 'Bonzo' Bonham and vocalist Robert Plant, for this new band. The story behind the choice of name (the original choice, 'the New Yardbirds', would have been disastrous) may be apocryphal, but my preferred version is that it has its origins with two disenchanted members of the Who – John Entwistle and Keith Moon.

Having returned from their controversial tour of Australia in February 1968, the Who's rhythm section let slip that they intended to leave the band and form their own group. Perhaps they could even join Page's new venture?

News of their possible defection would go down like a 'lead balloon' Page allegedly remarked. 'Like a lead zeppelin!' Moon replied. Page took the name for his own band – shortening 'lead' to 'led' so American fans would not pronounce it 'Leed Zeppelin' – and pissed off Entwistle and Moon in the process. But the name was apt; 'Led Zeppelin', both heavy and light – the dichotomy of rock-pop sensibilities of the time. Many bands would follow their lead, but few mastered both forms as well as 'Led Zep'.

Having recorded *Led Zeppelin I* (1968) and *Led Zeppelin II* (1969) on the road while completing back-to-back tours of America, the four members of the band returned home in 1970 to recharge and take stock of their newfound fame. Their new album, their third in as many years, would be a change of pace, 'a masterful union of ballads and bruising' as *Rolling Stone* later noted, although it would take the magazine decades to live down its lukewarm review of the album when it was originally released.

What prompted the shift? Perhaps something as simple as George Harrison's comment to John Bonham at a party: 'The problem with you guys is that you never do ballads,' the Beatle allegedly opined. Jimmy Page would show the former Beatle a ballad or two.

Although the resulting album confused the band's fanbase and was dismissed by critics, I doubt I would have become a Led Zep fan without listening to it. I was never a devotee of the white blues movement in England – it took me years to listen to the Stones; the Yardbirds were a mystery to me and I never gave Eric Clapton two thoughts until after he left Cream. When it came to the blues, I was decidedly in the John Lennon camp; 'Yer Blues', a parody of blues.

But Led Zeppelin changed all that.

In many ways, *Led Zeppelin III* was the band's first 'real' studio album. Jimmy Page and Robert Plant wrote and conceived the new batch of semi-acoustic, folk-inspired songs while on holiday in the Welsh town of Machynlleth, in Gwynedd, in the summer of 1970.

While Bonham and Jones returned to their respective families, Page and Plant talked about what they wanted to do on the next record at an informal get-together at Plant's home in the West Midlands before heading off on holidays. As a child, Plant had frequented a small cottage in Wales called Bron-Yr-Aur (pronounced *bron-yaar*) with his parents. The cottage had no electricity, sewerage or running water, but Page and Plant took in the pastoral surrounds, grew beards and mingled with the local town folk, all the while composing music on acoustic guitars and harmonica.

The retreat to a more rustic style of folk-infused music was a reaction to the Band's debut album, *Music from Big Pink* (1968). Eric Clapton, George Harrison and Van Morrison were also moved to return to their musical roots, so to speak, and Page and Plant were of a similar mind. Everyone from Crosby, Stills & Nash to Joni Mitchell had been affected by the Band's seminal release, and the early '70s was awash with folk-inspired imitators. Led Zeppelin was anything but that, but they would successfully fuse folk, blues, rock and heavy metal into this new album.

'There was more to us than being a heavy metal band,' Jimmy Page later said, and *Led Zeppelin III* proves it. 'I think we produced something really good: a courageous album, a band standing up for its convictions, doing what felt natural without being at the beck and call of record labels or A&R men. We were able, without any hindrance, to keep pushing the boundaries.'

Page was 'obsessed' with folk music – Celtic, Irish, Asian, African – and had much broader musical influences than just the blues. He knew *Led Zeppelin III* would 'shock' people, but he was determined to have something different on each successive album: jazz ('No Quarter'), doo-wop ('The Crunge'), reggae ('D'Yer Mak'er') on *Houses of the Holy;* funk ('Trampled Under Foot') and baroque-rock ('Kashmir') on *Physical Graffiti,* and even synth-rock ('All My Love') on *In Through the Out Door.*

After the stress of simultaneous touring and recording over the past two years, Bron-Yr-Aur presented Led Zep's chief songwriters with a completely different 'vibe' and the resulting songs showcased Page's considerable acoustic guitar skills and Plant's confident, folk-inspired lyrics. With them and their respective partners on this trip were roadies Clive Coulson and Sandy Macgregor, who helped heat the house and carry water in from outside. Nights were spent at a nearby pub – also the venue of the closest bathtub – mixing with locals unaware just who these young hippies were. When their partners returned to the city, Page and Plant spent several days recording the songs they had accumulated on a cassette recorder; 'one of the very first Sony cassette recorders and a bunch of Eveready batteries,' as Plant recalled.

It was the twilight time before Led Zeppelin became mythic rock gods. American audiences had taken them to their hearts as a hard-working live act with some 150-plus shows to their credit during the past two years. UK audiences and the hard-nosed British music press were still to be won over, however. In many regards, *Led Zeppelin III* was seen as a step backwards in the band's unconscious plan to rule the world, angering their solid core of blues fans. It would take almost another generation before the album would be regarded as the masterpiece it is.

The songs workshopped and recorded at the Welsh cottage were played for Jones and Bonham, and most would appear on the new album. An early attempt to record them the following month at London's Olympic Studios was quickly abandoned, however, with Page and Plant feeling the sterile studio atmosphere was not conducive to replicating the gentle, acoustic feel that had been achieved at Bron-Yr-Aur. With a new tour of America coming up in August, Page was keen to record the new album quickly, and so the band decamped to Headley Grange; an old mansion in Hampshire built in 1795 as a workhouse, where Genesis and Fleetwood Mac had recently recorded their albums with the assistance of the Rolling Stones' mobile studio.

Robert Plant later recalled that the mood at the renovated mansion was 'incredible'; the band recorded 17 songs during the sessions there. There were also early versions of 'Stairway to Heaven', which would become the centerpiece of the 'Runes' album (*Led Zeppelin IV*), 'Over the Hills' (which would not appear until three years later on *Houses of the Holy*), and also 'Down By The Seaside', 'The Rover' and 'Poor Tom'.

On 21 and 22 June, Led Zeppelin stopped recording to play two gigs in Reykjavik, Iceland, where they debuted a new blues song they had been working on called 'Since I've Been Loving You'. A press review of the gig paints a picture of band members in their youthful prime:

> Plant, like a lion with gilded mane, toned, young and elegant. He was dressed in a shirt, black with golden threads and very tight jeans. Adjacent to Plant, were two princes: Jimmy Page and John Paul Jones. Page, dressed in blue velvet; Jones in a white robe and green velvet trousers ... Bonham performed a clean, magnificent solo on drums, first with sticks and then with bare hands.

The first concert in Laugardalshöll was almost canceled when government civil servants went on strike, but the event was saved by the university students union, who banded together and got the hall ready for the concert. Unfortunately, the second concert in Essen had to be cut short when fans rioted after Plant prematurely announced the final song.

The following Sunday, Led Zeppelin showcased further songs from the unfinished album at the Bath Music Festival, including a song they had written about their experience in Iceland. On a bill that included American megastars Jefferson Airplane and Janis Joplin, Led Zeppelin's nearly three-hour set in front of 150,000 people defined the band's newfound position as the premier rock and roll act of their generation.

Paid £20,000 for their appearance, Led Zeppelin opened with a new song called 'Immigrant Song', as they would do with most of their shows for the remainder of the decade. The band started with that incredible beat laid down by Jones and Bonham, Page's staccato guitar riff in F#, Plant's 'battle cry' introduction and the words, 'We come from the land of the ice and snow'. Plant later acknowledged that the band wasn't trying to be 'pompous' (not many bands could sing 'Valhalla, I am coming …' and not be called pompous) but the song was a tribute to Iceland and its Viking heritage.

'Immigrant Song' would also open *Led Zeppelin III*, but while it's not representative of the other tracks on the album, that one song is arguably responsible for influencing a whole generation of 1980s heavy metal 'big hair' bands. The song reached a new cultural peak when it was featured in the 2003 comedy *School of Rock*, with actor-singer-comedian Jack Black personally appealing to the band (in character, on video) for permission to use the song in the film. Page and Plant had been reticent to license their songs over the years

('Tangerine' popped up in the Cameron Crowe film *Almost Famous* in 2000, but then Crowe was a former *Rolling Stone* journalist who had interviewed and even toured with the band in their 1970s heyday), but they were obviously swayed by Jack Black's novel approach.

Page came up with the open C tuning to 'Friends' when he demoed the song for Plant a few days before they went to Wales. During the mixing process, Page overdubbed strings on his intriguing acoustic guitar riff as Plant rails in his high-pitched falsetto, 'Mm-mmm, I'm telling you now / The greatest thing you ever can do now ...' Some people cite Crosby, Stills & Nash's 'Carry On', which was released on the *Déjà Vu* album in March, as an influence on Page, but he was actually going for an 'Indian feel' with the song. The result has a psychedelic, dream-like quality to it and it remains one of the few Led Zep songs to feature an orchestral arrangement (a move Page repeated on 1975's 'Kashmir').

'Friends' sonically devolves into the start of 'Celebration Day', which opens with another unique guitar riff from Page; this one played on slide guitar. The song has one of the more commercial choruses Led Zep recorded, with Page adding an equally accessible guitar hook after the chorus, 'My, my, my, I'm so happy / I'm gonna join the band / We gonna dance and sing in celebration / We are in the promised land ...'

Lyricist Robert Plant was indeed in a good place when he wrote this song – 21 years old, already a young father and the lead singer in the hottest band in the world – but 'Celebration Day' also cites life's winners and losers, the hard times left behind and the hard road ahead. When the band reconvened in 2007 to celebrate the life of Atlantic Records founder Ahmet Ertegun (1923–2006), playing live for the first time in 30 years and utilizing the considerable skills of

John Bonham's son Jason on drums, the resulting live CD and DVD was called *Celebration Day*.

'Since I've Been Loving You' started as a blues jam at Olympic Studios before being fully fleshed out at Headley Grange. Page didn't want a typical 12-bar blues tempo because the band had done that before on their previous album, but the song came together very quickly. Led Zeppelin played a shorter version of this song at Bath, but the finished version – all 7 minutes 25 seconds – stands as one of the band's greatest achievements. The blues never sounded so good.

'Since I've Been Loving You' was recorded live, with Jones contributing church-like Hammond organ. Plant's scatty, passionate vocal is particularly evocative on the lines, 'Workin' from seven to eleven every night / It really makes life a drag / I don't think that's right …' The lyrics may have their origins in a song called 'Never' by San Francisco outfit Moby Grape, but the finished song is pure Zep.

Jimmy Page's epic solo was overdubbed on a demo version but he was never really happy with it. He spent months trying to improve the solo – sometimes even splicing parts of different takes together – before settling on his original take. The countless videos on YouTube from young guitar guns who break down the solo into manageable parts so they can be mastered show Page's spontaneous genius on the track.

Side One closes with 'Out On the Tiles', which is credited to Bonham, Plant and Page. The song was originally referred to as 'the bathroom song' because Bonzo's drums sounded like they were recorded in a bathroom. The chorus is one of the more commercial on the album, Zeppelin mixing styles of heavy metal-blues and rock-pop. US fans scratched their heads for cultural references, with 'on the tiles' being an English expression for being out on the town for a drinking session.

Side Two opens with 'Gallows Pole', a reworking of the traditional English folk song 'The Maid Freed From the Gallows' (Page was a fan of Dorris Henderson's 1965 version, 'Hangman', and wanted to try his own arrangement). The tale of a condemned man pleading with the hangman to 'hold a while' so his friends and family can bargain with silver and gold (and carnal favors) to keep him from the 'gallows pole', Page's take imbues the song with much more menacing urgency. Page gives the folk tale some wonderful mandolin, an instrument he would use to great effect on *Led Zeppelin IV* ('Going to California', 'Battle of Evermore'). Plant adds banjo, but less effectively so.

The country-tinged 'Tangerine' started life as a potential Yardbirds song, 'Knowing That I'm Losing You', in 1968, but Page and singer Keith Relf never finished it before the band broke up. Robert Plant provided new lyrics after Page pulled it out of his repertoire during their Welsh holiday. Plant described the song as being 'about love in its most innocent stages,' later adding that the song was completely different to what the band was known for. Page added pedal steel guitar in the studio, with Plant's lyric ('I was her love, she was my queen / And now a thousand years in between …') elevating the chorus above the somber, minor key verses.

The melancholy 'That's the Way' was completed in Wales, sung with feeling by Plant and a wonderful acoustic feel rendered by Page in the recording studio. It even brought a tear to the glass eye of *Rolling Stone* critic Lester Bangs, who wrote of it: 'Son of a gun, it's beautiful. Above a very simple and appropriately everyday acoustic riff, Plant sings a touching picture of two youngsters who can no longer be playmates because one's parents and peers disapprove of the other ... the vocal is restrained for once.'

'Bron-Y-Aur Stomp' namechecks their Welsh quarters, where the song was written – even if it's spelt wrong (Bron-YR-Aur) on the final album. Starting as an acoustic jam, Page's open G# tuning makes the song stand out. Critics have commented on the song's similarity to Mississippi Fred McDowell's one-chord riff on 'Shake 'Em On Down' but Page takes this song to a whole new level – a psychedelic, acoustic stomp.

The final song of the album, 'Hats Off to Harper', is a tip of the hat to British folk singer Roy Harper's eclectic and often self-destructive career. Harper is perhaps best known today for singing on Pink Floyd's 'Have A Cigar' in 1975 but Jimmy Page first met the eccentric folkie at the Bath Festival in 1970. It was the start of a long collaboration between Harper and Page, the pair playing on each other's records and appearing at each other's shows. Harper would even open for Led Zep, introducing him to a much wider audience ... somewhere in the millions. The distorted reverb was achieved by playing the vocals and guitar through a vibrato amp and Page's frenetic slide guitar arrangement, which is credited on the sleeve to 'Charles Obscure'. Not so surprisingly, the song was never performed in public by the band.

Led Zeppelin moved to Island's No.2 Studio in Basing Street in Notting Hill Gate to finish the recordings. John Paul Jones' 'No Quarter' was also recorded there, but was not included on the finished album (it would also pop up on 1973's *Houses of the Holy*). With a US tour looming in the first week of August, Page was forced to mix the album in between tour dates, just as he had done with the first two albums. The album was completed in a series of sessions at

Ardent Studios, in Memphis, in time for an October release. There, Page had one last go at bettering his guitar solo on 'Since I've been Loving You', without success.

Jimmy Page conscripted graphic artist Zacron (born Richard Drew, 1943–2012) to design an innovative gatefold cover for their third album. Page had met the artist in 1963 when they were students together at Kingston College of Art (Eric Clapton was another classmate) and Zacron had decorated Page's guitars with experimental designs when he was playing with the Yardbirds. Zacron made his reputation making collage panels and graphic design effects he called 'Psychedelic Surrealism'. The pair decided on the concept of a die cut album cover with a rotating circular cardboard panel inside the vinyl sleeve that revealed various pop art images, including portraits of the band members; an interactive *Sgt. Pepper's* if you will.

According to Zacron's own website:

> Regardless of subject matter, each component [of the album cover] became a formal abstract element, interacting with all the images to make a unified whole. The work created a surrealist environment, changing relative concepts of scale and subject matter. The square format became a visual theater in which images could appear to move and have their own energy, some moved beyond the boundary.

Unfortunately, time was the enemy in the execution of the pop art masterpiece (this despite the fact that Zacron had first conceived the idea of a rotating disc underneath a pop art album cover as far back as 1965). Somewhat rushed to make the album pressing, many of the images on the internal wheel did not match up with the die cut circles, weakening the impact and novelty of the album cover. The collection of images was more random than surreal (butterflies?) with the odd zeppelin image thrown in for good effect. Page was unhappy with the end result, feeling that Zacron had 'disappeared with it' and had failed to nail the original concept. But it is unique to say the least, and the album cover is regularly cited as a premier example of album art at its most innovative.

The title lettering on *Led Zeppelin III* incorporated a bubble font popular of the period, while the back cover was dominated by four portraits of our heroes, with Plant's golden mane suitably colored. The internal gatefold is interesting, but static, while the only wording on the album is the list of songs and the following message: 'Credit must be given to BRON-Y-AUR (sic) a small derelict cottage in South Snowdonia for painting a somewhat forgotten picture of true completeness which acted as an incentive to some of these musical statements. August 1970.'

Jimmy Page worked with Terry Manning mixing the album in Memphis. The songs were simple and fresh, although the pair added a few production flourishes – the tape echo effect at the start of 'Immigrant Song', for example, and the distortion on 'Hats off to Harper'. The deliberate false start to 'Friends' was kept, along with the sound of the song winding down at the end and overlapping the slide guitar of 'Celebration Day' (and John Bonham's audible expletive at the beginning of the song). First pressings of the vinyl record included an inscription on the run-out groove of each side of the record: 'So Mote Be It' and 'Do What Thou Wilt', two quotes from occultist Aleister Crowley, of whom Page was a devotee. The inscriptions on the vinyl were not included on subsequent pressings, making the first run of *Led Zeppelin III* a collector's item.

Having helped in the production and mixing of the sound, Manning then assisted Page in determining the order of the songs and mastering of the album. 'It felt right for the album to have a rocky side and a folkie side,' Page reflected in 2011, 'and the rocky side clearly had to start with "Immigrant Song". With that hypnotic riff and Robert's bloodcurdling scream, I thought: "That's the way to open an album."'

After a meteoric rise for the band, *Led Zeppelin III* attracted the worst reviews of their career, and the album was largely considered a misfire at the time. Were they ripping off Crosby, Stills & Nash? *Melody Maker* asked. *Rolling Stone*'s erstwhile critic Lester Bangs damned it with faint praise:

> Much of the rest, after a couple of listenings to distinguish between songs, is not bad at all, because the disc Zeppelin are at least creative enough to apply an occasional pleasing fillip to their uninspiring material, and professional enough to keep all their recorded work relatively clean and clear – you can hear all the parts, which is more than you can say for many of their peers.

Years later Page and Plant would view the album as an important step in the band's development, 'our single most important achievement.' Modern reviews are just as glowing, with the BBC's Greg Moffett remarking in 2010:

> It's true that the bulk of the material doesn't favour rock, with even "Celebration Day" and "Out On the Tiles" lacking the sledgehammer weight of previous efforts, but this is no lightweight fluff. The slow blues of "Since I've Been Loving You" and the touching "That's

the Way" are other clear highlights which have earned their place on any genuine best-of collection. Elsewhere, the wistful folk rock of "Tangerine" and "Gallows Pole" – another Zep arrangement of a traditional folk song – bolster what is by any reckoning an underrated work.

Within two weeks of its release, *Led Zeppelin III* had reached No.1 in the US and would follow suit in the UK before Christmas. However, it was not a mega-seller and would quickly disappear from the charts in early 1971. 'Immigrant Song' was surprise choice for lead single in the US, the band not wishing to market themselves as singles artists. It reached No.16 just before Christmas 1970.

What to do next? 'Now we've done *Zeppelin III* the sky's the limit,' Robert Plant said in 1970, and he wasn't wrong. The following year, the band released arguably their career-defining album – *Led Zeppelin IV*, or the 'Runes' album as it became known – which for many is the starting point of fandom for the band. *Led Zeppelin IV* defies criticism and is almost the perfect album, although it tended to reinforce the basic problem that continued to hound the band even into the new millennium. Led Zeppelin was a different band on record than they were on stage, and their ability to consistently reproduce their albums live would be sorely tested for the remainder of the decade.

My older cousins caught the band when they toured in February 1972. They were somewhat disappointed by Plant's live vocal and his preference to sing under the melody rather than hit the high notes. The concert list was full of *Led Zeppelin III* songs, opening with 'Immigrant Song', reaching an early climax with 'Since I've Been Loving You' and an acoustic set including 'That's the Way',

'Tangerine' and even 'Bron-Yr-Aur Stomp', but also less than faithful versions of 'Black Dog' (tacked on to the end of 'Celebration Day'), a stop-start go at 'Rock and Roll' and a turgid rendering of 'Stairway to Heaven'.

As much as *Led Zeppelin IV* would be hailed as the band's masterpiece, there was the sneaking suspicion (brutally realized in the concert documentary *The Song Remains the Same* in 1976) that the record was over-produced and could not be played live. Zeppelin was effectively a three-piece band with vocalist, and the presence of Page's iconic double-necked Gibson guitar on stage may have allowed him to play rhythm and lead – but not at the same time. Page's ability as a producer, and his penchant for patching together the best bits from multiple takes and dub in seamless leads on his songs, would become a millstone around his neck.

Having conquered the world in the mid-1970s through constant touring of Europe and the US, Led Zeppelin were all but obsolete as a musical force by the time they released what would be their final album, *In Through the Out Door*, in 1979. Of all the 'supergroups' of the 1970s, Led Zep fared poorly in the wake of punk (the Who were adopted by the new generation, Neil Young tried tech music in the 1980s before Grunge discovered him, and Fleetwood Mac had gone all 'West Coast' and were already a parody of themselves). The death of drummer John Bonham in 1980, aged just 32, brought an end to a group that had already passed their peak. The original four members – Page, Plant, Jones and Bonham – could never play together again. The era was over.

Since the 2007 *Celebration Day* concert, Led Zeppelin has declined all offers to record or tour again because the weight of world expectations is just far too high. As successful as that one-off concert was, and Led Zep sounded great to me, having to produce that unique sound night after night is just too much for the original members, who are now in their 70s. Not even Led Zep can maintain the incredibly high standard they set on record.

And this is why *Led Zeppelin III* is such an underrated record; it's a true reflection of the band's musical sensibilities in the early 1970s – the 'heavy' and the 'light'– that helped open up the band's talents to a wider group of fans, including yours truly. As Kristopher Lenz noted in 2014 on the *Consequence of Sound* website:

> A new generation of fans may encounter this record and recognize some of the roots of rock and roll weirdness and experimentation that seem de rigueur today. While not the towering achievement of its brothers in numerology, *Led Zeppelin III* remains one of the great albums in rock and roll history, significant for its role in establishing the legend of Led Zeppelin that would become fact with *Led Zeppelin IV.*

Led Zeppelin III / **Led Zeppelin** (October 1970)   43:04

SIDE ONE   LENGTH
1.   Immigrant Song
      (Jimmy Page, Robert Plant)   2:26
2.   Friends
      (Jimmy Page, Robert Plant)   3:55
3.   Celebration Day
      (John Paul Jones, Page, Plant)   3:29
4.   Since I've Been Loving You
      (Jones, Page, Plant)   7:25
5.   Out On the Tiles
      (John Bonham, Page, Plant)   4:04

SIDE TWO
6.   Gallows Pole
      (Traditional, arr. Page, Plant)   4:58
7.   Tangerine (Page)   3:12
8.   That's the Way
      (Jimmy Page, Robert Plant)   5:38
9.   Bron-Y-Aur Stomp
      (Jones, Page, Plant)   4:20
10.   Hats Off to (Roy) Harper
      (Traditional, arr. Charles Obscure)   3:41

CHAPTER 4

All Things Must Pass

George Harrison 1970

'Watch out now, beware of the thoughts that linger ...'

I t is very hard to put into words the effect George Harrison's 'My Sweet Lord' had on people when it was released. The song cut right through to the audience, with a powerfully positive message, Harrison later remarked; adding not entirely facetiously that this one song was probably responsible for about half of the subsequent recruitment to the Hare Krishna movement. John Lennon, perhaps unhelpfully at the time, remarked to *Rolling Stone* editor Jann Wenner that the song was so omnipresent on radio that even he was starting to believe there was a God.

George Harrison recorded just 30 songs across 13 studio albums with the Beatles, from 'Don't Bother Me' on *With the Beatles* in 1963 to 'I Me Mine', recorded in January 1970 just as the band was disintegrating. Cast in the shadow of the 'the greatest songwriters since Schubert', the Lennon-McCartney songwriting juggernaut, George was often sidelined by the massive individual talents and egos of Lennon and McCartney in the selection of suitable songs for upcoming albums, his offerings relegated to the B-sides of singles and no more than one song on each side of an album.

But by 1969's *Abbey Road*, however, Harrison's two compositions were acknowledged by critics, the public and not least John Lennon, as the best songs on the album. 'Something' was George's first A-side single, and backed with Lennon's 'Come Together', topped the charts in the US (it was only No.4 in the UK; Shirley Bassey would match that with her 1970 cover of the song). Although 'Something' would garner some criticism for George's use of the line 'Something in the way she moves ...' (fellow Apple artist James Taylor had written a song with that exact same name), 'Here Comes the Sun' is acknowledged as one of the most original melodies in Harrison's music portfolio.

In May 1970, with the Beatles officially over as band, Harrison met with producer Phil Spector and a host of session players to produce not just his first commercial album (notwithstanding 1968's *Wonderwall*, an eclectic film soundtrack, and *Electronic Sound* in 1969), but a triple album. In stretching himself as far as he could go – and as thinly, it would transpire – Harrison was thrust to the very forefront of the post-Beatles breakup, with the 1970 album *All Things Must Pass* topping the charts around the world and spawning mega-hit single 'My Sweet Lord'.

In 1970, all four members of the Beatles released solo albums alongside the band's final offering, the almost posthumous *Let It Be*. In March, Ringo Starr offered a mawkish collection of pub songs on *Sentimental Journey*; in May, Paul McCartney released his under-produced, self-titled album and John Lennon released the comparatively non-commercial *Plastic Ono Band* in December, by which time Harrison's three-album tome had delivered his former bandmates a 'one-two-three' knockout punch. During the later part of the year, Harrison's mother Louise was battling a terminal illness in a Liverpool hospital and he was constantly visiting her in between recording sessions. That he was able to make such a strong musical statement during such a personally trying period speaks to both his passion for his music and his determination to get it out on record.

Phil Spector was perhaps a strange choice for Harrison to entrust with his first solo album. Spector was in London, 'looking for a gig' Harrison later remarked, after being assigned by then Beatles manager Allen Klein to produce the unreleased *Let It Be* tapes. The link between Spector and the Beatles goes back even further though. As fans of Spector's 'Wall of Sound' hits in the mid-1960s, the 'Fab Four' had invited Spector to travel with them on their 1965 Tour of America (Spector can be seen in photographs wearing his trademark sunglasses and talking to the band). Having apparently salvaged the *Let It Be* album (although the jury is still out on that one, with McCartney particularly unhappy with the addition of strings and choir voices on his song, 'The Long and Winding Road'), Lennon was keen to work with Spector again and tagged him as producer on his 'Instant Karma' single and his solo album that year.

Harrison became reacquainted with Spector when he attended the session for 'Instant Karma' and he revealed to Spector that he too was thinking of releasing his first solo album. Where Lennon opted for a stripped-down sound – piano, guitar, bass and drums – Harrison's album got the full 'Wall of Sound' treatment from Spector, a decision that would both elevate and severely date the album in the years ahead.

In light of the Beatles' recent demise, Harrison's selection of *All Things Must Pass* as the title of his solo album (Billy Preston actually released a version of the song on his album *Encouraging Worlds* before George), took on an even deeper context. Most fans thought the title referred to the end of the Beatles, although George clearly had his sights on more spiritual matters.

Harrison demoed his songs for Spector at his newly acquired home, Friar's Park, in Henley-on-Thames, in May 1970. There were so many songs (Spector later remarked that there were 'hundreds of them ... each one better than next') that after recording 18 tracks and various jam sessions at Abbey Road, Trident Studios and the newly constructed studios at Apple headquarters, the concept quickly expanded from single album to double album, and finally, a three-album box set including a 'jam' from the stellar cast of players used on the record.

The impetus and enthusiasm for his solo project came after Harrison's sojourn to Woodstock, New York, following the volatile 'White Album' sessions in November 1968. Harrison was hoping to work with Bob Dylan, who was also there at the time in semi-retirement following his injury in a motorcycle accident. Harrison mixed with members of the Band, who had just released their breakthrough album *Music from Big Pink*, but it took some time for Harrison to ingratiate himself inside Dylan's inner world – the song 'I'd Have You Anytime' is a paean to Dylan ('Let me in here ...') and the pair actually wrote the song together (take that Lennon-McCartney!). Another composition, 'Behind That Locked Door', can be viewed as a request to Dylan to open up to him, while Harrison would also cover Dylan's 'If Not For You' (which was released on Dylan's *New Morning* album in August 1970) on his own solo album.

Before the recording of the backing tracks started at the end of May at Abbey Road, Harrison and Spector collected an eclectic group of musicians, central to which was Eric Clapton, who would feature on most of the tracks. Because of contract restrictions, however, Harrison could only credit Clapton on the jam record, although his unmistakeable guitar work is evident on numerous tracks: the opening lead of the album, on 'I'd Have You Anytime', the lead on 'Wah-Wah', and the searing licks on 'Art of Dying'.

During that time Harrison, and Clapton in particular, had become enamoured by the American band Delaney & Bonnie (and Friends). Harrison had signed them to an Apple recording contract and Clapton had brought them to England as the opening act of his short-lived supergroup Blind Faith. A loose band of musicians and singers supporting husband and wife team Delaney and Bonnie Bramlett, the band had a minor hit with 'Never Ending Song of Love' in 1971, but it was their live performances featuring the talents of transient band members Leon Russell, Carl Radle, Bobby Whitlock, Bobby Keys, Jim Price, Rita Coolidge, Jim Keltner, Jim Gordon and the Allman Brothers, Duane and Gregg, that added to their growing legend.

Harrison and Clapton were joined by Radle (bass), Whitlock (keyboards) and Gordon (drums) on the *All Things Must Pass* sessions, with Clapton being so impressed with the players as a core unit that Blind Faith quickly became a thing of the past and a new band, Derek and the Dominos, was born. Horns specialists Bob Keys and Jim Price also featured prominently on Harrison's album, along with usual cohorts Ringo Starr, Klaus Voormann and Billy Preston, as well as Gary Wright (Spooky Tooth), Alan White (soon to join Yes), Gary Brooker (Procol Harum), Dave Mason (Traffic) and the entire rhythm section of Badfinger (Pete Ham, Tom Evans and Joey Molland).

Following the plaintive 'I'd Have You Anytime', which opens the album, three acoustic chords – Em, A and D – at the beginning of

'My Sweet Lord' announce to the world that George Harrison had indeed arrived as a solo artist. Spector recorded at least five players to get the right sound of that acoustic guitar burst – Harrison, Clapton, Ham, Evans and Molland – with Harrison's iconic slide guitar dubbed in. Harrison's newfound spiritual awakening was an obvious influence in the writing of the lyrics (and, it would later appear, the Phil Spector produced hit 'He's So Fine' was an influence on the chord structure and melody) but a not so obvious production influence was the Edwin Hawkin Singers, who had a world-wide hit in 1969 with 'Oh Happy Day'. This was the gospel feel Harrison was going for, and it is one of the few times on the album where Spector's production does not drown out the melody, perhaps unfortunately so. Instead of a choir, however, Harrison multi-tracked his own vocal and credited the chorus to the George O'Hara-Smith Singers.

'Wah-Wah', with its wonderful guitar lead from Clapton, is the third track of the album. The song was allegedly written in response to Paul McCartney's badgering of Harrison during the *Let It Be* sessions ('Wah-wah, you made me such a big star ...'). Spector gradually builds the song with guitar, drums and piano overdubs so that, by the time Harrison wails in with the opening line ('Wah-wah, you've given me a wah-wah ...') there is a whole avalanche of sound. Highlighted by Garry Wright's honky tonk piano, Jim Price's horn arrangement and Harrison and Clapton's guitar, the song is a powerhouse of simplicity. Ringo Starr is the only drummer credited on the track but one of the highlights of the *Concert for Bangladesh* documentary, in which 'Wah-Wah' opens the show, is Starr and Jim Keltner double-tracking the drumming in perfect unison to fill out the live sound.

The final track on Side One, 'Isn't it a Pity', dates back to at least 1966. Harrison wasn't happy with the longer, slower version that almost disappears in reverb over its seven-plus minutes, and so recorded it again with a slightly faster tempo at a shortened 4:45. Interestingly, Harrison includes both versions on the final album (shades of 1968's 'Revolution'?), burying the shorter take on Side Four. Is it just me or does the track also have a passing similarity to the chorus of Donovan's 1969 hit, 'Atlantis', in the opening chords and again on the chorus?

Side Two opens with the majestic 'What is Life', which also became the second single lifted off the album in some territories. Originally earmarked for Billy Preston's solo album, Harrison worked with Spector to flesh out a structurally simplistic song (similar to 'If Not For You'), adding the distinctive fuzz tone guitar opening. John Barham's string arrangement and Harrison's multi-tracked harmonies make the song an exuberant celebration of life. The song was quickly covered by Olivia Newton-John (who also mined 'If Not For You' from the album) and features prominently in Martin Scorsese's gangster flick *Goodfellas* (1990).

Following the aforementioned 'If Not For You', a straightforward cover of Dylan's song, 'Behind That Locked Door' is a rare country-themed waltz with the addition of pedal steel guitar from Nashville's Pete Drake. Another reach-out to a remote Bob Dylan, Harrison had supported Dylan upon his return to the stage, venturing to the Isle of Wight in 1969 with George and Ringo and their partners to watch him in concert, and again in New York the following May. Featuring Harrison's characteristic chord changes, 'Let it Down' is a long way from its acoustic origins, with some lovely slide guitar topped off with a raucous chorus. 'Run of the Mill' could easily be dismissed as a minor album track except that Harrison regarded it one of his favorite songs on the album. A pretty melody, if not slightly over-wrought, Harrison laments the factitious nature of relationships, most likely inside the Beatles bubble ('Tomorrow when you rise / Another day for you to realize me / Or send me down again …').

Side Three is arguably the strongest, opening as it does with 'Beware of Darkness'. On *The Concert for George* documentary, Eric Clapton says that George could take a weird chord and build a song around it, and he does this perfectly on the unique, non-pop song. Lyrically, Harrison explores familiar themes about the dangers of materialism ('Taxman', 'Within You Without You' and 'Living in the Material World'), utilizing some wry cynicism ('falling swingers', 'soft shoe shufflers' and 'greedy leaders') and building up into a rousing chorus on the back of some of his best slide guitar work. Leon Russell so liked the song when he heard the players rehearse it in the studio that he too recorded the song for his 1971 solo album, *Shelter*.

'Apple Scruffs' has a nice acoustic feel to it, with Dylan-inspired harmonica no less, and would not have been out of place on *Abbey Road*, if George could have squeezed it in there. The song was written in tribute to the fans who waited patiently outside the Apple offices in Saville Row in hope of a glimpse of their heroes ('Apple scruffs … how I love you'). The song is a surprisingly affectionate ode, given Harrison's open contempt for many of the trappings of Beatlemania, with Harrison playing all the instruments on the track, including harmonica.

'The Ballad of Sir Frankie Crisp (Let it Roll)' is one my favorite songs on the album. Similar in theme and style to 'Long Long Long' on The White Album (not so surprisingly, the tune dates back to 1968), the song is helped along by one of Harrison's better vocal performances and Pete Drake's pedal steel guitar. Gary Brooker's piano also features prominently in a song written about Friar Park founder, London lawyer and eccentric Sir Frank Crisp (1843–1919). The music was previously attached to a song Harrison called 'Everybody, Nobody' but was reworked to take the listener on a guided tour of his sprawling 33-acre property, Friar's Park.

'Awaiting on You All' is a gentle dig at the politics of organized religions with a burst of Harrison's dry humor ('You don't need no love in / You don't need no bed pan / You don't need a horoscope or a microscope to see the mess that you're in …'). The reverb is almost at breaking point on this song, and I much preferred the demo version included in the 30th Anniversary CD issue, which features a battery of descending chords (B, E♭m, B, A♭m, F#, E, E♭m, C#m, B) on the intro and, on which, all the words can be heard, especially in the outro ('And while the Pope owns 51% of General Motors / And the stock exchange is the only thing he's qualified to quote us …').

Side Three concludes with the title track 'All Things Must Pass'. A reflection on the transitory nature of life (also love, fame and material possessions), the song was written during Harrison's stay at Woodstock in 1968 and, as such, has a lilting country rock feel to it. Having failed to get the song past the Lennon-McCartney road block during the 'Get Back' session in January 1970, Harrison demoed the song on 25 February, his 26th birthday, at Abbey Road studios (a version was later included on the Beatles' *Anthology 3* album). Spector's 'wall of sound' is thankfully subdued on this track, although his important contribution was the addition of horns at the beginning of the song.

Side Four is the weakest on the album, not counting the 'Apple Jam' record that Harrison included as a bonus for fans. 'I Dig Love' is built around a single piano riff, and is not unlike Henry Mancini's 'Pink Panther' theme, with a boogie chorus tacked on. 'Art of Dying' is a cacophony of noise more suited to a James Bond theme, and thematically sounds a lot like Harrison's work on the *Yellow Submarine* soundtrack. Clapton's lead guitar is its one distinguishing feature although a teenage Phil Collins, soon of Genesis fame, is buried in the mix somewhere playing congas!

After 'Isn't it a Pity (Version 2)' Harrison finishes with 'Hear Me Lord', a somewhat self-indulgent reward for those fans who had gone the whole distance.

George decided that he needed a 16-track recording studio to complete the final album, which Abbey Road and Apple didn't have, so he moved to Trident Studios in London and oversaw the conversion of the master tapes from 8-track to 16. Although George was later critical of Spector's production, he took over much of the mixing of the album after Spector fell over and broke his arm (while drunk) and so responsibility for some of the 'dull' sound can be solely attributed to Harrison. John Barham's orchestrations were also added at this stage, with the final sequencing of the songs completed in New York in October.

Sessions had continued from May to October, with Capitol in the US unimpressed by missing their September, and then October, release dates. 'The accountant from Apple came down stairs one day while we were mixing the album at Apple Studios and asked when it was all going to end,' Harrison later recalled, and having recorded 18 songs he realized then they probably had enough for a double album. The addition of the jam sessions made it the first triple album by a solo artist (the Woodstock soundtrack had been released earlier that year but that was a compilation of different artists).

The 'Apple Jam' bonus album constitutes just under 30 minutes of music. Other than a vehicle for its star players, the only other historic issue of note on this disc is the inclusion of 'It's Johnny's Birthday' on Side Five. Yoko Ono had requested a recording to mark John Lennon's 30th birthday on October 9 and, having looked in the Abbey Road library for inspiration, Harrison produced this quick knock-off based on Cliff Richard's 1968 hit 'Congratulations'. The original album made no mention of this but a quick claim by songwriters Bill Martin and Phil Coulter rectified the problem and the pair were credited alongside Harrison on future pressings.

Grammy Award winning artist Tom Wilkes from Camouflage Productions was given the task of designing the album art and came up with the concept of a triple panel that folded in on itself and sat inside a box (something usually associated with classical music collections). The three record albums would be inserted in the top of each panel. Two of the panels would have the full lyric sheets, while a third displayed a pop art image of an 'Apple Jam' jar. Wilkes' initial idea of including a surreal painting of Harrison 'floating in the sky' inside a castle was replaced with a ghostly photo of a bearded Harrison standing in front of a window panel in a darkened hallway of his Friar's Park home.

For the cover art, George Harrison was photographed at Friar's Park by Barry Feinstein, who had taken equally evocative images of the Beatles, Bob Dylan, Janis Joplin and the Doors during his career. Harrison is pictured in a wonderful black-and-white image, wearing his gardening attire, sitting on a stool on the foggy lawns of Friar Park. Either by design or coincidence, Feinstein positioned four garden gnomes around the seated Harrison, with most fans seeing these as a direct reference to the demise of the

Beatles. Such symbolism may have appealed to Harrison's quirky sensibilities, but John Lennon was said to have been particularly peeved by the insult.

The original cost of *All Things Must Past* was a conservative £5.50, or US$12, at a time when most albums were discounted to under five dollars. Some critics pointed out the irony of the non-materialistic Harrison charging 'five quid' for an album – and at Christmas, no less – but the fear that *All Things Must Pass* would sink under its own massive weight proved unfounded when it went straight to No.1 on both sides of the Atlantic. Within a month, the album had gone platinum and it would eventually sell 6 million copies in the US alone – more than Lennon's *Imagine* and McCartney's *Ram*, both released in 1971, added together.

Harrison originally didn't want to release a single from the album, in line with his Beatles days, but bowed to label pressure, who rightly identified 'My Sweet Lord' as the standout track. He originally declined having the single released in his home territory of the UK (Billy Preston, who had input in the original construction of the song, namely the 'hallelujah' responses in the verses, released his version of 'My Sweet Lord' in Europe that September and the UK in December) but the former Beatle relented to public demand the following January. The song was a mega-hit around the world; the first solo Beatles No.1 and the biggest selling single in the UK in 1971.

With the release of *All Things Must Pass* it was if George Harrison had been released from his artistic shackles and reviews for the album were varied, with Ron Carr and Tony Tyler particularly criticizing the homogeneity of the production and the lugubrious, melancholy nature of Harrison's songs. *Rolling Stone*'s Ben Gerson called the album, 'Both an intensely personal statement and a grandiose gesture, a triumph over artistic modesty.' *Billboard* magazine called it 'a masterful blend of rock and piety, technical brilliance and mystic mood, and relief from the tedium of everyday rock'.

The sneaking suspicion that there was a great single album in there somewhere was not unfounded, with Sides One and Three being the standout moments (throw in 'What Is Life' on Side Two). Given subsequent events, Harrison may have been better off warehousing some of the songs from these sessions and keeping them for his next record. When John Lennon was pressed by the media about George's success he remarked wryly, 'Ah yes, but he has to back it up.'

George's immediate response to his worldwide hit was to organize a charity concert in support of the Bangladesh emergency appeal. As outlined in the song 'Bangladesh', Harrison's friend Ravi Shankar came to him to ask for help after a civil war, a flood and famine hit the inhabitants of Shankar's homeland (formerly West Pakistan). With the assistance of Allen Klein, Harrison organized two benefit concerts for 1 August, 1971 at Madison Square Garden. Both concerts would be filmed and recorded, with all proceeds from the resulting documentary and live album going to the Bangladesh appeal.

Harrison was supported on stage by many of the people who had worked on *All Things Must Pass* (Starr, Clapton, Preston, Voormann, Radle, Badfinger) as well as opening act Ravi Shankar, musical director Leon Russell (*Mad Dogs and Englishman*), guitarist Jessie Ed Davis, the Hollywood Horns and a choir under the direction of Don Nix. Casting a giant shadow over the whole enterprise, however, was the performance of Bob Dylan, with Harrison unsure whether the reclusive Dylan would even show up. Pressed to lend his considerable weight to the concerts, Harrison implored Dylan to play his hits rather than his 'new stuff' (Dylan facetiously asked Harrison if he was going to play 'I Want to Hold Your Hand'). Dylan duly showed, much to the surprise of the crowd and most of the performers on stage.

Of equal concern was whether Eric Clapton would show up, as his signature guitar sound was central to the success of the songs from the album. Clapton was in bad shape, battling drug addiction and alcoholism and nursing a broken heart for Harrison's wife, Patty Boyd, and it was uncertain whether he would use the plane ticket Harrison left in his name back in England. Clapton did in fact show, but was given an unfamiliar guitar to play and his presence on stage lacked the required punch the music needed.

Contractual issues that were always in the background regarding the rights of so many players to perform on *All Things Must Pass* later ground the *Concert for Bangladesh* documentary and live album to a halt. The album was released in December 1971 in the US, and January 1972 in the UK, but the Saul Swimmer-directed documentary was not released until March. The following August, I caught the film; a full year after the concerts were held. Many of the tracks from *All Things Must Pass* featured prominently – 'Wah-Wah', 'My Sweet Lord', 'Awaiting on You All' and 'Beware of Darkness' ('Hear Me Lord' was performed but not included in either record or film) – as well as several of Harrison's Beatles hits ('Something', 'Here Comes the Sun' and 'While My Guitar Gently Weeps'). For me, it was well worth the wait.

The Concert for Bangladesh was not only an historic moment for rock, setting the stage as it did for the Live Aid Concert in 1985, but it also confirmed the greatness of Harrison's work on *All Things*

Must Pass. Unfortunately, that record also represented the high water mark of Harrison's solo career, with each subsequent record representing a downturn in his musical fortunes. It was not until May 1973 that he was able to release his second solo album, *Living in the Material World.*

At the same time, Harrison was fighting a legal battle from the copyright owners of 'He's So Fine', the 1965 hit by the Chiffons that had originally been produced by none other than Phil Spector. As early as December 1970, Ben Gerson of *Rolling Stone* observed that Harrison had appeared to substitute the 'doo-lang, doo-lang, doo-lang' the Chiffons utilized on 'He's So Fine' with the 'Hare Krishna' responses on the chorus of 'My Sweet Lord'.

In February 1971 Bright Tunes Music, the publisher of 'He's So Fine', sued Harrison on behalf of the song's writer, Ronnie Mack, who had died in 1963, shortly after the Chiffons' tune became a No.1 hit in the States. A musicologist found the songs were similar in title (both had three syllables), tempo and two key phrases, called 'A' and 'B' during the court case. In the 'A' phrase, both song titles 'My sweet Lord' and 'He's so fine' which opened the respective songs, had a similar descending note progression. The 'B' phrase related to 'I really want to see you' and 'I dunno how I'm gonna do it' sections of both songs. During the court process, Harrison (and Lennon and Starr) severed managerial ties with Klein, who still went ahead with the purchase of Bright Tunes Music.

On 31 August 1976, Judge Richard Owen of the United States District Court found Harrison guilty of 'subconscious plagiarism' of Mack's song. 'It is clear that "My Sweet Lord" is the very same song as "He's So Fine" with different words,' Judge Owen found, 'and Harrison had access to "He's So Fine" (through Spector).' The penalty phase was delayed until February 1981 but Harrison was initially ordered to pay $1.6m (this was lowered to $600,000 when his former manager Allen Klein purchased Bright Tunes Music and negotiated the sale of the song to Harrison). Litigation continued until March 1998 before Klein and Harrison could come to an agreement. Because Klein had acted for Harrison at the beginning of proceedings, Harrison wryly observed that he was effectively 'suing himself' after Klein bought Bright Tunes Music and deliberately prolonged the court case.

George's 1976 album *Thirty Three & 1/3* was a return to form, with a not so subtle dig at his legal battles in the humorous 'This Song' (and accompanying film clip) and the whimsical 'Crackerbox Palace'. It would be another decade, however, before he was hot again, with 1987's *Cloud Nine*, his first collaboration with former ELO frontman Jeff Lynne. Harrison's work with the Traveling Wilburys quickly followed, and with his reconnection with Bob Dylan and Roy Orbison (with whom he had toured in 1963 with the Beatles) his career had come full circle. Harrison was back on top, not that he ever wanted to be.

In the 1990s, Harrison once again retreated from the spotlight, although he reconnected with his former Beatles bandmates to complete the *Anthology* documentary and record two new songs that were originally John Lennon demos ('Free as a Bird' and 'Real Love'). That experience should have taught him that it's hard to 'reheat a souffle', as breathing new life into the Beatles' past was once so eloquently stated. Harrison concentrated on his gardening, spent some time at his Hamilton Island hideaway, followed Formula 1 and was, for a time, content to leave his past behind. Having survived a bout with throat cancer in the early 1990s, and a vicious attack from an intruder at his Friar's Park home in the final days of 1999, perhaps his priorities changed.

In 2000, to mark the 30th Anniversary of *All Things Must Pass*, Harrison remixed the original album to rid production of the dreaded reverb, and even recorded a new version of 'My Sweet Lord' with a different melody line that skirted around the problematic 'A' and 'B' phrases on the original. Harrison added a new intro on slide guitar, acoustic guitar played by his son Dhani, along with Ray Cooper on percussion and Sam Brown on backing vocals, but the vocal is weak and the magic of the song is not just there. An outtake of a song called 'I Live for You' was included, as well as several other alternate demos. He also decided to have 'a bit of fun' with the album cover, sourcing the original album artwork from Barry Feinstein and colorizing the black-and-white cover photograph for the rerelease. Not being able to help himself, he changed the idyllic surrounds to add buildings and freeways to reflect the way he felt the planet was going.

Why did George Harrison tinker with the album? Regret perhaps; a perfectionist's desire to fix the past or an artist's prerogative to have another go at getting the music just right. 'I still like the songs on the album,' he wrote on the *All Things Must Pass* reissue box set, 'and believe they can continue to outlive the style in which they were recorded. It was difficult to resist re-mixing every track. All these years later I would like to liberate some of the songs from the big production that seemed appropriate at the time, but now seem a bit over the top with the reverb in the wall of sound.'

Within the year Harrison would be dead, succumbing to cancer in December 2001, aged just 58.

All Things Must Pass / **George Harrison** (November 1970)   105:59

All tracks written by George Harrison, except where noted*

SIDE ONE	LENGTH
I'd Have You Anytime (Harrison, Bob Dylan*)	2:56
My Sweet Lord	4:38
Wah-Wah	5:35
Isn't It a Pity (Version One)	7:10

SIDE TWO	
What Is Life	4:22
If Not for You (Dylan*)	3:29
Behind That Locked Door	3:05
Let it Down	4:57
Run of the Mill	2:49

SIDE THREE	
Beware of Darkness	3:48
Apple Scruffs	3:04
Ballad of Sir Frankie Crisp (Let It Roll)	3:48
Awaiting on You All	2:45
All Things Must Pass	3:44

SIDE FOUR	
I Dig Love	4:55
Art of Dying	3:37
Isn't It a Pity (Version Two)	4:45
Hear Me Lord	5:46

SIDE FIVE (*APPLE JAM*)	
Out of the Blue	11:14
It's Johnny's Birthday (Bill Martin, Phil Coulter, Harrison*)	0:49
Plug Me In	3:18

SIDE SIX (*APPLE JAM*)	
I Remember Jeep	8:07
Thanks for the Pepperoni	5:31

N.SMITH
GB.
GEORGE HARRISON
ALL THINGS MUST PASS
GOODBYE YELLOW BRICK ROAD
ELTON JOHN
Co-ordinated by STEVE BROWN

CHAPTER 5

L.A. Woman

Doors 1971

'Well, I've been down so very damn long / That it looks like up to me ...'

'Jim Morrison: he's hot, he's sexy and he's dead.' So heralded *Rolling Stone*'s controversial 1981 front cover to mark the tenth anniversary of the death of the enigmatic lead singer of the Doors. *Rolling Stone* was merely stating the bleeding obvious, of course. Morrison died in Paris in June 1971; and by the time I discovered *L.A. Woman* – the final record released by the original members and arguably their best – the album's lead singer was already dead. The band lasted just five short years, after forming in Los Angeles' famous Venice Beach, and yet, more than half a century later, the Doors still matter.

The Doors were never meant to be a mainstream band that achieved pop success. Starting out as a blues band before becoming pioneers of psychedelic or 'acid rock', the Doors were FM radio underground favorites on the west coast of the US. Their monster 1967 hit 'Light My Fire' introduced them to a worldwide audience. For many people, however, it was Jose Feliciano's 1968 cover of the song that introduced the Doors to that audience. I can still remember my father walking around our house, humming the insidious tune and asking no one in particular, 'light my fire?'

The Doors were dangerous, and Morrison was a troubled genius. One of the most compelling live acts of the era – theatrical, hard-rocking, uncompromising and unpredictable – no other band sounded like the Doors in the 1960s. The mixture of Ray Manzarek's Hammond organ, Robbie Krieger's blues guitar, John Densmore's jazz-influenced drumming and Jim Morrison's unmistakable baritone is why so many filmmakers – Francis Ford Coppola (*Apocalypse Now*, 1979) Oliver Stone (*Platoon*, 1986), Brian De Palma (*Casualties of War*, 1989) and Robert Zemeckis (*Forrest Gump*, 1994) – used the band's music as a soundtrack for their movies, especially Vietnam War movies. The Doors were unique in that they had that incredible capacity to define the times in which they lived with their music.

After their self-titled debut album in 1967, the Doors had left their underground status to delve into jazz, pop and even baroque-rock in ensuing albums *Strange Days* (1967), *Waiting for the Sun* (1968) and *The Soft Parade* (1969). *Morrison Hotel* (1970) saw them head back to their blues roots, a direction that was fully realized with the release of *L.A. Woman* in 1971. In the interim their label Elektra released *13*, the Doors' first compilation album, in November 1970, without any consultation with the band. Released for the Christmas market, it peaked at No.25 for two weeks in January and was off the charts by May. The album has never been issued on CD because, while it was the only compilation released before Morrison's death, it does not include any songs from *L.A. Woman*. That's how important that album is in the Doors' story.

'Our last record turned out like our first album: raw and simple,' drummer John Densmore reflected in his autobiography, *Riders on the Storm: My Life with Jim Morrison and the Doors*. 'It was as if we had come full circle. Once again we were a garage band, which is where rock and roll started.'

When the Doors started rehearsing the tracks that would end up on *L.A. Woman* the band was under enormous pressure. In 1969, Morrison had been charged with indecent exposure and 'public profanity' at a concert in Miami. In an attempt to incite a response from the audience, a usual Morrison ploy on stage, the lead singer asked, among other things, 'you wanna see my cock?' Although drummer John Densmore denied that Morrison exposed himself (it was just an invitation) on 20 September 1970, Morrison was found guilty over the Miami incident. He was sentenced to six months jail and fined $500. Morrison remained free on $50,000 bail while he lodged an appeal.

According to his bandmates, Morrison was not in good physical or mental shape at that time. Already an alcoholic, he had put on a lot of weight over the past year and was content to hide his pop-star features under unwashed hair and a large bushy beard. Morrison was tired of the rock-star lifestyle and was looking forward to getting away from LA. With the Doors coming to the end of their contract with Elektra, Morrison and girlfriend Pam Courson planned to go to Paris and write poetry. *L.A. Woman* would be his farewell to the 'city of nights'.

In November 1970, the Doors entered Sunset Sound Recorders in Los Angeles to demo early versions of 'L.A. Woman', 'Riders on the Storm', and 'Love Her Madly'. Long-time producer Paul A. Rothchild left the sessions abruptly after being critical of their new material, namely 'Love Her Madly', which he labeled 'cocktail jazz'. Rothchild later admitted that he was trying to shame the band into writing better material; despite three working songwriters in the band they just didn't have enough material for a new album. Rothchild was still in shock over the recent death of Janis Joplin, whose breakthrough second album, *Pearl* (1970) he had produced, and he was in no frame of mind to put up with Morrison's unreliability. He recommended that the Doors co-produce the new album with sound engineer Bruce Botnick, who had worked on the band's previous albums, because he felt they would probably do a much better job than he would anyway.

Botnick organized for the band to record in a makeshift studio at the Doors' Workshop, their private rehearsal space in a two-story building on Santa Monica Boulevard. It was a place where the band could chill out and relax. A mixing console was installed upstairs, while studio monitors, microphones and keyboards were set up downstairs. Morrison recorded his vocals in the bathroom doorway in lieu of an isolated vocal booth (he even used his favorite gold Electrovoice 676-G stage mic). Sessions were laid back and comfortable, incorporating improvised jams and tracks recorded live with minimal overdubs.

The Doors, of course, did not have a bassist (Ray Manzarek used the bass pedal on his organ to lock in with Densmore on drums). On previous Doors recordings, bass parts were often dubbed in after the backing track was nailed but, for *L.A. Woman,* the band wanted to record each song live. Elvis Presley's bassist, Jerry Scheff, and rhythm guitarist Marc Benno were hired to fill out the sound. Scheff worked well with Densmore on drums and slowed Ray Manzarek down on organ (even Morrison was impressed that Scheff had worked with 'The King', whom he regarded as kindred spirit). Scheff played on all songs except 'L'America'. Benno had worked with Leon Russell on two highly regarded albums, as the Asylum Choir in 1968 and 1970.

He supplied rhythm guitar for four tracks, 'L.A. Woman', 'Been Down So Long', 'Cars Hiss By My Window' and 'Crawling King Snake'.

Towards the end of the year, the Miami controversy had died down enough that the band was getting calls to do concert tours again. The Doors had lost close to a million dollars through canceled gigs in 1970 and were keen to get back on stage and play some of their new material. On 11 December, the Doors performed two sold-out concerts at the State Fair Music Hall in Dallas. The band opened the first concert with an extended version of 'Love Her Madly' but struggled with the older material as they had not played live since the Isle of Wight Festival the previous August. The set included 'The Changeling' and 'L.A. Woman' and closed with 'When the Music's Over', and recordings from the Doors' performances are included on the 2003 album *Boot Yer Butt: The Doors Bootlegs*. The Doors only performed 'L.A. Woman' live once, at their penultimate concert in Dallas.

On 12 December 1970 the Doors played the Warehouse in New Orleans for what turned out to be their last live performance with Morrison. Midway through the set, Morrison began slurring the lyrics to 'Light My Fire', sat in front of the drum platform in between Krieger and Manzarek's solos and did not stand up to finish the song. 'Jim wasn't even drunk,' Densmore says in his autobiography, 'but his energy was fading.' After prompting by his drummer, Morrison tried to continue, but after telling an off-color joke he finished the song by bashing the mic stand into the stage. It was a less than fitting finale for the band, although they didn't know it at the time.

L.A. Woman was recorded in less than a week – over just six days in December 1970 and January 1971 – with all songs completed in minimal takes on a portable 8-track recorder. According to band members, Morrison responded well to the informal surrounds and showed up on time and sober (he would, however, get drunk on Sundays and invariably crash his car). 'Crawling King Snake', 'Cars Hiss By My Window', and 'L.A. Woman' were even recorded on the same day, which Morrison dubbed 'Blues Day'. Mixing was completed at Poppy Studios between February and March 1971, by which time Morrison had already left for Paris.

Some of the songs the Doors recorded for the album were written well before 1971, specifically 'L'America', 'Crawling King Snake', and 'The WASP (Texas Radio and the Big Beat)'. Others were workshopped in the studio. Manzarek recalled they did not 'approach the album with one vision, but after we started working on the songs, we realized that they're talking about L.A. They're about men, women, boys, girls, love, loss, lovers-lost, and lovers-found in Los Angeles.'

L.A. Woman opens with 'The Changeling', based on a lyric written in 1968 in one of Morrison's notebooks. Author James Riordan noted the song may be another reference to Morrison's difficult childhood – a 'changeling' was traditionally believed to have been secretly substituted by fairies for the parents' real child in infancy. Morrison had a troubled relationship with his parents (when he sang 'The End' on stage he would improvise: 'Father, I want to kill you ...; mother I want to ...' well, you know the rest) and rebelled against his authoritarian career navy father, who disapproved of his career choices.

But the real meaning of the song might be something much simpler. Towards the end of his life when Morrison looked in the mirror, even he lamented that he would never look like the lithe rock-god figure of his 1967 'Young Lion' photoshoot with New York photographer Joel Brodsky. 'See me change ...' he sings. Morrison wasn't the same person any more.

Robby Krieger wrote 'Love Her Madly' about his future wife Lynne after one of their arguments ('Don't ya love her as she's walkin' out the door / Like she did one thousand times before ...'). The more commercial of the band's songwriters (Krieger also wrote the band's breakthrough hit 'Light My Fire' as well as 'Touch Me', the Doors' previous Top 40 hit released at the end of 1968), the song lacks Morrison's poetry but does possess a cool, detached lyric ('Don't you love her madly? / Wanna be her daddy?'). The title is a reference by jazz-fan Krieger to band leader Duke Ellington, who famously ended his concerts with the words, 'Love you madly.' Manzarek plays tack piano on the track.

'Been Down So Long' is a whiskey-soaked blues song inspired by the title of Richard Fariña's book *Been Down So Long It Looks Like Up to Me* and the Furry Lewis song, 'I Will Turn Your Money Green'. Folk singer Fariña was killed in a motorcycle accident in 1966 two days after his book was published, but Morrison borrows the title to describe his own mental state at the end of 1970, having battled alcoholism, been found guilty of public obscenity and now contemplating his future with the band.

'Cars Hiss By My Window' is the slightest of blues songs, and was composed in the studio. Manzarek recalled: 'Jim said it was about living in Venice [Beach], in a hot room, with a hot girlfriend, and an open window, and a bad time.' This would have been in 1965, when Morrison graduated from the University of California with a bachelor's degree from the UCLA film school. It was here that Morrison met fellow student Manzarek and the pair decided to form a band together to play and record the songs Morrison had already fully formed in his head, 'Moonlight Drive', 'Hello, I Love You' and 'Crystal Ship'. John Densmore and Robby Krieger completed the Doors, the name taken from the title of Aldous Huxley's book, *The Doors of Perception*.

'L.A. Woman' closes the first side of the record and is the longest song on the album. The title track paints a vibrant allegory of the period – Los Angles as a woman. What sort of woman would 'LA' be? Taking a cue from the song, LA is suburban, seductive, young, lonely, lost, sad. Morrison references many of the city's features: 'cops in cars, topless bars …', freeways and midnight alleys, hills on fire and freeway driving. One of the most intriguing lines in the song is 'motel money murder madness…' In one short line, he writes an entire movie script.

The highlight of the song is the deliberate slowdown of tempo by drummer John Densmore at the bridge, where Morrison introduces his anagram alter ego 'Mr Mojo Risin''. Densmore later remarked that before the widespread use of the dreaded 'click track' to keep drummers on the beat, he not only had to gradually slow down and then speed up the beat, but also finish the song at the same speed that he had started it. Morrison allegedly believed he would be reincarnated as Mr Mojo Risin', mojo being a well-known jazz term for 'magic charm' or a musician's 'personal magnetism or charisma'. More broadly, many people saw it as an extension of Morrison's sexuality; a pet name, if you will, for his masculine piece!

'L'America', which opens Side Two, was originally recorded in 1969 for the soundtrack of director Michelangelo Antonioni's film *Zabriskie Point* (1970). 'We played it for him, and it was so loud, it pinned him up against the wall,' Manzarek recalled in 2011.

'When it was over, he thanked us and fled.' Not surprisingly, the song did not make the final cut of the film, although Densmore wryly observed, 'it summarized his entire movie. No need to shoot the film!' Morrison said the apostrophe after the 'L' stood for 'Latin America, or Central America or Mexico, for that matter. Anywhere south of the border.' The only work done on the song during the *L.A. Woman* sessions were drum overdubs. The song has a haunting quality about it but takes a right turn into music hall in the middle.

'Hyacinth House' showcases the influence of Polish composer Frédéric Chopin's 'Polonaise in A-flat major' on Manzarek's solo on a Wurlitzer electric piano. This is my favorite track on the album, with some great guitar fills from Krieger and dark humor from Morrison. 'Why did you throw the jack of hearts away / it was the only card in the deck that I had left to play …' is a wonderfully enigmatic lyric. 'I see the bathroom is clear …' refers to the bathroom at the recording studio where the Doors were making the album. Morrison even took the door off the hinges so that he could get extra reverb off the bathroom tiles.

In Greek mythology, the hyacinth flower grew after the death of a beautiful youth at the hands of the god Apollo. Was Morrison foreseeing his own death? Not likely, just lamenting his mortality. His line, 'I need a brand new friend who doesn't bother me / I need a friend who doesn't need me …' is a poignant lyric for many reasons. Band members remarked that Morrison had surrounded himself with numerous hangers-on during his alcohol-fueled final year and it's clear that Morrison's paranoia was running rampant ('I feel that someone is following me …').

The Doors' take on 'Crawling King Snake' dates back to their early live shows, where it was sometimes coupled with Morrison's spoken word poem 'Celebration of the Lizard'. The poem first appeared on the inside jacket of the *Waiting for the Sun* (1967) album and contains the line, 'I am the Lizard King, I can do anything.' Morrison quickly adopted the 'Lizard King' persona on stage (the complete poem with musical backing can be heard on the 1970 album *Absolutely Live).* First recorded by Big Joe Williams in 1941, 'Crawling King Snake' was famously adapted by blues legend John Lee Hooker later that decade which, in turn, introduced the blues to a new generation of devotees in the 1950s and 1960s.

'The WASP (Texas Radio and the Big Beat)' is a reworking of Morrison's poetry that first appeared on the Doors' souvenir tour book in 1968. Morrison often recited his poetry in between songs at his concerts, and 'WASP' had been part of their live set for some time before it was decided to commit it to record. The band infuses the music behind Morrison's spoken word, the singer double-tracking his vocal, no small feat in itself, for extra emphasis. The real star, however, is John Densmore's inventive drumming. To highlight the poetry of the lyrics, Densmore devised an early use of synthesized drum sound to give Morrison's words extra punch and to accentuate the rhythm.

The final track on the album, 'Riders on the Storm', was a collective effort by the group. Beginning life as a rehearsal jam of the old Vaughan Monroe cowboy hit 'Ghost Riders in the Sky', Morrison contributed lyrics he had written down in his notebook, based on Hart Crane's poem 'Praise for an Urn' and his references to 'delicate riders of the storm'. The song taps into Morrison's 'hitchhiker' allegory, which featured in many of his own poetry projects. The inspiration for 'the killer on the road' may have been spree killer Billy Cook, who murdered six people – including a family of five and their pet dog – while hitchhiking to California in 1950. Cook was executed for his crimes in 1952.

In 1969, Morrison starred as a hitchhiker in a 50-minute experimental film called *HWY: An American Pastoral*. It was shot during the spring and summer in the Mojave Desert and in Los Angeles by Morrison and film colleague Paul Ferrari. Years later the film was set against the soundtrack of 'Riders on the Storm' and found a wide audience. Could Morrison have made it as an actor or even a filmmaker? Possibly, if could have found the discipline to learn his lines and show up on time. But then his whole rock career was an act. That's what destroyed him.

The band gathered at Poppi Studios early January 1971 to mix *L.A. Woman*. They added thunderstorm and rain sound effects to the song. Morrison's ghostly fade out singing the words 'riders on the storm' was the last recording he did with the band. Shortly after, he informed them that he was leaving for Paris with Pam. Although the album still needed to be mixed, Morrison had finished his vocals and left the band to finish the rest. Interestingly, 'Riders on the Storm' would later be released as the album's second single on 3 July, 1971 – the day Jim Morrison died.

Several additional songs were considered for *L.A. Woman*. Morrison recorded 'Orange County Suite' as a piano demo in early 1969, but it failed to make the cut for both *Morrison Hotel* and this final album. It was completed posthumously by the band and was later included in *The Doors: Box Set* in 1997. A blues medley called 'She Smells So Nice/Rock Me', which was recorded early in the sessions, was rediscovered in a tape vault and issued on the 40th-anniversary edition of the album in 2012. 'The alternate takes are all lesser versions interspersed with studio chatter and other audio vérité,' *Rolling Stone* noted in its review of the set, before adding, 'the sound of a band enjoying its work, unaware its time was nearly up.'

Another song, 'Paris Blues', remains unheard. The only known copy is a badly damaged cassette, on which portions have been accidentally erased. Considering the lyric, 'Goin' to the city of love / gonna start my life over again…' and especially, 'Once I was young, now I'm gettin' old / Once I was warm, now I feel cold / Well, I'm goin' overseas, gonna grab me some of that gold …' it's clear Morrison had already made up his mind about leaving LA.

For the cover art for *L.A. Woman*, the first pressing had a burgundy-colored, curved-corner cardboard cutout sleeve with a clear embossed cellophane insert, glued in from behind. According to Jac Holzman, chief executive officer of Elektra Records: 'I wasn't sure there would be another album ever, so I had Bill Harvey create a collector's cover. The Doors' faces were printed on clear film. The backing color of the inner sleeve could be changed and would affect the mood of the package. This is the first album in which Jim is bearded [on the cover]. His photo is on the right, no bigger, no smaller than the others, just another guy in the band.'

When Elektra released the album *Absolutely Live* in 1970, the label superimposed the image of a younger and thinner Morrison on the front cover. For the greatest hits compilation *13*, the label featured Morrison in a much larger image than his three bandmates, annoying him no end. They were not Jim Morrison and the Doors, they were the Doors! The group shot on *L.A. Woman*, which is credited to Wendell Hamick, shows the band as a single unit. What you don't see is Morrison clutching a bottle of whiskey just out of shot.

L.A. Woman was made on the cheap but it had something the

band's previous album, recorded at Elektra's premier recording studio at immense cost, didn't have. Hit singles. Jac Holzman chose 'Love Her Madly' as the lead single, the same song producer Paul A. Rothchild disliked so much. Even then the song's writer Robby Krieger thought the song was 'too commercial' and plumped for 'The Changeling'. Elektra overruled him and 'Love Her Madly', backed by the non-album B-side 'You Need Meat (Don't Go No Further)' with Manzarek on lead vocals, reached No.11 on the US singles chart, their best result since 1968's 'Hello, I Love You'.

L.A. Woman was released on 19 April, 1971. It reached No.9 on the Billboard charts, remaining there for 36 weeks, but reached only No.28 in the UK. An additional single was released in support of the album, a shortened version of 'Riders on the Storm', which peaked at No.14 in the US (No.22 in the UK) and was an immediate hit on FM radio. Despite enthusiastic reviews, the album was not a huge success and news of Morrison's subsequent death that July did not stop the album's gradual descent from the charts.

The album received mostly positive reviews. *Rolling Stone's* Robert Meltzer wrote, 'You can kick me in the ass for saying this (I don't mind): this is the Doors' greatest album and (including their first) the best album so far this year. A landmark worthy of dancing in the streets.' Robert Christgau stated 'the band has never sounded better', although he was disappointed with several tracks, including 'Been Down So Long' and 'L'America'. Robby Krieger reflected in a 2012 interview: 'I'm glad that *L.A. Woman* was our last album … It really captured what we were all about. The first record did, too, but *L.A. Woman* is more loose, it's live – it sounds almost like a rehearsal. It's pure Doors.'

Even before the final overdubs were finished and the record was mixed, Morrison had left LA for Paris. Girlfriend Pam Courson had found an apartment for them on rue Beautreillis on the Right Bank and Morrison was keen to follow the path of other American writers – Hemingway, Fitzgerald, Miller – to live and write there; to be a poet rather than a rock star. Although the timing of the decision surprised them, Morrison's bandmates thought that the move was a good idea – in Paris, their troubled friend could write, recharge his creative batteries and return to the US later in the year and tour the album. Perhaps even record again.

But the reality was, Morrison was in terrible shape in Paris. Apart from 'drinking wine for breakfast' as Manzarek later observed, Morrison had stumbled into Courson's drug hell – someone known to be afraid of needles, he had started snorting heroin with his girlfriend. They frequented the Paris nightlife, often partying at a nightclub called the Rock and Roll Circus, managed by John Bennett. According to Bennett's 2007 memoir, Morrison OD'd there one night and had to be helped from the premises by bouncers. Although Bennett is a reliable source (he later ran Disneyland Paris for the Disney company), his assertion that Morrison may have actually died in one of the toilet cubicles at his club – and was taken home and placed in the bath – cannot be corroborated.

According to her police statement, Pam Courson said that on 2 July, the couple went to the movies and out for dinner that night, later listening to records before falling asleep. Morrison awoke in the middle of the night feeling ill and took a hot bath. Courson said she found him dead in the tub early the following morning. A doctor was called and Morrison was pronounced dead from 'heart failure'.

Heart failure is not a heart attack, which is often attributed to the 27-year-old as cause of death. Courson's account tends to gloss over the finer details of what may or may not have happened that night – why did Morrison feel sick? Why did he take a hot bath, a known response for someone who has overdosed? She too would also succumb to a drug overdose in 1974.

Years after Morrison's death, Doors associate Danny Sugerman confirmed that Courson had told him that Morrison had OD'd on heroin that night. Perhaps the final piece of the mystery is provided by actress-singer Marianne Faithfull who, in her 2000 memoir, said that drugs were delivered that night to Morrison's apartment by her then drug dealer boyfriend Jean de Breteuil. The heroin was too strong, Faithfull admitted, and Morrison, a new user, overdosed. Breteuil died of an overdose in Tangier, Morocco, in 1971.

In an era before easy access international calls, Pam Courson contacted Doors manager Bill Siddons to tell him that Morrison had died. Siddons told an incredulous Manzarek the news and said he was on his way to Paris to confirm it. Morrison was buried in the cemetery at Père Lachaise, alongside fellow artists Georges Bizet, Frédéric Chopin, Honoré de Balzac, Marcel Proust, Georges Seurat, Oscar Wilde, Sarah Bernhardt, Isadora Duncan, Gertrude Stein and Edith Piaf, on 7 July 1971. No autopsy was performed and the casket was sealed. The only people at the funeral were Courson and Siddons.

Morrison died on 3 July 1971, two years to the day after the death of Rolling Stone Brian Jones, but by the time the news hit the American newspapers Morrison was already buried. Siddons told *Rolling Stone* the following month, 'The initial news of his death and funeral was kept quiet because those of us who knew him intimately and loved him as a person wanted to avoid all the notoriety and circus-like atmosphere that surrounded the deaths of Janis Joplin and Jimi Hendrix.'

In two short years, Jones, Joplin, Hendrix and Morrison had each died at the age of 27, a statistic that resonated for a new generation when Kurt Cobain committed suicide at that age in 1994. Morrison's early demise generated numerous theories, not least that he faked his own death and was living the life of an artist. That urban myth may have been the inspiration for the 1983 film *Eddie and the Cruisers,* about a charismatic rock and roll singer who disappears at the height of his fame. The less said about Oliver Stone's 1991 biopic *The Doors* the better; featuring a charisma-less performance from actor Val Kilmer as Morrison, the other members of the band are reduced to 1960s hippy caricatures and large sections of the narrative are fiction. The soundtrack is good though.

The remaining members of the Doors soldiered on without Morrison, releasing two more albums, *Other Voices* (1971) and *Full Circle* (1972), before calling it a day. They were offered a lot of money to continue on but as John Densmore so eloquently put it, 'we realized the front corner of our diamond was missing.' In 1978, Manzarek, Krieger and Densmore supplied music to Morrison's recorded poetry for the album *American Prayer,* which was attributed to the Doors. The resulting single, *Ghost Song,* is perhaps the best a Doors fan could ask for – evocative, poetic, a fully realized musical statement.

But the cult of personality surrounding Jim Morrison refused to die in the 1980s; starting with Francis Ford Coppola's use of 'The End' in *Apocalypse Now* (1979), the 1980 biography *No One Here Gets Out Alive* by Jerry Hopkins and Danny Sugerman, and *Rolling Stone*'s provocative 1981 cover alerted a new generation not to forget the legacy of the band. For me, it was the release of the live album *Alive, She Cried* in 1983 in the dying days of vinyl that confirmed just how good a band the Doors were. A compilation of recordings of various concerts during the band's peak years (1968-1970), the Doors' take on the Van Morrison hit 'Gloria', an extended version of 'Light My Fire' and especially 'You Make Me Real' led me and many others back to their album catalogue ... and *L.A. Woman*.

And what of the remainder of the band? In the new millennium, Ray Manzarek, Robby Krieger and John Densmore recorded songs with DJ and producer, Skrillex (Sonny Moore), and Manzarek and Krieger toured together for the best part of ten years. When they seconded Ian Astbury from the Cult as their lead singer and toured as the Doors of the 21st Century, however, this was a bridge too far for Densmore, who was joined in a suit by the Jim Morrison estate.

It just wasn't the Doors.

L.A. Woman / **Doors** (April 1971)   48:24

SIDE ONE   LENGTH

1.	The Changeling (Jim Morrison)	4:21
2.	Love Her Madly (Robby Krieger)	3:20
3.	Been Down So Long (Jim Morrison)	4:41
4.	Cars Hiss by My Window (Jim Morrison)	4:12
5.	L.A. Woman (Jim Morrison)	7:49

SIDE TWO

6.	L'America (Jim Morrison)	4:37
7.	Hyacinth House (Ray Manzarek, Jim Morrison) 3:11	
8.	Crawling King Snake (Anon, arr John Lee Hooker)	5:00
9.	The WASP (Texas Radio and the Big Beat) (Jim Morrison, Ray Manzarek, Robby Krieger, John Densmore)	4:16
10.	Riders on the Storm (Jim Morrison, Ray Manzarek, Robby Krieger, John Densmore)	7:09

CHAPTER 6

Ram

Paul and Linda McCartney 1971

'We believe that we can't be wrong ...'

Looking back on the early 1970s, most music critics, and indeed, many fans, had it in for Paul McCartney. It was Paul who had refused to sign a contract with new manager Allen Klein, despite the other three Beatles linking with the New York businessman; it was Paul who announced that he was leaving the Beatles, despite John telling his bandmates the previous September that he wanted 'a divorce' from them to work with Yoko; and it was Paul who launched High Court proceedings on 31 December, 1970, to dissolve the Beatles business relationship and release the four of them from their contractual obligations to Klein. By March 1971, London's High Court had ruled in McCartney's favor.

The future of the Beatles was untenable, but McCartney was forced to 'carry the weight' of not only millions of Beatles fans who blamed him for the breakup, but also music critics who dismissed his early post-Beatles efforts, and even his former bandmates, who attacked him on record.

In February 1971, Paul McCartney released his first solo single, 'Another Day'. Credited to both Paul and Linda McCartney, the song was a Top 10 hit in the UK (No.2) and the US (No.5) and was seen as a confident return to form after the savaging he received following the release of the *McCartney* album the previous year. 'Another Day' features a classic 'Macca' narrative, a wonderfully melancholy melody ('So sad, so sad …') and a singalong chorus ('it's just another day'), just like his best Beatles efforts (some even called it a sequel to 'She's Leaving Home' on the *Sgt. Pepper's* album).

Although it would not be included in the subsequent album that was released that year – all four Beatles would initially follow the successful formula of releasing singles for the Top 40 market and not short-changing their fans by dumping singles on albums – the song was recorded in New York at the beginning of the sessions for McCartney's new album, which would be called *Ram*.

The release of *Ram* in May 1971, however, was met with derision by many mainstream critics – but that did not stop it from topping the charts in the UK and reaching No.2 in the US. Again credited to both Paul and Linda McCartney (the only time in Paul's career that he would credit his wife as co-author and co-producer of his solo work), the album remains McCartney's most consistent and accessible solo album. What actually riled the rock media when the album was released, McCartney's 'happy domesticity' with his wife and young family, today constitutes the core of *Ram*'s brilliance and charm.

The songs were great and the production first class too, but still there were many doubters. The UK was in the midst of the glam rock movement ('Another Day' was kept off the top of the charts by T. Rex's 'Hot Love') and kids were buying records by Marc Bolan, David Bowie and Elton John in 1971. McCartney's audience, the millions of Beatles fans who had grown up with the group in the 1960s, were now in their 20s; they were marrying, having kids and settling down in the 1970s. The music Paul and Linda made was ideal for that market.

And credit where it is due; McCartney beat Lennon to the bat when he co-credited wife Linda on the cover of *Ram* (John and Yoko made experimental albums together but Yoko would not get an album co-credit until the disastrous *Some Time in New York City* in 1972). Rolling Stone Mick Jagger, who married first wife Bianca de Macias that same year (a wedding that the McCartneys attended), even remarked at the time that he would never put his 'missus' on one of his records. McCartney had no such concern.

Announcing he would no longer record with the Beatles, in April 1970 Paul McCartney holed up on his Scottish farm 'Kintyre' with wife Linda, her daughter Heather and newborn baby Mary (named after Paul's mother), making earthy, acoustic music to please himself and his family. Chastened by the criticism of his under-produced debut album in 1970, Paul and Linda relocated to New York in October to record their follow-up album and conduct secret auditions of local session musicians. Denny Seiwell was recruited on drums and 21-year-old David Spinozza on guitar. Spinozza had a prior booking for another session and so, after working on several songs, the group was augmented by the addition of guitarist Hugh McCracken.

Numerous backing tracks were recorded at CBS Studios in late 1970, consisting of just McCartney, Seiwell and Spinozza/McCracken; following on from his Beatles days, McCartney played guitar, not bass, preferring to overdub his bass parts once he had worked on them. 'The sessions were very organized and businesslike,' Spinozza would remember decades later. There was little improvisation, he said; they played what they were told to play, but they covered a lot of territory on the album: country, blues, '50s rock and roll and McCartney's unique brand of pop.

Orchestration and overdubs were added after shifting to A&R Studios under the direction of Phil Ramone and Dixon Van Winkle in the New Year. For two songs, McCartney called in long-time Beatles producer George Martin, who was more than happy to help with an orchestral score. Martin arranged strings for 'Back Seat of My Car', and 'Uncle Albert', which he inadvertently named 'Uncle Arthur' on the score sheets. McCartney conscripted the New York Philharmonic Orchestra to record the score under his direction, which meant that George Martin wasn't on hand to mentor his former pupil during the actual recording. Not that Paul needed mentoring.

The sessions were clearly prolific for the former Beatle, producing the single 'Another Day' and its B-side, 'Oh Woman, Oh Why'; 'Dear Friend', released on Wings' debut album later that year; 'Little Woman Love', the B-side of Wings' 1972 single 'Mary Had A Little Lamb'; 'I Lie Around', the B-side to Wings' 1973 single 'Live and Let Die', and an early version of 'Seaside Woman', a reggae-inspired song written by Linda, which would later be issued under the pseudonym Suzy and the Red Stripes in 1977.

Also recorded were three tracks used on Wings' 1973 album *Red Rose Speedway* – 'Get On the Right Thing', 'Little Lamb Dragonfly' and 'Big Barn Bed'. Of the three, the gentle ballad 'Little Lamb Dragonfly' is clearly the best of these and with its lush orchestration would not have been out of place on *Ram*. The first line of 'Big Barn Bed' ('Who's that coming round that corner / Who's that coming round that bend…') can be heard at the end of the 'Ram On' reprise on Side Two on the album.

McCartney also recorded 'Hey Diddle' (there is a great video on YouTube of Paul and Linda singing the song to their children on their Scottish farm), 'A Love for You', 'Great Cock and Seagull Race', 'Now Hear This Song of Mine', 'Sunshine Sometimes', 'When the Wind Is Blowing' and 'Rode All Night', which were included as bonus tracks on the *Ram* box set released in 2012. 'Rode All Night' has an interesting history; the song started out as a jam session involving McCartney and drummer Denny Seiwell and was later reworked and given to the Who's Roger Daltrey for his 1977 solo album, *One of the Boys*.

Although he clearly had more than enough material, rather than release a double album Paul chose the strongest songs for a single album, which made *Ram* a more cohesive musical unit. He later explained that the title not only reflected his determination to 'ram on' with his career post Beatles, but also reflected his current 'pastoral existence' on his farm. 'The name was strong, it had a double meaning and it's succinct and easy to remember,' he later opined.

Is the title *Ram* payback for what the Beatles put McCartney through? Perhaps, but Paul has never been overly vicious in his dealings with people and the title is more of a gentle nudge to keep going rather than a political statement. It would also prove an apt description of busting through the avalanche of criticism McCartney would endure as he fought to establish his solo music credentials.

It was Linda who suggested Paul hold a ram, a male sheep, for the front cover image. Paul tried out a number of different rams before settling on the farm's main breeding ram, which Linda photographed. Paul and Linda also oversaw the album art, with Linda taking many of the featured photos and both of them working on the garish, yellow marker trim to give it a 'homey' feel, as opposed to the slick production of the art studio. On the front cover, the letters L.I.L.Y. are written in the zigzag design, which stands for 'Linda, I Love You'. Other images are from the recording sessions in New York, while eagle-eyed Beatle-ologists did not miss the image on the back cover of two beetles fornicating … a subtle dig at his former bandmates.

There was nothing subtle about the opening track, 'Too Many People'. Relationships between the former bandmates were at an all-time low in the wake of McCartney's decision to launch the court proceedings to wind up their business dealings. It's clear Paul blamed John for the breakup of the Beatles – 'I love John, and respect what he does,' McCartney said in the infamous 1970 press release that came out with his debut album, '[but] it doesn't really give me any pleasure' – and the opening track of the album confirms it.

That Paul would open the album singing the words 'piece of (cake)' so that they become 'piss off' shows the depth of ill-feeling. Lennon had already gone on record saying Paul's first solo album, *McCartney*, was 'rubbish' (George Harrison's 'Wah-Wah' on his *All Things Must Pass* album is also a dig at Paul) so Paul fires an early broadside at his former writing partner on 'Too Many People'.

The first line of each verse, 'Too many people going underground …', 'Too many hungry people losing weight…' and 'Too many people preaching practices…' are direct references to John and Yoko. The chorus, 'You took your lucky break and broke it in two …' certainly got Lennon's attention (the original line was allegedly, 'Yoko took your lucky break and broke it in two'), setting off their tit-for-tat fight, on vinyl at least. And Lennon wouldn't miss McCartney either when his album *Imagine* was released later that year.

The second track, '3 Legs', can also be seen as a thinly veiled swipe at his former bandmates. 'My dog, he got three legs … but he can't run,' Paul sings on the blues-inspired song, with Linda echoing her husband's observations on harmonies. The Beatles were indeed a three-legged beast now that McCartney had left the band, and the subsequent court action meant the Beatles would not be able to record again as a three-piece, or any other configuration for that matter (there were rumors swirling around the world at the time that McCartney's place would be taken by long-time Beatles collaborator Klaus Voormann, or even Harry Nilsson!). The chorus rams home the point (excuse the pun); 'When I thought you was my friend (when I thought I could call you my friend) / But you let me down, put my heart around the bend …' '3 Legs' only gets moving with the up-tempo finish and then it's over, but it's a curious song coming so quickly after 'Too Many People'.

'Ram On' has the prettiest melody on the album and McCartney gives the tune a breezy, dreamlike quality with the use of ukulele and his whistling. The effect is so good, McCartney reprises the song on Side Two of the album (shades of *Sgt. Pepper's*?) but the magic of the gentle song is perhaps stretched too far by then. Interestingly, the ukulele was a bond McCartney shared with George Harrison, and there is a wonderful moment in the *Anthology* documentary in 1995 when George and Paul play ukes in a garden as Ringo listens contently. McCartney would also play the uke in the *Concert for George* in 2002, in the introduction to George's song 'Something', a year after the quiet Beatle's death from cancer.

'Dear Boy' was initially viewed as another attack on John and Yoko ('I guess you never knew, dear boy / What you had found …') but in a 1971 interview, McCartney says the song was autobiographical. '"Dear Boy" was my attempt at an autobiography about myself and how lucky I was to have Linda. I never realized how lucky I was to have her until I began writing the song.'

McCartney later cleared the air by saying that the song was directed at Linda's first husband, Joseph See, the father of Linda's daughter, Heather. After See committed suicide in 2000, McCartney respectfully suggested that maybe See never knew how much he missed in letting Linda go or what a good thing he had in marrying her in the first place (See is also referenced in another McCartney song; he is the inspiration for 'Jo Jo' in 'Get Back'). 'Dear Boy' features harmonies not unlike the Oscar-winning score Burt Bacharach utilizes in the 1969 film *Butch Cassidy and the Sundance Kid*. Lots of 'buda-buda-budas' here.

'Uncle Albert/Admiral Halsey' is like many of McCartney's Beatle novelty songs – 'Ob-la-di, Ob-la-da' and 'Maxwell's Silver Hammer' quickly come to mind. While many fans loved the song (it topped the US charts in September that year and won a Grammy for Best Arrangement), it's clear McCartney was trying to capture some *Abbey Road* magic here. Turning up to the studio with three different song parts, 'We're so sorry Uncle Albert…', 'Hands across the water …' and 'Live a little, be a gypsy …' McCartney did a 'George Martin' and joined the song together, glossing over the joins with the orchestral score. A little profanity in the lyrics didn't hurt its street cred either ('We're so sorry Uncle Albert / But we haven't heard a bloody thing all day …'); which had to be 'bleeped' for AM radio, such were the sensitivities of the times.

The song contains so many positive elements; Denny Seiwell came up with the groove at the beginning of the song when he started experimenting with his tom tom drum and high-hat cymbal. Paul came up with the idea of using a flugelhorn as a lead instrument in the middle of the song, humming the notes to jazz musician Marvin Strawn and instructing him to make it sound like it came from an old-time, 1930s radio broadcast. McCartney actually had an Uncle Albert in his family, and the key to the song is in the first line. 'We're so sorry Uncle Albert / We're so sorry if we caused you any pain …' was a tongue in cheek 'apology' to the older generation for McCartney's generation changing the world. 'But there's no one left at home / And I believe I'm gonna rain' is a typically enigmatic McCartney lyric, but I love the line, 'But the kettle's on the boil and we're so easily called away', because it's so 'old world' English.

'Admiral Halsey' is a random reference to US World War II Admiral, William 'Bull' Halsey, thus the 'hands across the water' section that links the two characters, one English and one American, across the Atlantic. McCartney repeated the same trick with 'Band on the Run' in 1973, linking two musical ideas together to form one memorable song.

The song segues to the count-in for 'Smile Away', which was recorded live in the studio. Denny Seiwell later stated that McCartney had the ability to 'smile' at his many detractors while glaring in their direction; easy inspiration for this song considering he was being painted as the villain in the Beatles' breakup. The lyrics contains examples of McCartney's more contemptuous humor ('Man I can smell your feet a mile away …') and the production has a real 'Sun City' feel, with great echo and faux 1950s backing vocals. Paul appears to be having a lot of fun with the band, the highlight being the sonic surge of production at 2:45.

'Heart of the Country' was one of the album's first songs to be picked up for promotion on TV, and subsequently on radio, because it came with an accompanying 'film promotional clip' directed by

Roy Benson. So much so, I thought the song was the opening side of the album when I got my hands on it and played that side of the record relentlessly. In the days before MTV and video clips, images of Paul and Linda riding their horses in the Scottish hills were shown around the world; a portent of the 'happy domesticity' that would permeate the album.

Featuring Hugh McCracken in support on guitar, McCartney performs a note-perfect scat vocal on 'Heart of the Country', which brings an element of cool to a song with lyrics as mundane as 'I want a horse, I want a sheep / I want to get me a good night's sleep …'

I scratched my copy of the album trying to write down the lyrics to 'Monkberry Moon Delight'. McCartney delivers one of his best vocal performances since *Abbey Road*'s 'Oh Darling!' on this song. Although the wordplay is impressive, the song struggles to sustain the same riff played in plodding, 2/4 time over five minutes. The title came from McCartney's infant daughter Mary trying to say the word milk ('monk'), with monkberry moon delight being a made up 'fantasy drink'. McCartney takes the lyric to the extreme, my favorite line being, 'When a rattle of rats had awoken / The sinews, the nerves and the veins …' What?

'Eat at Home' has an opening riff built around the C major chord that is perilously close to the lead in 'Day Tripper' (which, of course, McCartney also wrote). Reminiscent of Buddy Holly, especially in the chorus, the song descends into another '50s pastiche with a nice guitar lead from McCartney at the end. The song is cheeky, a 'winking sex song' as one reviewer describes it, but endearing in its inoffensiveness – much like Paul and Linda were in an era of John and Yoko's shenanigans.

Linda's subsequent musical contributions to Paul's band, Wings, have been mocked over the years but there is something very appealing – sexy, even – about her voice on this album. Content to sing harmony on most songs, Linda provides the perfect counterpoint to McCartney's faultless lead vocal on 'Long Haired Lady'. Paul says that he discovered that Linda could, in fact, sing during the 'Get Back' sessions, and he wasn't afraid to put her on his record.

Ram was a collaboration, albeit under Paul's direction. 'I gave her a hard time, I must say,' Paul later remarked, 'but we were pleased with the results. Elton John later said somewhere that he thought it was the best harmonies he'd heard in a long while. It was very much the two of us against the world at that point.'

Unfortunately, the recently sold Northern Songs Publishing drew the line at Paul and Linda being jointly credited as songwriters on 'Another Day' and six other songs on the album ('Dear Boy', 'Uncle Albert', 'Heart of the Country', 'Monkberry Moon Delight', 'Eat at Home' and 'Long Haired Lady'), thinking that McCartney was trying to circumvent his still operational songwriting partnership with John Lennon (they jointly owned the subsidiary, Maclen Music). Both music companies later sued the couple for being co-credited on *Ram*, but the matter was settled the following year.

McCartney later said that 'Ram On' was also meant as a pun of his pre-Beatlemania nom de plume 'Paul Ramon', the name he conjured when the fledgling band was briefly known as Long John and the Silver Beatles (Harrison was George Perkins, in honor of Carl Perkins, Stuart Sutcliffe became Stuart de Stael, after the artist, but Lennon refused to change his name). Paul had briefly returned to the name 'Ramon' when he was credited on Steve Miller's 1969 album *Brave New World*, so the name still resonated with him. Fast-forward to the end of the decade and a scruffy band of New York punks adopted the name as their own – the Ramones.

Following the reprise of 'Ram On' (why didn't McCartney just call the album 'Ram On'?), the album concludes with a production number to rival 'Uncle Albert/Admiral Halsey'. Initially written during the 'Get Back' sessions, 'Back Seat of My Car' is so calculated it could have been for a car commercial, except that it again goes for too long. A ready criticism of McCartney's work is that he often had too many musical segments in his songs and it tells here. The narrative is once again rooted in a 1950s dream – teenage lovebirds escaping from 'daddy' in a car – but it may as well be Paul and Linda escaping from the rest of the world. The refrain, 'We believe we can't be wrong…' was taken by many, including Lennon, as egotistical and self-serving on Paul's part, but who could blame him for using some positive self-talk in that immediate post-Beatles world?

Ram was mixed in Los Angeles, with final overdubs added under the control of engineer Eirik Wangberg. The album was released on 17 May 1971 in the US, and a week later in the UK, with the record label supporting the release with major ads and recorded radio spots (with the title 'Brung to Ewe By', which did not endear Paul any further with critics). The poor reviews were led by Jon Landau in *Rolling Stone* magazine: 'emotionally vacuous', 'incredibly inconsequential' and 'monumentally irrelevant' he wrote. Landau, and *Rolling Stone* for that matter, were firmly in the Lennon camp, and it shows. 'Lennon has created a music of almost monomaniacal intensity and blunt style,' Landau wrote in 1971, 'while McCartney creates music with a fully developed veneer, little intensity, and no energy.'

Alan Smith, in his review for *New Musical Express*, described the album as 'an excursion into almost unrelieved tedium,' he wrote. 'The melodies are weak, the ideas are stale, the arrangements are messy ... Suffice to say that *Ram* is the worst thing Paul McCartney has ever done.' And he was a long-time McCartney fan! 'Silly, laden down with caprice,' Robert Christgau opined in New York's *The Village Voice*, adding somewhat petulantly, 'I am infuriated by the McCartneys' modern young-marrieds image ... a major annoyance.'

But the fans didn't care. The album was a Top Ten hit around the world and a No.1 in Canada, Holland, Spain, Norway and Sweden. The first single, 'Uncle Albert/Admiral Halsey' was No.1 in the US but was not released in the UK. 'Back Seat of My Car' was released there as a single in August to drive album sales, but barely scratched the Top 40. 'Eat at Home' was released as a third single in some territories (No.21 in Australia).

McCartney, naturally enough, was hurt by the poor reviews. The first album had been a homemade effort, so he and Linda had approached *Ram* in a more conscientious manner, booking studio time, hiring session musicians and rehearsing the new songs to get them ready for recording. He had put himself, and Linda, into every note – even designing the album cover. 'I got caught up in [the criticism], so I assumed that a lot of stuff I did was no good,' he said in a recent interview before adding, 'I've learned not to care what they say, because [the critics] are just people: they're not God. So their opinion can often be wrong, or it can be different from the people who are going to buy the record.'

Instead of taking the time to learn from the experience, to write and reflect on what he wanted to do next and make an even better album, McCartney so enjoyed the collegiality of the New York studio that he started auditioning for a permanent band. David Spinozza demurred, wishing to remain a sought-after session player, but drummer Denny Seiwell joined former Moody Blues frontman Denny Laine and later, guitarist Henry McCullough, ex-Joe Cocker's Grease band, formed the new group Wings. McCartney would front the band, with Linda on keyboards and vocals, insulating himself from the personal criticism he copped. But first they would have to become a real touring band.

McCartney quickly followed up *Ram* with another homemade effort, *Wild Life*, Wings' debut album in December 1971, betraying a naïve willingness to get the band's new music out to the public. It was a momentary backward step in the snakes and ladders game that was McCartney's solo career. The band would not release another album for 15 months, *Red Rose Speedway*, by which time they were billed as Paul McCartney and Wings. McCartney would spend 1972 playing small gigs, releasing several singles that got a mixed response; 'Give Ireland Back to the Irish' (banned), 'Mary Had A Little Lamb' (panned) and 'Hi Hi Hi' (also banned).

Band on the Run (1973) was the album that proved to McCartney, and the world, that he had not lost his talent. He lost his band though, with Danny Seiwell and Henry McCullough declining to travel to Lagos, in Nigeria, to make their new album. That McCartney could pull a rabbit out of his hat under such immense pressure shows not only his brilliance, but also his tenacity. *Band on the Run* might be his greatest album with Wings, but I still prefer *Ram* and its organic charm and rough edges.

Today, *Ram* is revered as a rediscovered classic. 'Time has been kinder to *Ram* than its initial reception,' writes Neil Spencer on the *Ram* box set. 'The album's lack of cultural resonance no longer seems the sin it did during 1971. In fact it's a bonus; McCartney's family idyll rings truer today than Lennon's political musings, Harrison's heavy-handedness and Starr's lack of relevance.'

'Paul McCartney's *Ram* is a domestic-bliss album, one of the weirdest, earthiest, and most honest ever made,' Jayson Greene adds on Pitchfork.com.

'These songs may not be self-styled major statements, but they are endearing and enduring, as is *Ram* itself, which seems like a more unique, exquisite pleasure with each passing year,' says Stephen Thomas Erlewine on Allmusic.com.

How does one then explain the release of *Thrillington*? Riding the crest of a wave after conquering America on tour with Wings in 1975–76, McCartney threw jazz musician, arranger and former Apple staffer Richard Hewson a curve ball when he asked him to come up with an orchestral version of *Ram*. Hewson was given a free rein to interpret the album and recorded his jazz take on the ten songs over three days at Abbey Road. Why Paul felt this would be a good idea in the year of punk is anybody's guess, but he wisely didn't put his name to it and released it to little or no fanfare. One for the hard-core fans.

McCartney's attempts to turn Wings into a 'real band' drew mixed results in the late 1970s. A steady stream of replacement players came through Wings' ranks during the release of a series of well-received albums, but Macca's generosity in allowing band members to write, and then take the lead, on their own songs was misplaced. The public wouldn't buy songs written by Denny or Linda or anyone else for that matter. But Paul was looking for a musical partner, and while his bandmates did their best (Denny Laine co-wrote 'Mull of Kintyre' in 1977, which was a multi-million seller in the UK) they were not in the same league as McCartney. No one was, except perhaps John Lennon.

When Lennon was murdered in New York, December 1980, McCartney's former writing partner was granted almost universal sainthood, while he was relegated to the secondary role. McCartney did not help matters with his glib response to news of Lennon's death ('It's a drag, yeah') and to critics who labelled Lennon's body of solo work edgy, politically sophisticated and avant garde compared to McCartney's melodic, whimsical ballads. The truth is much more complex – McCartney was a lot more experimental with his music, in and out of the Beatles, and was open to incorporating musical innovation in his songs.

More importantly, where Lennon's solo albums dipped in quality, McCartney went from strength to strength, although he would have twice the lifetime to develop and showcase his talents. And his talents are indeed extraordinary, as the great Bob Dylan admitted to *Rolling Stone*: 'He's got the gift for melody, he's got the gift for rhythm, he can play any instrument. He can scream and shout as good as anyone, and he can sing a ballad as good as anyone. And his melodies are effortless, that's what you have to be in awe of.'

McCartney disbanded Wings in 1980, having aborted their Japanese tour after being arrested by customs authorities for drugs possession. Starting with *McCartney II* in 1980, Paul released 16 solo albums, up until 2018's *Egypt Station*, across almost four decades, as well as three electronic collaborations with the Fireman, five classical albums and various live albums. He also collaborated with numerous stars, such as Stevie Wonder ('Ebony and Ivory' in 1982), Michael Jackson ('Say, Say, Say' and 'The Girl is Mine' in 1983), Elvis Costello (the *Flowers in the Dust* album in 1989), Dave Grohl

('Cut Me Some Slack' in 2012) and even Kanye West and Rhianna ('FourFiveSeconds' in 2015), in an attempt to find that elusive magical partnership. There were several number ones but little magic.

Following the death of Linda McCartney from breast cancer in 1998, and then having to extricate himself from a disastrous marriage to Heather Mills in 2006, McCartney has toured widely in the new millennium and continues to do so well into his seventies. Having achieved the balance between his solo work and his Beatles catalogue in his live performances, he is seen today as the Fab Four's main standard bearer, showcasing a wonderful musical legacy to old and new generations alike.

Today, Paul McCartney is acknowledged as the most successful song-writer in the history of popular music, which incorporates his work with the Beatles and John Lennon, but also his considerable solo work. He has written or co-written a record 32 songs that have topped the US charts and is credited with more UK number ones than any other artist. Having won 18 Grammy awards, he is a two-time inductee to the Rock and Roll Hall of Fame (1988 with the Beatles, and 1999 as a solo performer) and a self-made billionaire.

Sir Paul McCartney, MBE, 'Macca' or just Paul ... a bloody marvel.

Ram / **Paul & Linda McCartney** (May 1971)   43:15

All songs written and composed by Paul McCartney,
or Paul & Linda McCartney where noted*

SIDE ONE		LENGTH
1.	Too Many People	4:10
2.	3 Legs	2:44
3.	Ram On	2:26
4.	Dear Boy *	2:12
5.	Uncle Albert/Admiral Halsey *	4:49
6.	Smile Away	3:51

SIDE TWO		
1.	Heart of the Country *	2:21
2.	Monkberry Moon Delight *	5:21
3.	Eat at Home *	3:18
4.	Long Haired Lady *	5:54
5.	Ram On (Reprise)	0:52
6.	The Back Seat of My Car	4:26

RAM

by

AUL AND LINDA McCARTNEY

	Side Two
People	Heart Of The Country
	Monkberry Moon Delight
	Eat At Home
...bert/Admiral Halsey	Long Haired Lady
...way	Ram On
	The Back Seat Of My Car

with

...enny Seiwell, Dave Spinoza and Hugh McCracken

Sound Engineering: Tim, Ted, Phil, Dixon, Armin and Jim
Mixing Engineers: Eirik the Norwegian
Cover Photography: Linda.   Art Work: Paul•

...TRIBUTED BY E.M.I. (AUSTRALIA) LIMITED. SYDNEY N.S.W.

CHAPTER 7

Sticky Fingers

The Rolling Stones 1971

'Let's do some living after we die ...'

In the 1960s, rock and roll fans were easily divided into two camps: you were either a Beatles fan or a Stones fan. For me the decision was easy; I was firmly in the Beatles' camp. The original Rolling Stones had none of the charm or style of the 'Fab Four'; they wore their own clothes on stage, they wore their hair long – hell, they didn't even bother to smile for the camera. Did Charlie Watts and Bill Wyman even talk? 'They are five young men of almost frightening aspect whose music is exciting but untuneful,' wrote Maureen Cleave, the same journalist who quoted John Lennon as saying the Beatles were 'more popular than Jesus'.

I was never a fan of the British 'blues' boom – what did affluent white boys from London have to be 'blue' about? Playing the music of unknown black American artists was as old as Elvis, and the Rolling Stones were merely following in those footsteps. They had the attitude, but not the songs.

In their original early '60s incarnation, which we will call Stones Mark I, the band were serviceable musicians with a frontman; the enigmatic Mick Jagger was a passable singer and an okay (just) dancer. Encouraged by their manager Andrew Loog Oldham, Jagger and bandmate Keith Richards learned the art of songwriting on the job. The results were identifiably their own – 'It's All Over Now' (1964), their first No.1; 'The Last Time' (1965) and especially '(I Can't Get No) Satisfaction', which was voted the best 45rpm single of the '60s by *Rolling Stone* magazine. But their early records lacked the musicianship and production of the Beatles' hits, and the Stones rarely gelled as a band on LP.

Truth be told, they were in the Beatles' shadow for the entire decade – albeit an interesting alternative to the 'Fab Four' ('The Beatles want to hold your hand,' writer Tom Wolfe famously wrote, 'but the Rolling Stones want to burn down your town!'). It wasn't until the departure of founding guitarist Brian Jones in 1969 that the Stones found their groove as a live band. As good as albums *Beggar's Banquet* (1968) and *Gimme Shelter* (1969) were, the transformation wasn't completed until the addition of 21-year-old guitarist Mick Taylor and the release of *Sticky Fingers* in 1971. The Stones Mark II were now the best band in the world.

Mick Taylor, who had performed with John Mayall's Bluesbreakers, joined the Stones in the middle of 1969, just before their free concert in Hyde Park. 'I just couldn't believe how bad they sounded,' Taylor said later, recalling when he joined the band for rehearsals. 'Their timing was awful. They sounded like a typical bunch of guys in a garage … playing out of tune and too loudly. I thought, "how is it possible that this band can make hit records?"' This harsh appraisal may also have been one reason why the band did not rush back into the studios to record an album. They had to become a 'real' band once again.

The Stones later joked they spent 'two million hours' recording the songs that would end up on *Sticky Fingers*. The first sessions commenced in December 1969 at Muscle Shoals Sound Studio, in Sheffield, Alabama, in between dates of their US Tour – the first with new guitarist Mick Taylor. The Stones wanted to commit some new songs to tape while they were playing so well on tour, but they did not have the necessary visas to record in the US and were originally turned away from studios in Memphis. They decided on Alabama Studios, the home of the legendary session players 'The Swampers' (backing stars such as Leon Russell, Boz Scaggs and Duane Allman), because it was out of the way and no one would know they were even there.

That the tracks did not see the light of day for another 15 months was the result of contractual disputes, on-going business issues and a variety of personal reasons. The sessions at Muscle Shoals produced three tracks in three days – the classic 'Brown Sugar', the ballad 'Wild Horses', and a cover of Mississippi Fred McDowell's 'You Got to Move' – but the songs would be overtaken by other releases in 1970 before the Stones debuted them on their new label, Rolling Stones Records, the following year.

The wait for new material to see the light of day was not unusual for the Stones. New boy Mick Taylor later conceded that working on Rolling Stones albums tended to 'overlap' one another and long after his departure from the band in 1975, the guitarist's stellar work would crop up on subsequent Stones albums, notably 'Waiting for A Friend' on the *Tattoo You* album, which was not released until 1981!

Mick Jagger began writing 'Brown Sugar' in August 1969, when he was in Australia with then girlfriend Marianne Faithfull to film *Ned Kelly*. If Jagger's selection to play Irish-Australian folk hero (and murderer) Ned Kelly was not controversial enough, his arrival with Faithfull at Sydney Airport – wearing a flop hat and attitude to match – sent the Australian media into overdrive. Faithfull's drug overdose in Sydney before the film had even started merely added to their notoriety. Faithfull's alleged response to Jagger urging her not to die ('wild horses wouldn't drag me away') provided the inspiration for another song recorded at Muscle Shoals. Jagger says that he came up with the barre chord progression that would form the basis of 'Brown Sugar' on guitar in the Australian bush trying to 'rehabilitate' the hand he injured filming *Ned Kelly*. It was arguably the only good thing that came from the experience, with Tony Richardson's film and Jagger's affected Irish accent receiving poor reviews.

Jagger and Richards worked on 'Brown Sugar' on the first day in the studio and recorded it the following day. Playing the song over and over until they were satisfied with it, engineer Jimmy Johnson was not happy with certain aspects of the backing track (Charlie Watt's drums were out of tune and Bill Wyman had his bass at low volume). Nevertheless, the rhythm track was finally nailed, but Jagger declined to do the vocal until the following day.

Jagger's ability to soak up the history and language of the South is best exemplified in his lyrics for 'Brown Sugar'. The song is sexually and racially provocative ('Ah, brown sugar / How come you taste so good …') and the first line sets the scene ('Gold coast slave ship bound for cotton fields / Sold in the market down in New Orleans …'). References in the remainder of the verse were cleared up in the booklet notes for the *Sticky Fingers* box set released in 2011. 'Scarred old slaver …' is actually 'Slydog slaver …' a reference to the nickname given to Allman Brothers guitarist Duane Allman, who also recorded at Muscle Shoals.

'Swampers' guitarist Jimmy Johnson, who engineered the songs along with the Stones, was the de facto producer at these sessions. Infuriatingly, especially for newly won Stones fans such as me, Jagger liked to bury his vocal in the mix so it was increasingly difficult to ascertain what exactly he was singing. According to Johnson, Jagger believed that if people wanted to know what he was singing, then 'mixing down his vocals would make fans more prone to buy the records!'

Jagger's vocal performance on 'Brown Sugar', ably supported by Keith Richards and a bottle of bourbon, was captured for all posterity by documentarians David and Albert Maysles, who joined the group to film the final concerts of the Stones' US Tour. The footage would later feature in the documentary, *Gimme Shelter*, which also documents the tragic events of the Altamont Concert held just three days later.

'Wild Horses' was recorded on the final day of their three-day session. Widely regarded as an ode to Marianne Faithfull – Jagger's relationship with his muse would run its course the following year – the plaintive melody was actually written by Keith Richards as a lullaby to his baby son, Marlon. Richards finalized the chords in the studio when the other members of the band took a lunch break. Jagger helped with the lyrics but later disavowed that the song is about Faithfull.

Stones everyman Ian Stewart refused to play piano on the song because it contained a minor chord (the superstitious Stewart did not play minor or 'Chinese' chords), and he was hurriedly replaced by session player Jim Dickinson so the session could be completed. Playing 'tack' piano, an ordinary piano in which thumbtacks or nails are placed on the felt-padded hammers of the instrument to give it a tinny, 'honky-tonk' sound, Dickinson tried his best to follow Bill Wyman's hurriedly drawn chord chart. Keith Richards and Mick

Taylor joined in on guitars, with Taylor playing the higher-tuned acoustic guitar.

After twenty or so takes, the song was completed and it features one of Jagger's most compelling vocal performances (and he followed straight away with his vocal for 'Brown Sugar'). Recording at Muscle Shoals re-energised the band – three songs recorded in three successive days was a great achievement for a notoriously slow and meticulous group like the Stones. That night, they flew to Atlanta, Georgia, and changed planes for their fateful date at Altamont on 6 December, 1969.

At the time, Keith Richards was hanging out with former Byrds frontman Gram Parsons, and critics thought Parsons may have had a hand in the writing of the song. Parson's 'country' background may have influenced Richards, especially with the unusual 'Nashville' tunings of the strings, but the lyrics are classic Jagger and Richards. Parsons actually released his version of the song with the Flying Burrito Brothers in 1970, before the Stones could get their house in order, three years before his death of a drug overdose.

The Stones played 'Brown Sugar' in public for the first time – 15 months before it would see the light of day as a single – at the Altamont Free Concert in San Francisco on 6 December, 1969. The concert is infamously remembered today as the scene of the death of 18-year-old Meredith Hunter, a young black man beaten and stabbed to death by members of the Hells Angels motorcycle club, who had been contracted to perform security on the night. The incident was captured on the *Gimme Shelter* documentary (Hunter had been rebuked by security for approaching the stage and was killed after he pulled out a revolver) and was seen as a shattering end to the '60's dream of peace, love and understanding.

That a murder occurred at a Stones concert (three other people died at Altamont; two in a hit-and-run accident and one from a drug overdose) added to the band's notoriety in living their lives outside accepted public norms. It had always been that way; from Jagger and Richard's 1967 drug bust, the increasing influence of the drugs culture on their songs, and Brian Jones' tragic death just after leaving the band in 1969.

After returning to London, the Stones met at Olympic Sound Studios just before Christmas to mix the three tracks recorded at Muscle Shoals under the direction of long-time producer Jimmy Miller. Jagger and Richards were so pleased with the songs they were keen to release 'Brown Sugar', with 'Wild Horses' as the B-side, but they decided to keep them for the album. Interestingly, both songs are the only two songs on *Sticky Fingers* to be credited to ABKCO-Decca, a remnant of their old recording deal negotiated by manager Allen Klein. The Stones still owed Decca an album before the contract ended in July 1970, so it was decided to give the label the tapes from their Madison Square Garden shows the previous July. The early months of the new decade were spent mixing those tapes under the watchful eye of Glyn Johns, with the resulting live album, *Get Yer Ya-Ya's Out!*, released in June.

The December 1969 sessions in London also produced the song 'Dead Flowers' (at one time the band considered calling the album *Dead Flowers*). Not the least bit representative of the songs on the completed album, the song has a faux country feel to it with Jagger and Richards wringing all the emotion out of the tune with their country-accented vocal. At the last moment, he changed the name of the girl in the song from Lily (get it, dead flowers) to 'Suzie', but the obligatory drugs reference ('I'll be in my basement room with a needle and a spoon ...') seems a bit forced. Ian Stewart provides 'swagger' with a nice turn on the piano so obviously there are no minor chords in this song.

'Dead Flowers' is saved from becoming a complete parody (the Stones would achieve that feat with the wonderful 'Far Away Eyes' on 1978's *Some Girls*) by Jagger's sardonic humor ('Send me dead flowers by the US mail / Say it with dead flowers at my wedding ...') but the whole thing is pretty turgid. At the time many critics were far from impressed. *Rolling Stone*'s Jon Landau wrote: 'Despite its parodistic intentions, the mere thought of the Stones doing straight country music is simply appalling. And they do it so poorly, especially the lead guitar ...'

Recording resumed in late March, alternating between Olympic Studios and Jagger's recently purchased mansion 'Stargroves', in Berkshire, with the aid of the Stones' mobile recording unit (Charlie Watts would set up his drumkit in the bay window). The band were about to undertake a European tour in August, so they had precious little time to add to the material already recorded. The sessions were fruitful, however, and by the time they finished recording at the end of the year they had another ten songs in the bag, some of which they held over to future albums.

The energetic Jimmy Miller, a New Yorker working in London who had started his relationship with the Stones with *Beggars Banquet* in 1968, oversaw the recordings alongside Glyn and Andy Johns. Miller had long realized that getting all five band members in the recording studio at the same time was like corralling lions; Richards was particularly unreliable at this time, having developed a drug problem that would reach rock bottom with his conviction in the late 1970s.

The Olympic-Stargroves sessions feature the ever-reliable Nicky Hopkins on piano with the addition of famed American session players Bobby Keys and Jim Price on brass. Keys (saxophone) and Price (trumpet) were in London at the time having been part of the Delaney & Bonnie Tour before being seconded by George Harrison to play on his yet to be released solo album *All Things Must Pass*. Keys, whom the Stones had first met on tour in the US in 1964, formed an integral relationship with the band (Keys and Keith Richards shared the same birthdate – 18 December, 1942) and toured with the Stones for more than 40 years before his death in 2014.

The song 'Sway' was pretty much written by Jagger in the studio at Stargroves in December 1970 and he also plays guitar on the track. Featuring one of the Stones' most underrated hooks ('It's just that demon life has got you in its sway …'), the song is also notable for its distinctive organ and piano runs by Nicky Hopkins, and alternate slide and lead guitar licks from Richards and Taylor. Interestingly, when the Stones invited Taylor to play with the band on their 50 and Counting tour in America in 2013, their former bandmate joined them on 'Sway'.

'Can't You Hear Me Knocking' has such a loose, 'jamming' feel to it and yet the playing is so tight. Jagger felt his vocal was a little too high, straining at times to reach the high notes on the chorus, but the urgency of the song comes through. In his 2012 autobiography, Keith Richards writes that when he locked in with that incredible opening lick, Charlie Watts instinctively hit his drums with that jazz-influenced beat. Originally the song was only as long as Jagger's vocal, which lasts just under three minutes, but Taylor (guitar), Bill Wyman (bass) and Rocky Dijon (on congas) kept a Latin-jazz-inflected vibe going for another five minutes. Bobby Keys joined in and nailed the sax solo on his first unedited take.

Producer Jimmy Miller, an underrated drummer in his own right, overdubbed further percussive instruments himself, as well as piano parts for Nicky Hopkins and Bill Preston (organ). Miller later resisted the temptation to edit the song (the only quibble I have is that it would have been the ideal way to close Side One – the long, meandering sax fade out providing the perfect ending). 'You Gotta Move', recorded in the Muscle Shoals sessions at the end of 1969, takes that role instead. The Stones had played the traditional blues song (first recorded in 1953 by the Blind Boys of Alabama) on their US Tour earlier that year. Mick Taylor's slide guitar makes the song.

When the sessions finished at the end of July 1970, the album was far from ready for release. *Sticky Fingers* would miss its Christmas window because the band and its management would be involved with setting up their own label, Rolling Stones Records. Atlantic Records signed the band to distribute six new albums in the next six years for just under US$6 million (RCA offered more money but the band thought CEO Ahmet Ertegun and Atlantic were more 'sympathetic, musically' to their cause).

The Stones performed some of the new material on their European Tour, notably 'Brown Sugar' and 'Dead Flowers'. In October 1970, twelve days after their European Tour finished, the band were back at Stargroves to finish the album. Having survived a baptism of fire on their US Tour and refined their sound on their highly successful 1970 European Tour, the Stones discovered that rare ability to 'lock in' as a band and create magic in the recording studio. Taylor's fluid playing style meshed with Richards' lead guitar and provided a sail for Jagger's vocals to soar above the beat.

The first song the band worked on during these sessions was 'Bitch'. If the media thought 'Brown Sugar' was provocative, then 'Bitch' more than matched it in opening Side Two. The song also came out of an impromptu jam session (was it Jagger on guitar or Richards? Accounts differ) but the song was given its much needed 'groove' by Richards' distinctive guitar riff and a beat accented by Bobby Keys and Jim Price on brass.

'Bitch' was worked over by Jagger and Richards in the garden at Stargroves before being recorded, with Richards' guitar solo a counterpoint to Jagger's sneering vocal. While feminists might arch up at the song, perhaps a better title would have been 'It's a Bitch' (as on the lyric '… must be love / It's a bitch, yeah'). The song features some of Jagger's best wordplay, reusing the structure of the opening line ('Feeling so tired, can't understand it / Just had a fortnight's sleep …') to address themes of drunkenness, hunger and lust, in a three-minute pop song.

'I Got the Blues' features Billy Preston on Hammond organ, with Keys and Price again contributing brass. As the song suggests, this is another take on the Stones' particular brand of 'white soul', with Jagger later acknowledging the influence of Otis Redding and the early Stax blues records on this track. Preston later augments the Stones' live performance on their 1975 US Tour, although the keyboardist was constantly reminded by Richards to tone down his playing. Played in unusual 6/8 time, the song slows the pace of the record somewhat, a vibe that continues on with the next track, 'Sister Morphine', which has an equally interesting history.

'Sister Morphine' is the oldest track on the album, pre-dating even the Muscle Shoals sessions. Credited to Jagger, Richards and Marianne Faithfull, the song was written while Jagger and Faithfull were on holiday in Italy in 1968, before Mick Taylor joined the band. Jagger constructed the chord sequence and Faithfull helped with the lyrics. An early version of the song was recorded in LA's Elektra Studios, with studio producer Jack Nitzsche on piano and young guitar prodigy Ry Cooder on guitar. Faithfull recorded her version over Jagger's guide vocal and then released it as a single in 1969. The song (credited to Jagger and Richards only) was banned on radio and withdrawn for sale by her record label, the ABKCO-owned subsidiary London Records.

In March 1969, Nitzsche and Cooder were in London to write the score to the Donald Cammell/Nick Roeg film *Performance*, which starred Jagger as an idealized version of himself – a decadent rock star who had withdrawn from society. Jagger took the opportunity to use the pair to record a slightly faster version of 'Sister Morphine' featuring his vocal. Nitzsche, who had played piano on several Stones tracks for Decca in the mid-1960s, was Neil Young's long-time collaborator and would later be nominated for an Academy Award for his *One Flew Over the Cuckoo's Nest* score in 1976, before winning an Oscar as the co-writer (with Will Jennings and Buffy St Marie) of the song 'Up Where We Belong' for 1983's *An Officer and A Gentleman*.

It goes without saying that 'Sister Morphine' is the 'druggiest' song on the album. Although the lyric starts out routinely, a patient lying in his/her hospital bed, waiting for their next dose of morphine, drug references are at the forefront of the song ('Ah, can't you see, Sister Morphine, I'm trying to score ...'). The line 'Sweet Cousin Cocaine, lay your cool cool hand on my head ...' moves the song into the (non-medical) drug sphere.

'Moonlight Mile', the final track on the album, is Jagger's song, having worked out the chords on acoustic guitar before the band laid down a basic backing track. Writing the lyrics in the studio, Jagger recorded multiple vocal tracks before he achieved the right 'dreamy' affectation to his voice in the early hours of the new dawn. Strings were added by Paul Buckmaster closer to the album's release in early 1971. Jim Price takes the distinctive piano part on this song, gently exploring the melody, and also arranged the brass parts that mimic Mick Taylor's stellar guitar work.

'Moonlight Mile' does not feature Keith Richards at all. The guitarist later admitted that he was 'very out of it' in the final months of the album's completion and missed the recording session completely. Recording wrapped up on 18 December, 1970; Keith Richards and Bobby Keys' 29th birthday. Understating the hard labour needed to complete the album, Keith Richards would later admit, somewhat surprised, '*Sticky Fingers* – it pulled itself together.'

In early 1971, future Oscar-winning movie producer David Putnam conscripted American photographer Peter Webb to photograph his friends the Rolling Stones for a possible album cover, the shoot taking place in Webb's Regent Park studio. Wearing their street attire, the Stones were photographed as a group, with the one of a yawning Mick Jagger standing apart from his bemused bandmates deemed the best of the bunch. A 12 by 12 inch black-and-white copy of the image – a wonderfully evocative shot of the band in their early 1970s heyday – was included as a giveaway in early pressings of the album.

Sticky Fingers was the first album released on Rolling Stones Records, and the first time the band had total control of both the music and its packaging – the perfect collaboration between music and art. The *Sticky Fingers* cover is included in every book published about album art, not only because it was somewhat controversial for the time but also because it incorporated work by celebrated American pop artist Andy Warhol.

As early as April 1969, Jagger had asked Andy Warhol to design the album cover – leaving it in the artist's 'capable hands' to do what he wanted to do. Warhol's fee was an astronomical £15,000 pounds (£220,000 in today's money, or about US$350,000). The album title was yet to be been finalized, so Warhol came up with the concept of the image of a pair of jeans focused on the crotch of a young man. 'Unzipping' the zipper revealed the man's underwear, imprinted with Warhol's name and the enigmatic message – 'This Photograph May Not Be ... Etc.' (artist Ernie Cefalu came up with the concept of giving the cover a 'real' zipper).

Warhol took numerous test shots on polaroid film before choosing the best image for the 'zipper' feature. Rather than being a new concept, Warhol may have already had the images on file. Many fans believed (or fantasized) the crotch belonged to Mick Jagger, but it was one of several young men who featured in Warhol's avant-garde films who posed for the shot (perhaps even 'Little Joe' Dallesandro or Jackie Curtis, the cross-dressing actor, later immortalized in verses of Lou Reed's 'Walk on the Wild Side').

Warhol did not object to cover supervisor Chris Baum stamping the band name and album title in red on the revolutionary cover (subsequent printings dispensed with the 'customs' style stamp and merely printed the words in red at the top of the front cover). Nor did Warhol object to the newly minted 'lips & tongue' logo – with the song titles displayed on the tongue – being printed on his reverse jeans image on the back cover. The design duly offended almost everyone and was even banned in some territories (notably Spain, where it was replaced by an equally suggestive image of fingers sitting in an oil-filled can!).

The 'lips & tongue' logo has since become one of the most recognizable images in popular music. In April 1970 John Pasche from London's Royal College of Art was asked to design the poster for the Stones' UK Tour and 'to create a logo or symbol which may be used on note paper, as a programme cover and as a cover for the press book.' By the time of the album's release, 'lips & tongue' merchandise was also hitting stores – on sweat shirts, scarves, hats, belt buckles, key chains, embroidered patches and posters – and the logo was suddenly everywhere.

The inspiration for the image came from Jagger, who wanted something 'anti-authoritarian' to represent the Stones. Jagger gave the 24-year-old Pasche a photo of Kali, the Hindu goddess of Time, Change, Power and Destruction, visually portrayed with her tongue sticking out. Pasche made various sketches before deciding upon the slightly side-on version of red lips and tongue. The stylized image, which could be reproduced simply and added to items of merchandise, had more in common with Jagger than the goddess Kali, and quickly became synonymous with the band. Pasche's fee was just 50 guineas, with a £200 bonus paid to him at the end of 1972. In 2008, he sold the original artwork to London's V&A Museum for £50,000.

Sticky Fingers was mixed during the first two months of 1971 and the order of songs finalized under the supervision of Jimmy Miller. Mick Jagger and Keith Richards were the only Stones involved in the process, perhaps showing the pecking order in the band but, in truth, the others just weren't interested in the laborious process.

'Brown Sugar' was released as a single in March, backed with 'Bitch' and the bonus track, a cover of Chuck Berry's 'Let it Rock', and it quickly climbed to No.2 in the UK (it reached No.1 in the US and in other territories). The Stones promoted the release with a mini UK Tour, augmented on stage by Keys, Price and keyboardist Nicky Hopkins.

Sticky Fingers was released on 23 April 1971 during a period of intense controversy for the band. Mick Jagger's film *Performance* had been released in January and the documentary *Gimme Shelter*, featuring the tragic events at Altamont, was released soon after. The Stones-Atlantic deal was signed on 1 April, but by the time the album was released the band had left for France (the album release party was held there, at the Port Pierre Canto Club). With the new contract putting the Stones into a higher tax bracket, members of the band would become tax exiles, living and working in France. Their next album, *Exile in Main Street*, would be recorded there in 1972.

Sticky Fingers was a No.1 hit on both sides of the Atlantic, bringing an immediate return on Atlantic's investment in the band. As far as fans were concerned, the album was well worth the wait, with *Sticky Fingers* selling 3 million copies in the US alone. Unsurprisingly, *Rolling Stone* magazine was effusive in its reviews: '[The Rolling Stones were] not only alive,' wrote editor Jann Wenner, 'but were kicking the shit out of everything else being done in rock and roll music … it's the latest beautiful chapter in the continuing story of the greatest rock and roll group in the world.' Jon Landau, though, was a dissenting voice: '… middle-level Rolling Stones competence. The low points aren't that low, but the high points, with one exception [Brown Sugar] aren't that high.'

Sticky Fingers was the start of a new era for the Stones, but after the release of the well-regarded double-album *Exile in Main Street* in 1972 – a not too subtle observation that they might be the best band in the world but they couldn't live in England and enjoy the rewards – each subsequent album lost a little of the band's luster. The production of *Goats Head Soup* (1973) was disappointing, and *It's Only Rock and Roll* (1974) was threadbare, by which time Mick Taylor left the band. The pace of life in the Stones had become much too dangerous, and nursing an increasing drug problem, Taylor suddenly quit.

The Rolling Stones Mark III would welcome the addition of former Faces guitarist Ronnie Wood in 1975. I saw the Stones play live, some 20 years later, on their 1995 Voodoo Lounge Tour and could only marvel at the way Richards and Wood seamlessly weaved their music together (Bill Wyman had retired by this stage), but perhaps the band had lost some magic along the way. I couldn't put my finger on it; Jagger was in great form, Charlie Watts still didn't smile and Bobby Keys was back on sax (Keys was banned by Jagger from touring with the Stones for a time in the early 1980s, because of certain 'lifestyle choices'). It was different from the sound the band had in the early 1970s. Was Mick Taylor the missing element?

'The Mick Taylor period was a creative peak for us,' drummer Charlie Watts has admitted. 'A tremendous jump in musical credibility.' Richards was in awe of Taylor's playing – 'the melodic touch, a beautiful sustain and a way of reading a song,' he admitted – but also accused him of being 'very distant'. Richards and Taylor did not hit it off, and that was that. 'He was a very fluent, melodic player … and it gave me something to follow, to bang off,' Mick Jagger said of Taylor's years in the Rolling Stones. 'Some people think that's the best version of the band that existed.'

Sticky Fingers / **The Rolling Stones** (April 1971)   46:43

All songs written by Mick Jagger and Keith Richards, except where noted.

SIDE ONE   LENGTH
1.   Brown Sugar   3:48
2.   Sway   3:50
3.   Wild Horses   5:42
4.   Can't You Hear Me Knocking   7:14
5.   You Gotta Move (Fred McDowell/Gary Davis)   2:32

SIDE TWO
6.   Bitch   3:38
7.   I Got the Blues   3:54
8.   Sister Morphine (Jagger/Richards/M. Faithfull)   5:31
9.   Dead Flowers   4:03
10.   Moonlight Mile   5:56

imagine the clouds dripping. dig a hole in your garden to put them in. yoko '63

imagine
john
lennon

PAS 10004   (1E 064 o 04914)   stereo

CHAPTER 8

Imagine

John Lennon 1971

'All I want is some truth, just gimme some truth ...'

J ohn Lennon, saint or sinner? Troubled genius or lucky bastard
to have met Paul McCartney at a Woolton Church fete in 1957?
'Man of the Decade', or not even 'Father of the Year'? Opinions
differ, but this is the problem in trying to reconcile real people,
even talented ones like Lennon who die tragically young, with their
historical and cultural legacies. What would popular music have
been like – hell, what would the world have been like – if Lennon
had lived? These are all unanswerable questions.

In December 1980, I was 21 years old and had just finished my
first year as a school teacher. Returning to my car, having just bought
a copy of Alan Aldridge's *Illustrated Beatles Lyrics*, I was thumbing
through the pages, listening to the car radio. As one Beatles song
played after another, I became engrossed in the book, enjoying the
serendipity of the music playing and the pop art images in front of
me. A voice on the radio then announced, 'playing a solid hour of the
Beatles in honor of John Lennon, who was shot and killed in New
York City today.'

I was still sitting there an hour later.

Almost forty years after his death, the crowning glory of John Lennon's post-Beatles career is the song 'Imagine' from the 1971 album of the same name. Since 1980 especially, the song has become a much-loved anthem for (former) hippies, dreamers and idealists, and has been embraced by subsequent generations who only have Lennon's music to know him by. The song's message, with Lennon's gentle piano and vocal, has since taken on a life of its own and is regarded across many countries and cultures as the world's favorite 'peace' song.

How did this happen?

After the release of several experimental electronic albums, and the sparse *Plastic Ono Band* (1970), *Imagine* was a case of Lennon giving fans what they wanted. *Imagine* sounded like a Beatles album, with its balance of ballads, rockers and political statements, wrapped in some of Phil Spector's best production work (before he went crazy!). '"Imagine" is a big hit almost everywhere,' Lennon later observed. '[An] anti-religious, anti-nationalistic, anti-conventional, anti-capitalistic song, but because it is sugar-coated it is accepted. Now I understand what you have to do.'

The album *Imagine* was released in September 1971 and quickly climbed to the top of the charts around the world. The single, which was not released in the UK, was No.1 in Australia and Canada, but only No.3 in the US. In December of that year, the UK release of 'Happy Xmas (War Is Over)', credited to John Lennon and the Plastic Ono Band with the Harlem Community Choir, stopped at No.2 in the charts. The single 'Imagine' would not be released in the UK until 1975, to promote the *Shaved Fish* compilation, stalling at No.6. After Lennon's death, it finally became a posthumous No.1 in the UK in 1981. Of course, it would.

I received a copy of *Imagine* from my parents for my 13th birthday in December 1971. I was experiencing Beatlemania again, albeit second-hand through the release of the Beatles' solo albums. Although John was going through his rebellious phase with Yoko – posing nude on the cover of their album *Two Virgins* (1968); spending their honeymoon in bed and inviting the world media to interview them in 1969; cutting off their hair in 1970 and auctioning it off for 'peace' – my parents had no idea how subversive the album was. 'Imagine there's no religion …' was an incredibly confronting concept for a Catholic school kid at that time.

This was no 'Top of the Pops' material, nor was it unfamiliar territory for Lennon. In March 1966, he was quoted in an interview with journalist Maureen Cleve as saying:

> Christianity will go. It will vanish and shrink. I needn't argue about that; I'm right and I'll be proved right. We're more popular than Jesus now; I don't know which will go first – rock 'n' roll or Christianity. Jesus was all right but his disciples were thick and ordinary. It's them twisting it that ruins it for me.

The article did not raise eyebrows in the UK, but in the lead up to the Beatles' US Tour, America's 'Bible Belt' took offence, banned Beatles songs on local radio, burned their records and promotional material on public bonfires and generated a lot of hate for Lennon and the band. It was a PR disaster for manager Brian Epstein but the Beatles rode out the controversy and their careers actually went from strength to strength.

At the beginning of 1971, John and Yoko were living at Tittenhurst Park Estate in Ascot, having installed an eight-track recording studio in its premises (which they called Ascot Sound Studios). Working with the Beatles, Lennon had grown to hate recording, and yearned to make the process simpler and quicker. *Plastic Ono Band* had been recorded there the previous year (Yoko Ono simultaneously released her album, also called *Plastic Ono Band*, although it not surprisingly failed to chart). The single 'Power to the People' was recorded there too and was released as a single in March 1971. An unrelenting barrage of raw power 'searching for a melody' as one reviewer noted, 'Power to the People' was a minor Top 10 hit in the UK (No.6) and struggled to make a dent in the US charts (No.11).

The real concern at the time was that the new album from Lennon and Ono would be like 'Power to the People': an unrelenting attack on the establishment, as they saw it; blunt, harsh and aggressive. But Lennon, Ono and producer Phil Spector showed an astute change of pace and the peaceful ballad 'Imagine' set the tone for the rest of the album; melodic, orchestrated, yes, even 'sugar-coated'. It was also the last album that Lennon would write, perform and produce in his native England.

Although John Lennon would receive sole credit on the cover, the inner sleeve credits the album to John Lennon and the Plastic Ono Band. Always meant to be fluid group of players, the band included Yoko, regular sidemen Klaus Voormann (bass) and Alan White (drums), as well as session drummers Jim Keltner and Jim Gordon; Joey Molland and Tom Evans from Badfinger, Ted Turner from Wishbone Ash and Mike Pinder from the Moody Blues; premier session keyboardist Nicky Hopkins and sax legend King Curtis (whose work on several tracks was later dubbed in in New York). Lending a hand to proceedings, especially on the track 'How

Do You Sleep?' was George Harrison, whose presence on the final album would give it a heightened context.

Lennon was very keen to use musicians he had not played with before, which conformed to the ad hoc nature of the Plastic Ono Band. Former Beatles roadie Mal Evans was friends with Rod Linton, who brought along John Tout, Steve Brendell and Andy Davis to the sessions. The players would start the morning with breakfast around a large table before working on each song. '[Yoko] was actually very nice and very friendly towards us all,' Tout recalled in a 1998 interview. 'We all used to eat in a big room. They would serve up lunch and dinner. It was a nice atmosphere. People were just lounging around smoking joints as it was in those days.'

The 'behind the scenes' action in making the album was revealed with the belated release of a documentary, filmed by the Lennons' PA Daniel Richter in the summer of 1971. Released briefly on TV the following year, the film was not widely seen until the mid-1980s, well after Lennon's death, when it was mass produced on video as *Gimme Some Truth*. It is not only a window into how the album was made but also to the different dynamics at play in that first full year after the Beatles breakup.

The home studio was constructed adjacent to the kitchen and there is a great scene in the *Imagine* documentary when George Harrison materializes at the breakfast table one morning and jokes with Lennon that he had not seen the other Beatles for a while but that 'Beatle Ed' was 'No.5 in Sweden' (Lennon likes the joke so much he repeats it for the camera, taking the punch line for himself). The laconic Harrison then looks across the table at producer Phil Spector eating breakfast and observes, 'I see Beatle Phil's making a pig of himself though.' Harrison is at the top of his game here, and his playing shows it.

Spector's 'Wall of Sound' production is limited to a just a couple of songs ('Gimme Some Truth' and 'I Don't Want to Be A Soldier') while he lends his background vocals to 'Oh Yoko'. Only three of the songs on the album were written in 1971, 'Imagine', 'Crippled Inside' and 'How Do You Sleep?'. The rest were songs Lennon had written or partially developed over the previous three years. Besides the tracks that would end up on the album, the unreleased 'San Francisco Bay Blues', a demo of 'Aisumasen (I'm Sorry)' that would later turn up on Lennon's *Mind Games* (1973) album, and a demo of 'I'm the Greatest' that he would give to Ringo Starr in 1973, were also recorded during the sessions.

The inspiration for the lyric, 'Imagine there's no heaven …' was Yoko Ono's poem 'Cloud Piece', part of which was reproduced on the back cover of the album ('Imagine the clouds dripping, dig a hole in your garden to put them in'). Simply structured around a C major chord, Lennon stated at the time that he composed the song on piano to stop himself from repeating familiar chord sequences on guitar. Lennon liked to use the same four 'pop chords' – F, G, C, E – in many of his songs, starting in different keys but always including minor chords into the progression (even the novelty song 'You Know My Name (Look Up the Number)' has a similar chord structure). 'Imagine' would be no different.

Lennon was clearly still going through his 'white phase' during 'Imagine' and plays the song on a white 'baby grand' piano, a photograph of which was inserted in the album as a giveaway poster and has since become iconic. His playing is simple; Lennon, of course, was a self-taught pianist, but he was determined to play the song himself rather than hand the duties over to Nicky Hopkins, who doubles on piano but is hardly audible in the mix. In the *Imagine* documentary, Lennon demoes the song for Hopkins and Klaus Voormann, talking through the lyrics, which are already fully formed.

'That's the one I like best,' Lennon remarks, ultimately making it the lead track on the album, which he also called *Imagine*. The sound was sparse, piano, bass and drums, so Spector later added strings, which gives the song an almost hymn-like quality. But the incongruity of a millionaire pop star singing about a world with 'no possessions' was not lost on some critics; the former Beatle and his eccentric wife were easy targets. Elton John famously sent a 40th birthday message to Lennon shortly before his death, 'Imagine six apartments / It isn't hard to …', but the simplicity and humility of the song defies parody.

'Crippled Inside' is Lennon at his most sardonic. The song also marks the first appearance of George Harrison's unmistakable slide guitar on the album and Nicky Hopkins on wonderful, honky-tonk piano. John Tout also plays piano on the track (he is wrongly credited as a guitarist on the sleeve notes), while Jim Keltner takes on drumming duties. Lennon used three different drummers on the record (also Alan White and Jim Gordon, of Derek and the Dominos fame), but Ringo Starr was not one of them, the former Beatle working on the film *Blindman* in the summer of 1971.

Although the song is plainly metaphorical ('One thing you can't hide / Is when you're crippled inside …'), early in his career Lennon did have a somewhat cruel sense of humor when it came to disabled people. There are ample images of Lennon mugging for the cameras, stamping his feet on stage and generally goofing around during his career 'like a cripple', with George confirming in the *Anthology* documentary, 'You could see he had a thing about them; I think it was a fear or something … We'd come out of the band room to go to the stage and we'd be fighting our way through all these poor unfortunate people.'

Lennon's experience with 'primal scream' therapy opened a window for him about his own emotional shortcomings and this newfound mindset led to him writing 'Crippled Inside', 'Oh My Love' and 'How?' as well as finalizing 'Jealous Guy', one of the stand-out tracks on the album. Dating back to the White Album sessions, when the song was called 'Child of Nature', Lennon changed the clunky lyrics to a more honest refection of his relationship with women. 'Jealous Guy' is Lennon at his most honest, and vulnerable ('I began to lose control …'). The string arrangement is stunning, complementing Lennon's wonderful vocal, which finishes with his gentle whistling of the melody before the final verse. Alan White plays the vibraphone on this track while musical arranger John Barham (*All Things Must Pass*) works the harmonium.

The song would have made an ideal single to follow 'Imagine', matching that song in simplicity and unvarnished beauty, but was strangely overlooked. Following Lennon's murder, English band Roxy Music covered the song in February 1981 and had their only No.1 UK hit. Tribute or gross opportunism, take your pick, but you just can't beat the original.

With its obvious double-entendre title, 'It's So Hard' is a straightforward blues number with a choogling beat. One of the first songs recorded in the sessions, Lennon was keen to have King Curtis, the New York saxophone legend who had featured so prominently on such early rock and roll songs as the Coasters hits 'Yakety Yak' and 'Charlie Brown', play on it. A virtuoso player and underrated composer and arranger of soul music, Curtis had supported the Beatles on their 1965 Shea Stadium concert (the King Curtis Band backed Brenda Holloway). Lennon was in awe of Curtis' talent and couldn't believe he had agreed to play on the record.

The final track on Side One, 'I Don't Wanna Be a Soldier', is Lennon's most direct political statement ('I don't wanna be a soldier mama I don't wanna die …') with sparse lyrics echoing across Spector's 'wall of sound' production. Not so surprisingly, the song started out as a jam session during the 'Power to the People' sessions in February and has a similar feel to that song, but Lennon was apparently unhappy with the end result and re-recorded the song later.

Side Two of the album opens with the blistering 'Gimme Some Truth'. Featuring some of Lennon's best wordplay ('No short-haired, yellow-bellied, son of tricky dicky's gonna mother hubbard soft soap me with just a pocket full of hope …') the song also showcases arguably Lennon's best vocal performance and a wonderful guitar solo from George Harrison. Most contentious was the line, 'money for dope, money for rope …' coming so quickly after the reference to 'tricky dicky' (the nickname for then American President Richard Nixon). The line tapped into the early 1970s conspiracy theory that the US government-sanctioned CIA were trafficking cocaine into the States from Latin America (a theory later to prove correct) but the song works on so many levels … protest song, rock song and political manifesto.

Many people at the time, however, saw the song as Lennon supporting drug use (or perhaps, suicide) and although this was not true, the line is still confronting. When Pearl Jam's Eddie Vedder sang the song during the band's post 9/11 concerts in New York in

2001, he copped out and only mumbled the words about 'dope' and 'rope', apparently not wanting to be seen to support either. I respect Eddie Vedder a lot as musician, but it just shows how brave John Lennon was thirty years before him.

The next track, 'Oh My Love', is a gentle ballad elevated somewhat by Nicky Hopkins' delicate piano. The song is reminiscent of Lennon's 'Julia' on 'The White Album' and is prayer-like in delivery. 'Yoko helps me a lot on lyrics,' Lennon said in a 1971 interview, and his wife is credited as co-writer on this song, the only co-credit she was given on the album at the time. More about that later.

'How Do You Sleep?' is the most controversial song on the album. A direct attack on former writing partner Paul McCartney, the glee on Lennon's face is clearly evident in the *Gimme Some Truth* documentary when he demoes the song on piano for George Harrison. 'That's the nasty one,' Lennon laughs. He later justified the attack as being payback for Paul's album *Ram* (especially 'Too Many People') and consolidated the view by posing with a pig (as Paul did with a ram) and putting a photograph of it inside the record sleeve as a giveaway.

Rather than being clever or insightful, the lyrics in 'How Do You Sleep?' can be dismissed now as Lennon trash talk ('You live with straights who tell you you was king …'). The finished song is quicker, and funkier, than the original demo, with a nice hook at the end of each line of the chorus ('How do you sleep …') that is picked up by Harrison on slide guitar and again in the orchestration. Lennon leaves lots of clues about his relationship with Paul along the way ('The only thing you done was yesterday / And since you're gone you're just another day …') and hurls a 'c-bomb' in McCartney's direction during the demo.

McCartney's response was all class. 'How do I sleep?' he answered journos at the time. 'Quite well, thank you.'

That no one close to Lennon – Yoko, Harrison, Spector or even Klaus Voormann – had the nerve to say to him, 'Do you really want to do this?' speaks a lot for Lennon's star power personality. This was the one song the press picked up on when the album was released, even more than the peaceful 'Imagine', and fueled stories about the band's animosity for years to come. And in another example of Lennon's apparent hypocrisy, critics asked how he could be advocating for a peaceful utopia on one track and spewing such hatred on another? Or were fans reading far too much into it?

'When I heard *Ram*, I immediately sat down and wrote my song which is an answer to *Ram*,' Lennon later clarified. 'It's as simple as that. It's also a moment's anger. But it was written down on paper and when I sang, it wasn't quite as angry as when I sang it in the studio, because it was four weeks later and we were all writing it, you know. It was like a joke. "Let's write this down." We didn't take it that seriously.'

But Lennon regretted the lyrics almost immediately. 'The only thing that matters is how he and I feel about these things and not what the writer or commentator thinks about it. Him and me are okay,' he said in 1974. Lennon would later rework the song for the *Walls and Bridges* album that year, renaming it 'Steel and Glass' and aiming any vitriol towards his former manager Allen Klein ('There you stand with your L.A. tan / And your New York walk and your New York talk…').

'How?' is one of my favorite songs on the album, and features some of Lennon's most heartfelt lyrics ('How can I give love when love is something I never had …'). I particularly like the chorus

('You know life can be tough / Sometimes I feel I've had enough …'), especially when Lennon sings under the melody the second time around, as if defeated by life. John Barham plays the vibraphone and does a wonderful orchestral arrangement on this track.

'Oh Yoko!' is a great way to finish the album, with Lennon's signature harmonica harking back to his early Beatles days with 'Love Me Do'. The overall feeling is one of joy and happiness – a statement of their love – but the recording of the song was the source of much frustration back in 1971. With Phil Spector assisting John in singing back-up harmonies, it was left to Yoko to direct recording engineer Phillip McDonald in finding the right verse on the tape playback for the pair to dub the vocals. Yoko suggests to an increasingly frustrated Lennon that they 'forget about it for today' but Lennon presses ahead and drops the c-bomb on the hapless 'Phil' when he again fluffs the playback. The sight of Yoko directing Lennon and Spector (of all people) to 'sing into the mic' is quite galling, especially given that they are actually singing her name in the song. The effect is strangely similar to Yoko helping John write a love letter to herself.

Lennon and Spector mixed the record in New York in June 1971, adding King Curtis' sax to 'It's So Hard' and 'I Don't Wanna Be a Soldier' and string arrangements by the New York Philharmonic Orchestra (credited as the Flux Fiddlers on the album). In August, a month before the album's release, Curtis was stabbed to death in an unprovoked attack outside his New York apartment and would never hear the finished album. Interestingly, Jack Douglas, the Record Plant engineer on *Imagine*, would produce Lennon's final album, *Double Fantasy*, in 1980.

For the cover of the album, the Lennons originally considered a somewhat garish portrait of John with die cut eyes – revealing clouds(!) – and opening up into images from his childhood. Clouds were a recurring theme for John and Yoko at the time; a single cloud features on the *Live Peace in Toronto* album, in 1969, and also the *Plastic Ono Band* album in 1970. Instead, they opted for Iain Macmillan's photograph of Lennon looking up at the sky, which ended up at the last moment being placed on the back cover. For some obscure reason, the Lennons substituted a less flattering polaroid taken by Andy Warhol in 1969 with a cloud superimposed over it (the same cloud is superimposed on the back cover) for the front cover. Not that Warhol got the credit, like he did on the Rolling Stones' *Sticky Fingers*; Yoko Ono is credited for all artwork on the album.

Imagine was one of the most critically acclaimed albums of 1971. 'It's the best album of the year, and for me it's the best album he's done, with anything, or with anyone, at any time,' Roy Hollingworth wrote in *Melody Maker*. 'The album is superb,' Alan Smith agreed in *NME*. 'Beautiful. One step away from the chill of his recent total self-revelation, and yet a giant leap towards commerciality without compromise … I have no criticism at all.'

Ben Gerson, however, wrote an incongruously poor review in *Rolling Stone* in its October 1971 issue:

> In its technical sloppiness and self-absorption, *Imagine* is John's *Self-Portrait* [referencing Bob Dylan's poorly received 1970 album] … on the heels of Plastic Ono Band it only seems to reinforce the questioning of what John's relationship to rock really is. 'Imagine', for instance, is simply the consolidation of primal awareness into a world movement. It asks that we imagine a world without religions or nations, and that such a world would mean brotherhood and

peace. The singing is methodical but not really skilled, the melody undistinguished, except the bridge, which sounds nice to me.

Rolling Stone had been Lennon's champions since its first edition, in 1967, so what was the issue now? Just before the release of *Imagine*, editor Jann Wenner had a major falling out with Lennon regarding the rights to an extensive interview he conducted with John and Yoko, which was meant as a 'one-off'. The *Rolling Stone* editor then published the interview in book form as 'Lennon Remembers'. Lennon did not speak to Wenner for the rest of the decade, ceding only to give an interview shortly before his death in 1980, after giving *Playboy* the exclusive. Did this affect Lennon's review?

In a November 1971 interview for *Melody Maker*, McCartney spoke positively about *Imagine*, commenting on the fact that it appeared to be 'less political' than Lennon's previous work. Lennon was quick to chide his former bandmate, saying, 'So you think "Imagine" ain't political? It's "Working Class Hero" with sugar on it for conservatives like yourself!'

By the time of *Imagine*'s album release, the Lennons had relocated to New York and started to absorb the anti-establishment politics of the period. Having lived inside a fame bubble for much of his adult life, Lennon proved to be easily influenced, pliable even, and the radical lives of David Peel, Abbie Hoffman, John Sinclair and Angela Davies found their way into his music. Yoko Ono was now John's legitimate music partner, and the next album recorded in New York would be jointly credited to John and Yoko.

Some Time in New York City (1972) has many high points musically – Spector's production on some tracks, the orchestration on

'Angela', the dobro guitar on 'John Sinclair' and the general playing of the band Elephant's Memory (especially the sax playing of Stan Bronstein) is exceptional – but the lyrics quickly alienate (especially 'Woman is the Nigger of the World') and come across as forced and naïve. The album undid much of the goodwill generated by *Imagine* and, in retrospect, Lennon's solo career never fully recovered. He temporarily split from Yoko in 1973 and released two albums under his own name (*Mind Games* in 1973, and *Walls and Bridges,* in 1974) as well as a recording a collection of old songs for *Rock and Roll* (1975), part of the settlement for his plagiarism of a Chuck Berry song on *Abbey Road*'s 'Come Together'.

Having reconciled with Yoko, Lennon retired from recording following the birth of their son, Sean, on 9 October 1975 (which was also Lennon's 35th birthday). For the next five years, he retreated to his Dakota Building apartment, content to be a 'house husband' and raise his son; watching the wheels go 'round and round' as he later eloquently put it. Lennon only decided to go back into the recording studio when he thought he had enough good songs for an album, but even then, he only signed a contract with Geffen Records on the proviso that Yoko be given equal space on the album, which would be called *Double Fantasy* (1980).

On 13 September 1980, Elton John held a free concert in New York's Central Park, ending it with 'Imagine'. Elton told the audience, 'This is for a dear friend of mine who doesn't live too far from here, so let's sing it loud enough for him to hear it.'

Three months later, John Lennon was doing the publicity rounds after the release of his first album in five years when he was gunned down in the entrance to the Dakota Building. The killer had asked for his autograph earlier that night (I will not mention the man's name in these pages). The tragedy of Lennon's senseless murder was not that it robbed the world of a unique artist, or even a music 'genius', but that it took the life of a man who was just finding himself as a father and a husband.

Since then, 'Imagine' has become an important part of Lennon's legacy. A mosaic that spells out the word 'Imagine' in a section of Central Park is dedicated to Lennon. The memorial is called Strawberry Fields and is located across from Lennon's apartment, where he was murdered. In 1999, a BBC poll named 'Imagine' as Britain's favorite lyric and, in 2002, a survey by the Guinness Book of Records voted it second (behind Queen's 'Bohemian Rhapsody') as the UK's favorite song of all time. In 2012, *Imagine* was voted 80th on *Rolling Stone* magazine's list of the '500 Greatest Albums of All Time'. The following year, 'Imagine' was No.3 on *Rolling Stone*'s list of the 500 greatest songs, the reviewer calling it Lennon's 'greatest musical gift to the world.'

'Imagine' has also been the focal point of many peace campaigns, beginning in 1971 when the album was released. The 'Imagine' message was more powerful than the 'War is Over' slogan John and Yoko promoted around the world and would prove to be a lasting memory after Lennon's death in 1980.

Following the 9/11 attacks on New York in 2001, Ono paid for billboards in New York, London and Tokyo with the simple message, 'Imagine … living life in peace.' Not that all decisions about the song have been so altruistic.

In the 1990s, Ono first allowed a version of the song to be used in a Japanese TV commercial for a telephone company and was allegedly paid US$400,000. More recently, Lennon's original recording has been used to advertise values.com, 'the foundation for a better life' and UNICEF (World Vision). Lennon's main heir and executor of his estate, Ono could license the song's use, but she still didn't have industry recognition as co-writer of 'Imagine'.

In an interview with *Rolling Stone* in the late 1970s, Lennon claimed that the main inspiration for the song was a 'prayer-book' written by the comedian and political activist Dick Gregory, which he was reading at the time. But he also acknowledged that the song was originally inspired by Yoko's 1964 book *Grapefruit*. 'In it are a lot of pieces saying, "Imagine this, imagine that",' Lennon said. 'Yoko actually helped a lot with the lyrics, but I wasn't man enough to let her have credit for it. I was still selfish enough and unaware enough to sort of take her contribution without acknowledging it.'

In more recent interviews, Ono says 'Imagine' was mainly written in the bedroom she shared with John at Tittenhurst Park in the early 1970s, but she was at first reticent to confirm the part she played in the writing of the song 'because I have been a figure that was not necessarily loved.' She adds, 'I was worried that the fact that I had anything to do with the song would have been considered as interference to its popularity.'

Having unfairly been blamed over the years for taking John from his first family, for the breakup of the Beatles and for trading on Lennon's fame for her own artistic purposes, Ono would receive a belated honor. On 14 June 2017, the National Music Publishers' Association announced that Yoko Ono would finally be credited as co-songwriter of 'Imagine'. This took place at a ceremony where Yoko was given a Centennial Award for her contribution to 'Imagine', which was followed by a performance of the song by Patti Smith.

'Imagine' is a Utopian ideal that millions of people around the world bought into and continue to aspire towards. As Yoko Ono once put it, the song is 'the crystallisation of our dream'. As simple as that.

And perhaps that is the key to the song's enduring popularity. Its simplicity.

Imagine / **John Lennon** (September 1971)   39:29

All songs written by John Lennon, or John Lennon & Yoko Ono*

SIDE ONE		LENGTH
1.	Imagine*	3:01
2.	Crippled Inside	3:47
3.	Jealous Guy	4:14
4.	It's So Hard	2:25
5.	I Don't Want to Be a Soldier	6:05

SIDE TWO		
6.	Gimme Some Truth	3:16
7.	Oh My Love*	2:50
8.	How Do You Sleep?	5:36
9.	How?	3:43
10.	Oh Yoko!	4:20

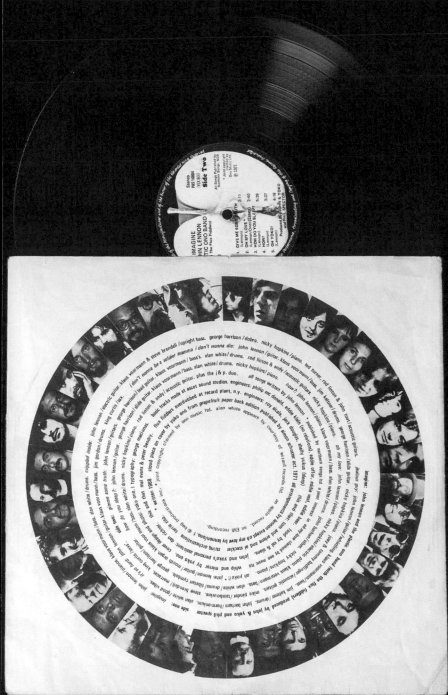

CHAPTER 9

American Pie

Don McLean 1971

'There we were all in one place, a generation lost in space ...'

Don McLean had many heroes growing up. An asthmatic child in affluent New Rochelle, in New York, he missed a lot of school because of his illness and spent his teenage years immersed in pop culture staples, radio, TV and popular music – any music. Not only rock and roll, but music from the 1920s and 30s, bluegrass, country and western, and most importantly, folk music.

Hopalong Cassidy was an early hero. On the inner sleeve of the *American Pie* album, McLean includes a free-form poem honoring actor William Boyd, aka Hopalong Cassidy (1895–1972), the star of many B-grade movie westerns who found fame on fledgling black-and-white TV in the 1950s. 'The black and white days are over,' McLean writes. 'So long Hopalong Cassidy.'

Taking up the guitar as a teenager, McLean was a natural talent with an angelic voice. Pete Seeger (1919–2014) became another hero. Soaking up the influences of folkies like Seeger, Woodie Guthrie, and the Weavers, McLean could be heard playing music at Caffe Lena, the Bitter End and the Newport Folk Festival in the mid-1960s. The New York State Council for the Arts invited him to be their Hudson River Troubadour, traveling from town to town and sharing his music. McLean then spent a year sailing with Pete Seeger's ecology-promoting *Clearwater* sloop up and down the Atlantic Coast, playing folk music to a willing audience.

But most importantly, the singer Buddy Holly (1936–1959) was an important presence in McLean's early life. In 1971, McLean found international stardom with a song that charted the pop culture history of the volatile decade that came after Holly's tragic death in a plane accident at the age of 22. 'I dedicated the album *American Pie* to Buddy Holly,' McLean wrote in an open letter to fans in 1993, '… in order to connect the entire statement to Holly in hopes of bringing about an interest in him, which subsequently did occur.'

In 1961, when Don McLean was just 15 years old, his father suddenly passed away, which left him hurt, bitter and, at times, angry. Coming so quickly after Holly's death, it's not too hard to see that McLean somehow configured the grief of his father's death with that of Holly the year before. When McLean laments the passing of a simpler time in 'American Pie', he may just as well be talking about his own life as much as pop culture history.

'"American Pie" is a death song, really,' McLean admitted in a 2012 interview. Buddy Holly, McLean's father, John Kennedy, Martin Luther King Jr, Robert Kennedy, thousands of Vietnam vets, and even 18-year-old Meredith Hunter, the fan beaten and stabbed to death in front of the stage at a Rolling Stones concert at Altamont Speedway in December 1969, all died within that period.

I was turning 14 when 'America Pie' was climbing the charts around the world – about the same age McLean was when he delivered 'bad news on the doorstep' as a paperboy in February 1959 – so this one song had just a big an impact on me as the news of

Holly's death had on McLean. I pored over the record looking for clues, listened to the record and learned.

My first glimpse of Don Mclean was grainy, black-and-white film of him singing 'American Pie' in concert at Wollman Auditorium, Columbia University, which was shown on TV in early 1972 – the compère of the program mispronounces his name as Don Mc-*clean*. Not only was McLean's voice totally unique, but the way he played the guitar was mesmerizing; gently moving his shoulders as he strummed, raising the neck of the instrument high like a matador in a bullfight. With a mass of hair swept across his face, he actually starts out with the chorus of the song and then gets his college student audience to sing along before launching into the introductory verse.

'American Pie' was already deeply iconic and performing the song was a cultural event.

The early 1970s was a wonderful era for singer-songwriters; performers who did not require the backing of a band but could sit alone on stage – naked, in a performance sense – with only a guitar, piano or their voice for accompaniment. They were songwriters who largely wrote their own material, idiosyncratic to their own style. In that milieu, a diverse group of performers including James Taylor, Carol King, Tim Buckley, Arlo Guthrie, Randy Newman, Joni Mitchell, Paul Simon, Melanie Safka, Cat Stevens, Gordon Lightfoot, Judy Collins, Harry Chapin, Laura Nyro, Van Morrison, Harry Nilsson and Jim Croce had various degrees of success – and these are only the ones I listened to.

That a non-descript troubadour named Don McLean would have arguably the longest popular success is in no small part due to the release of his *American Pie* album in 1971. The epic single of the same name became a worldwide hit early the next year and, in 8 minutes and 33 seconds, perfectly encapsulated the relatively short journey rock and roll had taken since Buddy Holly's death a little over a decade before.

Upon hearing the song and surveying the LP dedicated to Holly, I was keen to learn more about the tragedy that befell the 22-year-old music sensation in February 1959. Born Charles Hardin Holley in Lubbock, Texas, Holly was traveling on the Winter Dance Party Tour of the American Midwest with a host of other rock stars of the era. Ritchie Valens, a 17-year-old Latino who had back-to-back hits with 'Donna' and 'La Bamba', former DJ 'The Big Bopper', J.P. Richardson, who had a novelty hit with Chantilly Lace, and Dion and the Belmonts were also on that tour. Having split with the Crickets, Holly's backing band on this tour comprised Waylon Jennings and Tommy Allsup on guitars, and Carl Bunch on drums.

Holly was reluctant to go on the tour; his wife Maria was expecting their first child and, now based in New York, he did not want to go off and play 24 dates in 24 consecutive days in the middle of winter. On the other hand, having spent his recent time as an in-house producer for the Coral record company, Holly's own records had stopped selling; 1957's 'That'll Be the Day' was his only No.1 hit, and following the release of 'Peggy Sue' the same year, none of his subsequent singles had reached the Top 10. The tour would reignite interest in his music, he was told, so Holly signed on.

After each concert, the performers continued on to their next venue by bus, often driving throughout the night. Later described as 'the tour from hell', the group zig-zagged back and forth across four states without a single day's break. The tour bus had only minimal heating and drummer Carl Bunch was hospitalized with frostbite as the party traveled into Clear Lake, Iowa, to play the Surf Ballroom on 2 February. Richie Valens actually played drums for Holly that night, in what would be their final, fateful concert.

Rather than travel the 400 miles by bus to their next venue in Moorhead, in northwest Minnesota, a tired Holly asked the owner of the Surf Ballroom to charter a small plane to take him and his two bandmates to nearby Fargo (North Dakota) so they could get a good night's sleep and do their laundry.

When he heard of Holly's plans, J.P. Richardson asked Waylon Jennings if he could take his spot in the plane because he was battling the flu. Ritchie Valens then asked Tommy Allsup for his seat, but the guitarist originally said no. As the trio were leaving for the airport around midnight, Valens asked Allsup to reconsider and the pair decided to toss a coin. Valens won the toss and lost his life. Allsup also gave his wallet to Valens so the teenager could us his ID to check into his motel room. The wallet was later recovered from the crash site.

The trio of rock and roll stars took off from Mason City Municipal Airport in a 1947 Beechcraft 35 Bonanza flown by 21-year-old pilot Roger Peterson at 12.55am as a snow drift hit the area. Aircraft owner Herb Dwyer stood and watched the tail-light of the plane bank left for the northwesterly turn to Fargo. Dwyer then waited for his pilot to radio in his flight plan, but despite repeated attempts he heard nothing from the pilot for the remainder of the night. Concerned, later that morning Dwyer took off in another plane and retraced the plane's movements. Within minutes, he spotted the wreckage in a cornfield just 6 miles (10km) from the airport.

Deputy Bill McGill was the first to arrive at the crash site. The light plane had hit the frozen ground at high speed, wrapping the plane into a tight ball of metal with only one wing sticking out from the wreckage. The body of the young pilot was trapped inside but all three passengers had been thrown from the wreckage, which had come to rest on a barbed-wire fence, and they were killed on impact. The body of Buddy Holly, who was sitting next to the pilot when the plane took off, was found 17 feet (5m) southwest of the plane. Of the two backseat passengers, Valens' body was near Holly's but Richardson had been thrown into an adjoining paddock some 40 feet (12m) away. All three had suffered multiple body fractures and traumatic brain injuries.

The identities of the victims were identified by Caroll Anderson, the owner of the Surf Ballroom, who also cleared up why Tommy Allsup's wallet was among the victims' belongings. By then local media, including a TV film crew, had arrived at the scene to document the tragedy. A subsequent coroner's inquest found that the young pilot did not have the instrument training to fly in the poor weather conditions and may have inadvertently driven the plane into the ground after being confused by the plane's older gyroscope (the instrument that displays pitch altitude information). Tragically, that model Bonanza displayed information in a graphically opposite manner to what pilot Peterson had been used to.

The death of the three young rock and roll stars made news around the world. Holly had already toured England, Europe and Australia during his short life and one can only speculate what he would have achieved during the rest of his lifetime, if not as a performer then certainly as a producer. Holly had already inspired a generation of young Britons, including those teenagers who would later form the Beatles, the Rolling Stones, the Hollies, the Searchers and countless other bands of the 1960s. In America, the impact of Holly's death was a deeply personal one too for teenager Don McLean.

A member of the New York folk scene for much of the 1960s, Don McLean had the great misfortune to name his 1970 debut album *Tapestry*, which was swamped by the Carol King album of the same name released the following year. Although the album did not make the Top 100 in the US, it did produce two hit songs – 'Castle in the Air', which was later re-released with an added strings arrangement, and 'And I Love You So', which was a hit for Perry Como some three years later.

Signing with United Artists Records, McLean's next offering catapulted him to worldwide success in October 1971. Both the *American Pie* album and single were No.1 hits in the US, UK and Australia in early 1972, and the word quickly spread among music journalists and a growing number of loyal fans that something special was happening with the title song. Deciphering just what the song was about became a worldwide obsession.

McLean started writing the verses to 'American Pie' as early as 1969, but it would take a good 18 months for him to nail down exactly what he wanted to say (and how he wanted to say it). There was an entire underground industry in operation at the time, interpreting lyrics to pop songs (especially by the Beatles), and a whole generation took great pleasure in analyzing the lyrics to 'American Pie'. Here's my take on it.

'American Pie' might just have been called American Dream, because it is a lament for the passing of a gentler age characterized by sock hops, beauty queens and rock and roll. 'Miss American Pie' is the personification of the popular term 'as American as apple pie' and is the hook each chorus hangs from (there's just so much happening in the song; the melody even has a passing resemblance to Holly's 'I'm Gonna Love You Too'). 'Levee was dry' and 'whisky and rye' is an easy rhyme, as is 'Chevy' and 'levee', having also been used in a popular Chevrolet car commercial of the 1950s. 'The Levee' was also a dance venue in McLean's native New Rochelle, so perhaps this is a personal reference as well.

The final line of the song, 'This'll be the day that I die ...' is a play on Holly's breakthrough hit, 'That'll Be the Day'. The title of that song has its origins in the 1956 John Wayne film *The Searchers*; Wayne's character Ethan Edwards responds to his nephew's taunt, 'I hope you die!' with the laconic line, 'That'll be the day.' Interestingly, the English band the Searchers later took their name in honor of Holly's song (the Beatles chose their name – a clever spelling of 'beetles' – in honor of Holly's band the Crickets).

In 'American Pie', McLean portrays the death of Holly and his friends as 'the day the music died' but he observes that popular music in the 1960s had drifted too far away from its fundamental purpose – to make you want to dance! Roughly charting the decade between Holly's death and the Rolling Stones' disastrous Altamont concert in December 1969, the song includes six verses, including an 'intro' and 'outro'.

The intro to the song ('February made me shiver ... bad news on the doorstep') references the fate of Holly, Valens and the 'Big Bopper' in the early hours of 3 February 1959. The reference to Holly's 'widowed bride' is all the more poignant given that Maria Holly miscarried the baby she was carrying in the aftermath of her husband's death. Even allowing for his clunky rhyming ('Bad news on the doorstep, I couldn't make one more step ...') credit must be given to McLean for coining the phrase 'the day the music died'. Sixty years later, it is a term that continues to be used to describe these events.

In the second verse, McLean references the Monotones' 1958 hit 'Book of Love', a song later featured in the hit movie *American Graffiti*. He then cleverly draws the comparison between this book and the 'good book' (Gospel singer Don Cornell had a 1950s album called 'The Bible Tells Me So') before asking the question all of us who love rock and roll ultimately ask ourselves ('Do you believe in rock and roll? / Can music save your mortal soul …').

Ultimately, though, it's about the demise of dance music. McLean refers to oft-felt teenage angst ('I know that you're in love with him / 'Cause I saw you dancin' in the gym…') experienced at 'sock hops' – dances in the school gymnasium where kids had to remove their shoes so as not to mark the parquetry floor. He then refers to the origins of rock and roll ('Man, I dig those rhythm and blues …') before giving a shout out to Holly's country origins, with a reference to Marty Robbins' 1957 hit 'A White Sport Coat' ('… with a pink carnation and a pickup truck').

In the third verse, McLean fast forwards a decade with the contrary statement '…and moss grows fat on a rollin' stone…', portraying a society now turned on its head (Buddy Holly also referenced the idiom in his song 'Early in the Morning'). McLean then refers to various 1960s heroes: Elvis ('the king'), Bob Dylan ('the jester' who wears a jacket on the *Freewheelin' Bob Dylan* cover similar to the one James Dean wore in *Rebel Without A Cause*), a politicized John Lennon ('Lenin read a book on Marx') and the Beatles ('the quartet practiced in the park …'). The jester stealing the 'thorny crown' of the king may refer to Elvis' stint in the army and the rise of folk music in the early 1960s. Does 'no verdict was returned' refer to the 1964 murders of three civil rights activists in Mississippi? It makes sense when McLean signs off with the line,

'... and we sang dirges in the dark / The day the music died'; a dirge being a funeral rite.

Verse four continues the themes of change and social unrest: 'Helter Skelter in the summer swelter...' refers to the Manson Family murders in the summer of 1969 (the murderers wrote the title of the Beatles song in blood at one of the crime scenes). The Byrds' misfire single 'Eight Miles High' in 1966 'landed foul on the grass', moving popular music further and further away from its dance origins. Dylan's semi-retirement in upstate New York after a motorcycle accident is referenced in the line 'the jester on the sidelines in a cast'. 'Sweet perfume' could only mean the growing drug culture, while 'the sergeants' references the Beatles' immense success with the *Sgt. Pepper's* album. 'The players tried to take the field' is, perhaps, a commentary on the 1968 Democratic National Convention when anti-war activists tried to storm the proceedings. The next line, 'Do you recall what was revealed...' may be homage to the growing number of Beatle-ologists interpreting lyrics, but it is clear McLean is teasing the listener to take a closer listen to his song too.

In verse five, the generation of fans who attended concerts at Woodstock, the Isle of Wight and Altamont in 1969 is aptly described in the line, 'There we were all in one place / A generation lost in space ...' As a product of the first 'TV generation', I would like to think the sci-fi cult classic *Lost in Space* is referenced here, but I'm not so sure – 'lost in space' probably refers to the era's drug culture or the lack of leadership being experienced at the end of the decade. 'Jack' is introduced into the narrative – most likely Mick Jagger, as referenced in Rolling Stones hits 'Jumpin' Jack Flash' ('Jack Flash sat on a candlestick', a clever pun about San Francisco's famous

Candlestick Park) and 'Sympathy for the Devil' ('no angel born in Hell'). The 'sacrificial rite' may allude to the murder of the young fan at Altamont but McLean does not hide his disdain for the Stones' brand of 'stadium rock' ('… as I watched him on the stage / My hands were clenched in fists of rage …') which is a world away from the 'sock hops' of the 50s.

For the outro, the song slows down considerably. 'I met a girl who sang the blues …' may be Janis Joplin, who died of a drug overdose in October 1970. The 'sacred store' could be the local record store, with the current state of rock and roll reflected by the missive 'the man there said the music wouldn't play'. The chaos of the late 1960s is clearly evident ('… the children screamed, the lovers cried, the poets dreamed…'). The 'three men I admire most' would clearly reference Holly, Valens and the Big Bopper were it not for the line, 'they caught the last train for the coast' (why not 'plane'? Too obvious?). There was speculation at the time that the 'three men' were JFK, his brother Robert (as per the familial relationship of 'father/son') and Martin Luther King Jr, who died within five years of each other in the 1960s. The end of the song represents the end of an era.

McLean recorded *American Pie* at the Record Plant in New York City during May-June in 1971. Ed Freeman, who had produced fellow folkie Tim Hardin's album, was asked by McLean to produce the record, but he immediately had misgivings. Freeman says he found McLean's sound 'too commercial' and his songs 'overly poetic', and relations between the pair became quite testy during the recording. McLean rarely sang a song the same way twice, and with the producer wanting to capture a live quality in the material, he assembled a backing band made up of local session musicians that would keep the singer anchored in the music. Having never played with a band before, McLean rehearsed his songs with the group for a week before recording them.

Freeman liked the intro to 'American Pie' that McLean played him on guitar and thought the song was a surefire hit – right up until McLean launched into an up-tempo version of the chorus, thrashing his rhythm guitar as his vocal sailed all over the melody. The singer was still tweaking the lyrics in the studio but Freeman got what he was trying to say, 'the loss of American innocence', if only they could record how best to say it. It was Freeman's idea, however, to use piano on 'American Pie', and Paul Griffin's gospel-inspired piano changed the whole tone of the song. Although the band is playing live and the rhythm slowly builds to a crescendo (you can tell it's live because the tempo is all over the place), McLean's final vocal is a combination of 24 different takes because the singer was 'too fluid' in style.

The title track also features Rob Rothstein (bass), Ray Markowitz (drums) and David Spinozza (on guitar, recently of Paul McCartney's *Ram* sessions) with other musicians substituting on different songs. The last chorus on 'American Pie' features the 'West Forty Fourth Street Rhythm and Noise Choir', with Freeman later confirming the 'choir' was actually Pete Seeger, James Taylor and then girlfriend Carly Simon, and Taylor's brother Livingston.

McLean could have made his reputation on that one song but he actually has two classics on the album. 'Vincent' is the rarest of pop ballads, an intelligent ode to a troubled genius, the artist Vincent van Gogh. Apparently, McLean wrote the lyrics on a brown paper bag while working in the American school system in 1970, after reading a biography of the tragic Dutch artist, who committed suicide in 1890. Although he was certainly famous, Van Gogh was yet to reach pop culture status at the time of the song's release. I had seen Kirk Douglas' portrayal of Van Gogh in the film *Lust for Life*, so I knew who the artist was (a faded laminated copy of his most famous artwork, 'Starry Night', hung in our high school classroom) but the song 'Vincent' brought the artist to life for me and millions of others.

The song is beautifully constructed, with a writer's pallet of word pictures ('Swirling clouds in violet haze / Reflect in Vincent's eyes of China blue ...'); the lilting final verse wrings out the emotion of the song ('When no hope was left inside on that starry, starry night ...') and the subtle change on the last line ('... perhaps they never will') leads to a wonderfully wistful finish.

'Vincent' was released as the album's second single (with 'Castles in the Air' as the B-side) and was largely responsible for McLean achieving an almost cult-like following in the UK after reaching No.1 there in June 1972. 'Vincent' is played daily in the Van Gogh Museum in Amsterdam and a time capsule buried there contains some of Van Gogh's brushes and McLean's sheet music of the song.

Of the remaining songs on Side One, 'Till Tomorrow' meanders along like a bubbling stream. It's the perfect musical antidote to the busyness of the title track and sets the tone for the listener to fully take in and appreciate the next song, 'Vincent'. The contemplative 'Crossroads' has a gentle piano melody (played by Warren Bernhardt); and the breezy love ballad 'Winterwood' closes that side of the album.

McLean later revealed that when he wrote 'Empty Chairs', which opens Side Two, he had the painting 'Van Gogh's Chair' in mind, but that too is just a symbol for emptiness. McLean had recently gone through a marriage breakup so the song is also about his own personal experience ('Never thought you'd leave, until you went ...').

'Everybody Loves Me, Baby' is McLean at his most ironic,

cynical even, and it's similar in tone to the rollicking pace set by 'American Pie'. It's important not to look too much into the meaning of the song, which is basically a rampant ego trip, but McLean was obviously able to tap into his dark side on this one ('I've used my talents as I could / I've done some bad, I've done some good / I did a whole lot better than they thought I would …').

'Sister Fatima' (originally misspelt 'Faima' on the album cover) is an atmospheric piece of music with some lovely chord changes on a drop D tuning let down by an ambiguous ending. The song was dropped from some pressings of the vinyl after 1980 and then reinstated for the CD release.

In an era when the Vietnam War had scarred the psyche of the American public, 'The Grave' is the most political song on the album. As with many war songs, the themes are universal. A soldier hides in his trench and covers himself with the earth to hide from the war until it becomes his grave. McLean's vocal is emotive, but straightforward, and the message is clear and unambiguous ('I'll cover myself! I know I'm not brave! / The earth! the earth! the earth is my grave').

The final track on Side Two is the traditional, 'Babylon', sung as an overlapping round. The Melodians made a reggae recording of the song in 1970 called 'Rivers of Babylon' which was later covered by German disco group Boney M at the end of the decade, but it has little in common with McLean's gentle, multi-tracked round that closes the album. McLean later said that he once hoped the song would have been released as a single from the album, but by the time 'American Pie' and 'Vincent' had run their races as singles, McLean was ready to release his follow-up album, the strangely-titled *Don McLean* (1972). Most of the world knew who Don McLean was by then.

The iconic front cover design, with the stars and stripes of the US flag painted on McLean's thumb, was photographed by Lee Hays, the former bass singer with the Weavers and co-writer (with Pete Seeger) of the folkie hit 'If I had a Hammer'. Hays also helped with some musical arrangements on the album, notably 'Babylon'. He had been blacklisted in the 1950s because of his political activities but McLean had befriended him years before and Hays was another mentor to McLean's fledgling career.

Released on 24 October, 1971, 'American Pie' is the longest song ever to top the Billboard Hot 100. The 45rpm single was split on either side of the vinyl, with respective fade out and fade in effects, but due to the song's growing popularity many DJs just played the full album track to give fans the whole story.

'American Pie' caught the nostalgic mood in America just at the right time. In 1973, George Lucas made his breakthrough film *American Graffiti*, set in 1962. Paul Le Mat's character wryly observes, 'Rock and roll's been going downhill ever since Buddy Holly died.' Many fans agreed.

'American Pie' entered the prevailing pop culture, spawning a cover from no less than Madonna (who, as a point of difference, starts her dance mix cover with the outro verse), inspiring a parody from 'Weird' Al Yankovic ('The Saga Begins') and lending its name to a teen-sex movie franchise from which McLean smartly kept his distance but collected a royalty nonetheless for owning the copyright to the title. The song enjoys a perennial presence on 4th of July celebrations (and is also featured in countless movies, including Oliver Stone's *Born on the Fourth of July*) and is regularly murdered at karaoke bars around the world.

And the song led to a rediscovery of Holly's legacy too. When former Beatle Paul McCartney was told by his father-in-law, New York lawyer Lee Eastman, to invest his millions in publishing (having lost his stake in the Beatles' publishing house, Northern Songs), McCartney was quick to buy Buddy Holly's entire catalogue. It also led to *The Buddy Holly Story* being filmed in 1978 which, if not for the Oscar-nominated performance from an almost unrecognizable (but extremely good) Gary Busey, could be dismissed as one of the most erroneous biopics ever made. In September that year, McCartney hosted the UK premiere of the movie in London, which was attended by Who drummer Keith Moon on what was to be his final night on the planet. Moon died the following morning from an accidental drug overdose.

McLean himself would become part of the mythmaking when it was widely reported that Roberta Flack's 1973 hit 'Killing Me Softly' was inspired by one of his performances. It would take writers Charles Fox and Norman Gimbel decades to correct the record – they had written the song in 1971, independent of any knowledge of McLean, but when folksinger Lori Lieberman casually remarked to them that she knew what they were writing about, having recently seen Don McLean in concert, the story took on a life of its own.

'I must say I'm very humbled by the whole thing,' McLean remarked at the time, and who wouldn't be? 'He was strumming my pain with his fingers / Singing my life with his words ...' But McLean, of all people, should know the power of myth.

McLean always found discussing 'American Pie' difficult. 'If something makes you feel a certain way then there's no reason to analyze it to decide why,' he said in 1972. 'I'm a firm believer that people find out what they want to find out.' At its best, 'American Pie' summarizes a whole decade of youth consciousness and provides a musical history lesson for post 'baby boomer' generations.

Whenever people asked Don McLean what 'American Pie' really meant, he'd reply somewhat flippantly, 'It means I never have to work again.' He was partially right; in 2014, 16 pages of handwritten notes he had hidden away in a box in his home for more than four decades were sold for $1.2m (£800,000) at Christie's in New York, to an anonymous buyer.

But McLean was no one-hit wonder; having released an album with two certified classic songs he followed with a series of well-received albums in the 1970s – but the singer admits he 'cracked up' under the pressure of having such a huge hit. History has been a little kinder; *Chain Lightning*, which was released in 1978 but would take another three years to find an audience, confirmed not only was he a talented songwriter with one of the finest voices in popular music but he was also one of the more masterful interpreters of other artists' music (McLean's stellar cover of Roy Orbison's 'Crying' topped the UK charts in 1981).

When his songwriting slowed in the 80s, McLean's clear tenor voice and virtuoso playing never deserted him as he constantly toured the world. In 1998, he came to my home town where my wife and I caught him in concert at a small theater. Although he apologized for having a slight cold, McLean's singing and playing was exquisite that night, with his four-piece band belting out faultless versions of his most well-known songs. When one punter yelled out, somewhat prematurely, for 'American Pie', McLean dryly replied from the stage, 'Yes, you'll get your pie. But first you have to eat some spinach.' He then launched into a long, bluegrass number I and everyone in the auditorium had never heard before, rendering everyone speechless with his spirited playing.

That's the real power of Don McLean as a performer.

American Pie / **Don McLean** (October 1971)   36:24

All songs written by Don McLean except where noted*

SIDE ONE   LENGTH
1.   American Pie   8:33
2.   Till Tomorrow   2:11
3.   Vincent   3:55
4.   Crossroads   3:34
5.   Winterwood   3:09

SIDE TWO
6.   Empty Chairs   3:24
7.   Everybody Loves Me, Baby   3:37
8.   Sister Fatima   2:31
9.   The Grave   3:08
10.   Babylon*   1:40

*Traditional; arranged by Lee Hays and McLean

CHAPTER 10

Harvest

Neil Young 1972

'Drink up, drink up, let me feel your cup with the promise of a man ...'

Neil Young's *Harvest* (1972) is Modern Americana on a music canvas; more Dylan than Dylan, it's the album that introduced country-rock to a wide audience, and in the process, paved the way for the Eagles, the Doobie Brothers, America, and even Lynyrd Skynyrd to find mainstream success. *Harvest* was original, influential and timely, coming out as it did in the post-Sixties hippy glow, but the impact of the multi-million-selling album so rattled its creator that Young deliberately drove his career into a two-decade ditch before returning as the 'godfather' of a new music generation.

Before the release of *Harvest,* I was aware of Young without knowing who he was. I knew that he had been a member of Buffalo Springfield, who had a hit with 1967's 'For What It's Worth', but it wasn't until it was pointed out to me by my cousins that Young was also a peripheral member of supergroup Crosby, Stills & Nash, and had been involved in the best-selling *Déjà Vu* album in 1970, that the penny dropped. *That* Neil Young.

When a lot of punters not familiar with Young's solo work heard the first single from his new album, 'Heart of Gold', on the radio in

January 1972, it certainly turned heads. Was it Dylan? The harmonica on the intro certainly pointed in that direction, and although there was the same high-pitched nasal quality to Young's voice that Dylan had, there was a smoothness and sincerity to the production that was all his own.

Harvest's nod to a Dylan record wasn't lost on the master, either. 'The only time it bothered me that someone sounded like me was when I was living in Phoenix, Arizona, in about '72 and the big song at the time was "Heart of Gold",' Dylan told journalist Scott Cohen in 1985. 'I used to hate it when it came on the radio. I always liked Neil Young, but it bothered me every time I listened to "Heart of Gold". I think it was up at number one for a long time, and I'd say, "Shit, that's me. If it sounds like me, it should as well be me."'

'Heart of Gold' became Young's first No.1 hit in the US, the UK and his native Canada. The song was ironically knocked off the top of the charts by the band America, whose song 'Horse With No Name' many people thought *was* Neil Young when it was released. Neil Young, the Dylan 'copyist' was being copied himself – a sure sign that Young had long since made the grade as a musician. Interestingly, at one stage in the 1970s Young, Dylan and America were all managed by Young's mentor, Elliot Roberts.

And how did Young deal with his hard-won, newfound success? As he famously wrote in the liner notes of his 1977 compilation, *Decade*, the hit single, and the entire album for that matter, 'put me in the middle of the road. Traveling there soon became a bore so I headed for the ditch. A rougher ride but I met more interesting people there.'

It would take Neil Young 20 years to come to terms with the enormous success *Harvest* brought him. The albums that immediately followed confounded his critics and confused his fans; the live album *Time Fades Away* (1973), *On The Beach* (1974) and *Tonight's The Night* (1975) later became known as 'The Ditch Trilogy'. After forays into electronic music and retro-rock in the 1980s, he was adopted by a new generation of 'grunge' rockers and returned from the music wilderness to release his sequel to *Harvest*, 1992's *Harvest Moon*, using many of the same musicians on that album. Having come full circle, Young has continued to play and record *his* music ever since. One thing is for certain, he has never been guilty of repeating himself.

Neil Young has both disavowed and lauded *Harvest*, but he never wanted to be defined by the record, or by its success for that matter. It was 'a mellow trip, where my life was at the time, but only for a couple of months,' he later recalled, before adding. 'It's probably the finest record I ever made but that's really a restricting adjective for me.' Young has always cared about capturing the moment rather than perfecting the song, and my favorite quote from him, in answering criticism after a particular live concert with his band Crazy Horse, is when he said they didn't play the song but 'played what the song was about'. That sums up his entire career for me.

His first band was the Squires, and after enjoying some success with the Mynah Birds (with a young Rick James as lead singer) he followed fellow traveler Stephen Stills' suggestion to move to Los Angeles. The famous story goes that Young was driving with Canadian Bruce Palmer on a busy Sunset Boulevard and spotted Stills traveling with his friend Richie Furay. The four started a band, after securing fellow Canadian Dewey Martin on drums, and called themselves Buffalo Springfield after a tractor company. The band generated a lot of hype on the LA scene, but their debut album was poorly produced and, despite their best-selling single, the band fell apart after Young quit and rejoined several times.

Part of Young's problem at the time was his insecurity concerning his singing voice, a high-pitched nasal falsetto. Fortunately, he also had the songwriter's knack of being able to compose songs that suited his range, and he was determined to sing his own compositions. Producer Jack Nitzsche helped him in that pursuit, starting with the Buffalo Springfield track 'Expecting to Fly' in 1967, which was effectively a Neil Young solo effort. Young did not like compromising his musical vision in the interest of band unity, and his unreliability and intractability would also characterize his participation in Crosby, Stills, Nash & Young.

Young 'found' his voice and style in three solo albums leading up to the release of *Harvest*: the self-titled debut *Neil Young* (1969), *Everybody Knows This Is Nowhere* (1969) and especially *After the Gold Rush* (1970). Songs such as 'Cinnamon Girl', 'Down by the River', 'Cowgirl in the Sand', 'After the Gold Rush', 'Only Love Can Break Your Heart' and 'Southern Man' marked Young as a guitarist *par excellence*, with a melancholic, country-rock edge to his music – Dylanesque, but with a simple, more straightforward appeal. Young still liked the idea of being in a band, though, and after jamming with a local group called the Rockets, he renamed them Crazy Horse and recorded and toured with them, on and off, for the next forty years.

Originally, Crazy Horse comprised Danny Whitten on guitar, Billy Talbot on bass and Ralph Molina on drums. The band backed Young on two solo albums before releasing their self-titled debut album in 1971 with producer Jack Nitzsche. Whitten's worsening drug issues may have warned Young off from using the band on what would become *Harvest*, and Whitten would succumb to his addictions the following year. Young did not play with Crazy Horse again until *Tonight's The Night* and *Zuma* (both 1975), with guitar prodigy Nils Lofgren taking Whitten's place as lead guitarist.

Joining Crosby, Stills & Nash in 1969 gave Young a national, even international prominence, starting with their appearance at Woodstock that August, though he was ambivalent about the album they made (Young plays on only three songs on *Déjà Vu*: 'Helpless' and 'Country Girl', which he wrote, and the Joni Mitchell cover 'Woodstock'). Young wanted spontaneity in the music; 'Ohio', which he wrote in response to the Kent State University massacre in May 1970, was written in a day and released by Crosby, Stills, Nash & Young only weeks after the actual event.

Young was now in demand as a solo artist, and his next album was highly anticipated. That it did not come out until February 1972 was due to a number of issues, not least Young's poor health and complicated private life. In August 1970 his first marriage, to Susan Acevedo, ended and he moved from Topanga Canyon in the hills above Los Angeles to a ranch at La Honda, outside San Francisco. Having injured his back moving wood on his ranch, he spent a long time in and out of hospital combating a debilitating spinal condition brought on by his childhood polio. During that time he formed a relationship with Oscar-nominated actress Carrie Snodgrass, who later moved into the ranch with her extended family.

Neil Young recorded several concerts live on tour, including two songs with the London Symphony Orchestra under the direction of Jack Nitzsche in late 1970 and two concerts at Massey Hall in Toronto recorded by David Briggs in January 1971. The new record was first going to be a double album, made up of live recordings and studio tracks but, not for the first time in Young's unpredictable career, this idea was eventually shelved in favor of the Crosby, Stills, Nash & Young live album *4 Way Street* (1971). Young refused to even listen to the Massey Hall tapes (they would not be released for 25 years), and while he continued to accumulate new material he had no real idea what the new album would be.

In February 1971, Young went to Nashville, Tennessee to appear on *The Johnny Cash Show* and he ended up recording several tracks there, at Quadrafonic Sound Studios (now Quad Studios) with producer Elliot Mazer. Bob Dylan had recorded in Nashville in the late 1960s, and the Stones in Alabama in 1970, so the idea of a counter-culture hero like Young going to the home of the conservative South was not as cutting edge as it may seem. Although he was not as overtly political as Dylan, like many artists of the era he took a keen interest in the Civil Rights movement. Young had even criticized the South in 1970's 'Southern Man' on the *After the Gold Rush* album ('Southern man better keep your head / Don't forget what your good book said …') but he always had a strong country sensibility to his music, despite being Canadian, and the mood moved him to record there.

Young appeared on *The Johnny Cash Show* along with Linda Ronstadt, James Taylor and Tony Joe White, playing solo piano versions of 'The Needle and the Damage Done' and 'Journey Through the Past'. Elliot Mazer had produced Ronstadt's *Silk Purse* album the previous year and invited Young, his manager Elliot Roberts and Linda Ronstadt to dinner. Young told Mazer that he had a batch of songs that he wanted to record and Mazer organized a band to support him that weekend – Kenny Buttrey on drums, Tim Drummond on bass, Teddy Irwin on electric guitar and Ben Keith on pedal steel guitar. Young played acoustic guitar because his weakened spinal column did not allow him to stand for very long or carry the weight of his 'Old Black' Gibson electric.

Where Crazy Horse became infamous for their lack of proficiency – they played the way Young wanted them to play, raw and 'in the moment' – Nashville had the best session players in the country. Ben Keith gave the songs a melancholy, country feel; his pedal steel guitar filling out the sound and punctuating the space Young and Mazer left in the production. But, somewhat frustratingly for the talented session men, Young instructed them to keep it simple, causing Kenny Buttrey to later remark: 'He hires some of the best musicians in the world and has 'em play as stupidly as they possibly can.'

Quad Studios was a renovated two-story, Victorian-era house, with the control room on the porch and the living rooms and dining rooms connected by sliding doors to form the playing studio. Young placed himself between the players, near the drums. The songs he brought to the session were fully formed and needed little or no arrangements. Although the studio had a 16-track recording facility, there was no way the sound of each instrument could be isolated, because the tracks were recorded live. Mazer was not fazed by this: 'Leakage gave the record character and we knew we weren't going to replace anything.'

For the first session in Nashville, Young invited Linda Ronstadt and James Taylor to sing back-up and produced two songs that would drive the new album to the top of the charts and quickly become classics. The melody in 'Heart of Gold' is said to have been inspired by Paul Mauriat's instrumental 'Love is Blue', which was a No.1 hit in the US in 1968. The first song recorded for the *Harvest* album, everyone from Elliot Mazer to James Taylor said 'Heart of Gold' was a hit as soon as they heard it. Some critics described the lyrics as banal, but they're simple and the allegory is accessible ('I want to live, I want to give / I've been a miner for a heart of gold …').

The first song Ronstadt and Taylor contributed to was 'Old Man'; Taylor plucked away on a six-string banjo while James McMahon played piano (a third song, 'Bad Fog of Loneliness', did not make the final cut). Each song was only played for a few takes, with Young determined to maintain a 'live' feel to the music. 'Less is more,' was the phrase Young used over and over to describe the music he wanted played.

'Old Man' is one of Neil Young's most popular and insightful records. Amazingly, someone who was only 24 years old (the line, 'Old man, look at my life / 24 and there's so much more…' places the writing of the song firmly in 1969) could compose a lyric that summed up the generation gap with the words, 'Old man, look at my life / I'm a lot like you were …' Young would tell his BBC audience later that year that the song was about his ranch foreman, Louis Avila and his wife, 'who came with the place when I bought it.' In his autobiography, *Waging Heavy Peace* (2012), Young writes that his absent father Scott Young thought the song was about him until his son informed him that it wasn't, and that Young Sr was hurt by the misunderstanding.

'Old Man' ponders issues of life and death, love and loss, youth and age ('Give me things that don't get lost / Like a coin that won't get tossed / Rolling home to you …'). Here Young is clearly in pain after the end of his first marriage, wailing to anyone willing to listen ('I need someone to love me / The whole day through …'). Released as the second single off the album, with 'The Needle and the Damage Done' on the B-side, the song made the Top 40 in the US (No.4 in Canada).

Young did not make it back to Nashville until April, after traveling to London to play Royal Festival Hall and appear on the BBC program *The Old Grey Whistle Test*. On stage, Young played several songs that would end up on *Harvest* (though he forgot the words to 'Out on the Weekend' or hadn't finished them yet, which would be the opening cut on the new album). While in London, Jack Nitzsche organized for the Rolling Stones Mobile Unit to record two of Neil's songs – 'A Man Needs a Maid' and 'There's a World' – with the backing of the London Symphony Orchestra, conducted by David Meecham, at Barking Town Hall. Young sang both songs live while playing the piano, and they were recorded by Abbey Road engineer Glyn Johns.

'There's A World' is a slight song given an elaborate, heavy-handed arrangement by Nitzsche. The first verse is promising ('Look around it, have you found it / Walking down the avenue?') but the song goes nowhere and the lush production on such a simple ballad attracted a lot of criticism at the time. Perhaps Young was going for something experimental here – orchestrated simplicity? Although it's probably the weakest track on the album, he would write and record much worse during his career, sometimes deliberately so.

'A Man Needs A Maid' addresses Young's marriage breakdown and his new relationship with Carrie Snodgrass ('I fell in love with the actress / She was playing a part that I could understand …'). Decidedly old-fashioned by today's standards ('Just someone to keep my house clean / Fix my meals and go away …') it nevertheless has its poignant moments and gives an interesting insight into the singer's frame of mind at the time, especially on the lyric, 'There's a shadow running through my days / Like a beggar going from door to door …'

Young had first seen Snodgrass in the 1970 film *Diary of A Mad Housewife* and had got a message to her asking if she would like to meet. Snodgrass had no idea who he was or about his music but she did visit Young when he was recuperating in hospital. Within weeks she had moved into his ranch at La Honda, along with her mother and father. Young and Snodgrass' son Zeke was born there in September 1972, partially paralyzed and with brain damage. The relationship did not last long, with Snodgrass later moving in with Young's producer Jack Nitzsche and suing her former partner for maintenance in the early 1980s. Snodgrass later returned to acting, and died in 2004.

When Young reconvened at Quad Studios in April, he recorded 'Harvest' and 'Out on the Weekend'. An early version of 'Alabama' was also recorded at this session, but a new song called 'Words' needed further work. Young plays acoustic guitar and harmonica on 'Out on the Weekend' and later remarked that although the song was 'bleak and desolate' he was actually expressing his elation at being in love with Snodgrass, it's just that he was trying to hide it.

'Harvest' was written in London in February 1971, and was first performed at the concert Young played at Royal Festival Hall the following day. Played as a slow tempo waltz, session man John Harris plays piano on the final recording, which is a live, two track mix. The song was Young's favorite from the Nashville sessions, so much so that he named the album *Harvest*. The line, 'Did I see you down in a young girl's town / With your mother in so much pain?' refers to Carrie Snodgrass's mother, with whom he was to have a somewhat strained relationship. The lyrics were inspired by Snodgrass' stories about her mother's threats to kill herself.

Young's back problems became so bad over the summer that

he was unable to play guitar for any great length of time, and in August he finally went under the knife to correct the problem. Several discs were removed from his back during a laminectomy and he was ordered to rest at his San Francisco ranch, doped up as he described it on 'copious amounts of painkillers'. Elliot Mazer set up a recording studio in a barn, utilizing the Wally Heider recording truck to complete the remainder of the album. The Nashville session players joined them there, along with Jack Nitzsche on piano and slide guitar, with Young naming the band 'the Stray Gators' – a musician's term for side players.

Dubbed 'Broken Arrow Studios', the barn setting proved ideal for recording the 'noisier' songs on the album – 'Are You Ready for the Country?', 'Words (Between the Lines of Age)' and a louder version of 'Alabama'. Mazer set up microphones outside the barn to record the natural reverb and set up speakers so that the sound of the songs ran across the lake and up into the hills. Young slowly recovered from his operation and played a Gretsch White Falcon electric guitar he got from Stephen Stills while wearing a back brace for extra support.

'Are You Ready for the Country?' features Neil Young on piano while Jack Nitzsche plays a Howlin' Wolf-inspired lick on an old Kay slide guitar that Young bought for him on spec but which he barely knew how to play. Back-up vocals were provided by Graham Nash, who was visiting Young at his farm when the song was recorded. The song is mainly the same riff being punched out over and over again, but country singer Waylon Jennings liked it enough to cover the song, expand the lyrics and name his solo album after it in 1976.

'Alabama' continues the themes from Young's 1970 song 'Southern Man'. The metaphor 'Your Cadillac / Has got a wheel in the ditch /

And a wheel on the track ...' may have been the inspiration for Young's 'ditch' narrative about his own music, but while the song is also hopeful ('Can I see you and shake your hand? Make friends down in Alabama / I'm from a new land ...') it led to one of the most written about and misunderstood feuds in rock and roll.

In 1974, Florida band Lynyrd Skynyrd wrote 'Sweet Home Alabama' in response to what many people saw as Young's sweeping generalizations about people in the South. Co-writer and lead singer Ronnie Van Zant even mined the chord progression (D / C / G) for the song from 'Heart of Gold' (Em / C / D / G). But far from being a vicious take-down of Young (despite the line, 'Well, I hope Neil Young will remember / A Southern man don't need him around anyhow ...') Lynyrd Skynyrd were also critical of the South; they 'boo' racist Alabaman Governor, George Wallace, and declare 'Montgomery has the answer ...', supporting the Civil Rights movement that guaranteed voter rights in the South. Van Zant was even photographed wearing a Neil Young t-shirt on the cover of the 1977 album *Street Survivors*. They were fans of Young's music, responding in kind to one of their heroes.

When Ronnie Van Zant, Steve Gaines, back-up singer Cassie Gaines and their assistant road manager were killed in a plane accident in October 1977, Young sang 'Sweet Home Alabama' at a concert in Florida to honor the band. That Young *loved* being put in his place by Lynyrd Skynyrd says a lot about him. In his autobiography, Young wrote, 'My own song "Alabama" richly deserved the shot Lynyrd Skynyrd gave me with their great record. I don't like my words when I listen to it. They are accusatory and condescending, not fully thought out, and too easy to misconstrue.'

The longest song on the album, 'Words (Between the Lines

of Age)' meanders through almost seven minutes of angst but is rescued by Young's great guitar work. In the first verse Young sings about his ranch, the people who work there and those who visit him, before he heads off into 'Dylan' territory with mixed results and mixed metaphors. There is a 16-minute version of the song on the soundtrack to Young's 1974 experimental film *Journey Through the Past*, but it's no better than the album track. The song is a typically enigmatic way for Young to finish his album.

The ten-song album list was finalized by the addition of the acoustic ballad 'The Needle and the Damage Done', which had been recorded on 30 January 1971, at Royce Hall at the University of California, a week before Young went down to Nashville. The concert had been taped by Henry Lewy in the Wally Heider mobile truck. No other songs from that concert were included on the album, but Young was suitably satisfied with this particular recording to include it on *Harvest*. It was a masterful addition, a song full of dread and painful resignation.

Young's most direct statement about the perils of heroin addiction, 'The Needle and the Damage Done' is also one of his most personal songs. Singing in the first person ('I hit the city and I lost my band / I watched the needle take another man…') makes the message more direct; so much so that later fans thought the song was about Danny Whitten, the lead guitarist of Crazy Horse. Although Whitten was battling his demons when the song was written, he did not succumb to a drug overdose until November 1972, after the album was released. The last image Young draws, 'Every junkie's like a setting sun …', to the polite applause of his Californian audience, should have been enough of a warning for a whole generation of fans not to do hard drugs. I know it was for me.

Mixing the album took the remainder of 1971, with Mazer conscious of matching the diverse sound from the San Francisco 'barn' recordings, the gig with the London Symphony Orchestra, the University of California track and the Quad recordings from earlier in the year. David Crosby and Stephen Stills added backing vocals in New York, but Christmas would come and go before the album finally saw the light of day. The criticism that *Harvest* was actually 'three different albums' did not escape Young, with the strings especially seen to be out of place, but the album reflects his musical range and ambition and the record would be regarded as a classic. It works.

Artist Tom Wilkes from Camouflage Productions designed the front cover for *Harvest*. Having coordinated the cover art for almost a hundred records over the past five years, including the Rolling Stones' *Beggars Banquet* (1968), George Harrison's *All Things Must Pass* (1970) and Joe Cocker's *Mad Dogs & Englishmen* (1970), Wilkes opted to write the title 'Harvest' above Neil Young's name in swirling, ornate lettering across a red sunset set against a wheat-colored background. The cover was finalized by the end of September 1971, but Young was not completely satisfied with print tests, finally opting for cardboard obtained from the cellulose of oat fibers to give the album just the right texture. Originally, he wanted the album cover to biodegrade after the plastic shrink-wrap was removed, but this was overruled by the record company head, Mo Ostin, as being impractical.

The back cover image by Joel Bernstein shows the five main players on the album inside the makeshift barn studio – Young, standing upright, his hair covering his face; rhythm section Drummond and Buttrey; Ben Keith sitting at his pedal steel guitar with Jack Nitzsche behind him at the piano. The internal gatefold had a large close-up of Young's reflection in a doorknob, also taken by Bernstein, with the five songs on each side of the album listed on the left. No less than four producers are credited – Mazer and Young, Lewy and Young, and Nitzsche by himself.

The album is unique in that it didn't need a photo of Young on the cover to sell it (Joel Bernstein took an iconic shot of Young sitting with his guitar, his long hair giving what the artist himself describes as a 'simian' look; the photo was used on the *Harvest* sheet music and the cover of Young's 2004 *Greatest Hits* compilation). Young would let the music do the talking; he didn't need to sell it. As journalist David Fricke later wrote, 'You look at something like Neil Young's *Harvest*, the texture of the cover and that very simple, almost antique lettering, and you get a feel of what Neil was trying to do in that record, the honesty and the grit and the deep Americana of what that record represents now.'

Not that every critic was as kind upon its release. *Rolling Stone*'s John Mendelsohn panned *Harvest*'s 'half-assed baloney ... flatulent and portentous nonsense and weariest clichés ... He's all but abdicated his position as an authoritative rock-and-roller for the stereotypical laid-back country-comforted troubadour role, seldom playing electric guitar at all anymore, and then with none of the spellbinding economy and spine-tingling emotiveness that characterized his playing with Crazy Horse.' But over the years, especially when compared to Young's subsequent releases, *Harvest* continued to grow in stature. In 2003, *Rolling Stone* named *Harvest* as No.82 in its Top 500 albums of all time.

'I can't even remember if I enjoyed it,' Young recalled of the album's success. 'It was very intense. People saw something in me

I didn't see in me ... the producer of Crazy Horse [David Briggs] felt like that was a sellout record. I did this for everybody else because this is what everybody wanted.' Upon its release, Young went into seclusion, made a movie nobody saw (*Journey Through the Past*) and continued to write the songs he wanted to play and sing.

In 1972, Neil Young and the Stray Gators recorded several other songs, notably 'Lookout Joe', which appears on 1975's *Tonight's the Night*, and 'War Song', which was a Neil Young and Graham Nash single released in support of George McGovern's presidential campaign, and *Journey Through the Past*, the title of his small, indie film. The Stray Gators backed Young on his 1973 tour (sacking Kenny Buttrey mid tour and replacing him with John Barbata), which produced the poorly received live album, *Time Fades Away* (1973). Young wanted to give Danny Whitten a lifeline and take him on this tour, but his friend was too drug-addled and was sacked (he died soon after). Young blamed himself for Whitten's death and was not in a good space on that 1973 tour, berating his audience, dissing his band and becoming increasingly erratic. His mood would darken further with the death of Crosby, Stills, Nash & Young roadie Bruce Berry from a drug overdose in June 1973.

At age 27, a dangerous age in rock and roll, Neil Young could have been accused of hitting his artistic peak with the release of *Harvest*, but he has had several artistic peaks throughout his career and just as many troughs. *Comes a Time* (1978) charted similar country (Young even referred to it as *Harvest II*) but, in many ways, it was more daring in that it came out at the height of the '70s punk movement. By the time *Rust Never Sleeps* was released in 1979 with Crazy Horse, music critics were already talking about 'Neil Young's comeback' record.

In the 1980s, Young was lost. Signing with Geffen Records, he released two electronic albums – *Re·ac·tor*, with Crazy Horse (1981) and *Trans* (1982) – before suffering the ignominy of his own label suing him for releasing records deemed to be 'uncommercial' and even 'unlike Neil Young'. *Everybody's Rockin'* (1983) was a half-hearted return to his rock roots, *Old Ways* (1985) was the country album Young wanted to make, but the songs on *Landing on Water* (1986) were nothing more than rejects and outtakes from previous sessions. *Life* (1987), credited to Neil Young & Crazy Horse, ended his contract with Geffen and saw him return to his old label, Reprise.

Young rediscovered his sense of humour with the 1988 release of *This Note's for You*, backed by a band he called the Bluenotes. A blistering attack on the growth of commercialism in popular music with a not so MTV friendly video clip lampooning the real-life incident when Michael Jackson set his hair on fire while filming a Pepsi commercial, Young's 'fuck you' attitude hit the right note (excuse the pun) with a much younger 'grunge' audience. His next album, *Freedom* (1989), marked his musical return from the wilderness and produced the hit, 'Rockin' in the Free World', that resulted in Young touring with Pearl Jam in the early 1990s. Neil was back!

While Young would never achieve the same mainstream success that *Harvest* afforded him, his eclectic career has served him well over five decades. He remains an icon, a music maverick content to dance to his own beat and tune rather than follow the fashions of the day.

Neil Young, the great contrarian, doing things his own way.

Harvest / **Neil Young** (February 1972)   37:11

All songs written and composed by Neil Young.

SIDE ONE	LENGTH
1. Out on the Weekend	4:35
2. Harvest	3:11
3. A Man Needs a Maid	4:05
4. Heart of Gold	3:07
5. Are You Ready for the Country?	3:33

SIDE TWO	
6. Old Man	3:24
7. There's a World	2:59
8. Alabama	4:02
9. The Needle and the Damage Done	2:03
10. Words (Between the Lines of Age)	6:40

CHAPTER 11

School's Out

Alice Cooper 1972

'Don't make a stranger of yourself ... remember the Coop'.'

It is the last day of high school, 1972. I am standing outside the principal's office holding a copy of the Alice Cooper album *School's Out*. My sole aim that summer afternoon is to persuade my principal, a notoriously stern man with no sense of humor, to play the song 'School's Out' over the public-address system when school finishes for the holidays. 'He's a very busy man,' the school secretary explains when she notices that I'm still standing there during the final period of the day. 'I'll wait,' I tell her. I'm still waiting there when the dismissal bell rings and my friends rush for the school gates.

By 1970, the only things the band Alice Cooper had achieved were bad publicity, underselling records and huge debts. Their lead singer, a young man also called Alice Cooper (more about that in a minute), had killed a live chicken on stage, the press said (incorrectly, as it would turn out); the other band members hanged their frontman on stage, locked him into an electric chair, dressed him in a straightjacket, even decapitated him. They were blood-thirsty Satanists, 'sick things' the lot of them. 'Alice' even draped himself in a large snake as blood poured from his eyes and mouth.

The reality was, Alice Cooper were pioneers of 'performance theater' rock and roll, with its origins in 1960s punk and garage rock, who had become the darlings of the glam rock movement in the UK. And 'hard hearted' Alice, the lead singer? He was an asthmatic kid from Arizona, born Vince Furnier in 1948. He was about as threatening as 'Fonzie' on TV's *Happy Days* ... and, ultimately, just as popular.

Alice was in it for the fun, and the theater, but his act was more burlesque than satire. At a time when America was involved in the Vietnam War, civil unrest was at its height and violence was on display in family living rooms, not only on the nightly news but also with the prevalence of crime shows on TV, it was Alice Cooper that became a *cause célèbre* in the US, and finally around the world.

Alice Cooper – Alice (vocals), Michael Bruce (guitar), Glen Buxton (guitar), Dennis Dunaway (bass) and Neal Smith (drums) – were an outrageously cocksure band who lived and eventually died by the maxim, 'Give the public want they want.' The release of the concept album *School's Out* in the summer of 1972 encapsulated the spirit of teenage defiance in the early 1970s. The album was a No.2 hit in the US, while the single topped the UK charts, solidifying Alice Cooper – the singer and the band – as avant-garde provocateurs of teenage pop culture.

Alice Cooper found a willing fanbase in the UK, which readily adopted the band at the height of the glam rock movement. Alice admitted to British pop mag *New Musical Express*, 'There's actually no point whatsoever to our act,' but kids around the world lapped it up. They audience was in on the joke – we knew it wasn't real, but we applauded the way Alice Cooper did it with wit, style and even a wink. Many others would follow in their footsteps – there would be no KISS without Alice Cooper, and certainly no Marilyn Manson – but these bands lacked the personality, the humor and, dare I say, the talent of the five original members of the Alice Cooper band.

First, some big questions need to be answered. How did the Spiders, young Arizona wannabes, become the Nazz and then the band, Alice Cooper? How did Vince Furnier become the singer Alice Cooper? And finally, in the mid-1970s, how did Alice Cooper the singer usurp the career of the band and become a bona fide rock and roll icon?

Vince Furnier, Dennis Dunaway and Glen Buxton were school friends at Cortez High School in Arizona in 1964 when the Beatles conquered America. The friends formed a 'parody' band called the Earwigs for a school talent show and, miming Beatles songs of the day, duly won the competition. The group decided to become a real band and recruited local guitarist Michael Bruce from the Wildflowers (a band that featured future Alice Cooper contributor Mick Mashbir). Drummer Neal Smith was the last to join (having gone to school with Mashbir at nearby Camelback High School), replacing original drummer John Speer in 1968.

The band were first called the Spiders, and they had a hit on Arizona radio in 1966 with their original single, 'Don't Blow Your Mind'. They then changed their name to the Nazz, in honor of Jesus of Nazareth (aka 'the Nazarene'; the future Alice was the son of a pastor and would become a committed Christian), but when the band relocated to LA in 1968 seeking fame and fortune they were forced to change their name because there was already a band there called the Nazz (featuring future star Todd Rundgren).

The origin of the name 'Alice Cooper' is clouded in myth and misinformation – one story propagated in the media was that the name was selected by Ouija board during a paranormal session; another was that they were named after a female wrestler or that the name was found on the TV show *Mayberry R.F.D* (a wonderful urban myth at the time was that Alice was actor Eddie Haskell, 'Beaver' Cleaver's nemesis on the *Leave It To Beaver* TV show, grown to adulthood – he wasn't). Whatever the truth, giving the band a female persona not only gently bent accepted gender roles of the era but also became an essential point of difference in a crowded rock and roll landscape and an obvious talking point with a perplexed media. The band needed the publicity too, because they weren't that good on stage. The change in name worked, and lead singer Vince Furnier quickly adopted the 'Alice' persona as well.

Alice Cooper were an LA oddity in the late 1960s. Stylistically, they were like many of the 'psychedelic' bands of the era, playing songs that resembled long, extended jam sessions, and they found work supporting the likes of the Doors, Love, the Grateful Dead and Jefferson Airplane at various Sunset Strip venues. Frank Zappa offered the group a recording deal in 1969 when he saw the band empty a room after just one song – any band that had such a dramatic effect on their audience had to have something going for them, he reasoned. The two albums Alice Cooper released on Zappa's Straight Records, *Pretties for You* (1969) and *Easy Action* (1970), lacked any discernable tunes and made no impact in the charts.

The highlight of this period was the band's appearance at the Toronto Rock and Roll Revival festival in September 1969. Signed to play in Canada's answer to the Woodstock concert, which had been held the previous month, Alice Cooper supported numerous rock and roll greats, including Chuck Berry, Bo Diddley and Gene Vincent. The main attraction on stage, however, was the appearance of John Lennon and Yoko Ono, backed by Eric Clapton, Klaus Voormann and Alan White, in his first solo appearance without the Beatles, immortalized on the record *Live Peace in Toronto* (1970).

Alice Cooper's set is infamous for the supposed death of a chicken, which was thrust on stage by a member of the 25,000 strong crowd. When Alice gently threw the chicken back to the audience, it was torn apart. This is how urban legends are made.

Having failed to make an impact in LA, Alice Cooper relocated to Detroit and focused on honing their musicianship and songwriting. One of the things that made the band so endearing for Zappa, their ability to play so many different chords within the same song, was their Achilles heel on record; the band had a hard rock attitude but were unfocused and didn't play as a unit. Signing with Warner Bros. Records, the band hooked up with producer Bob Ezrin who, according to Alice, 'taught us how to play as a band'. Their first album under Ezrin's musical leadership, 1971's *Love it to Death*, produced the band's first hit, 'I'm Eighteen', as well as live favorites 'Is It My Body' and 'Ballad of Dwight Fry' (which Alice sang in a straightjacket).

I first became aware of Alice Cooper early in 1972 when I discovered *Killer*, with its bright magenta cover, the eponymous 'killer' snake and child-like scribble of the titles 'alice cooper' and 'killer' (sans caps). *Killer* represents the first time the band managed to produce a musically integrated and coordinated concept album, with mini-epics 'Halo of Flies', 'Dead Babies' and 'Killer' quickly becoming staples of the band's live performances. As confronting as a song called 'Dead Babies' was in 1971, Alice later explained that the song was actually about child abuse, with 'little Betty' neglected by her parents. The title track allowed the band to fully explore different forms of theatrical execution on stage and added to the growing 'Alice' legend.

Killer is a great album; future Sex Pistol Johnny Rotten (born John Lydon in 1956) thought so too and it remains one of his favorites. *Killer* also features 'Be My Lover' ('She asked me why the singer's name was Alice / I said, "listen baby you really wouldn't understand…"'), 'Under My Wheels' (featuring a blistering solo by guest guitarist Rick Derringer) and 'Desperado', a tribute to the Doors' Jim Morrison, who died that year aged just 27 (not to be confused with the Eagles' classic of the same name and period).

Curious to find out more about the band behind *Killers,* I found out that they had been featured in the 1970 movie *Diary of a Mad Housewife,* starring future Neil Young muse Carrie Snodgrass. I caught the film on late-night TV and so, when *School's Out* was released later that year, I was a step ahead of the hype that accompanied Alice Cooper as the single and album climbed the record charts.

The songs that finished up on *School's Out* were worked on at the Galesi Estate, in Greenwich, Connecticut, which the band used as a rehearsal studio. As concept albums go, there was an air of deliberate commercialism about the title track and Alice knew the band were on a winner. 'If you can capture the two happiest moments in a year, what would they be?' Cooper later asked journalist Glenn Burnsilver, explaining the motivation behind the song. 'Christmas morning, when you're getting ready to open all the presents, because of the anticipation, and the last day of school … It was the only song out of [my] 14 hit records that I was absolutely sure of.'

Early versions of the songs featured in the *School's Out* Box Set in 2012 show just how much each song had to be workshopped before they were deemed ready to record. The recording itself was done at The Record Plant in New York, under the direction of producer Bob Ezrin, the acknowledged 'sixth member' of the band. Whereas *Killer* was dominated by guitarist Michael Bruce, who had a hand in writing all eight songs, the new album also features key contributions from Buxton ('Gutter Cat vs. the Jets'), Dunaway ('Luney Tune') and Smith ('Alma Mater').

In his autobiography *No More Mr Nice Guy*, Michael Bruce laments that he had to share songwriting credits with all five members on the title track, 'School's Out'. Sometimes maligned as a guitar player and lambasted for his lack of enthusiasm for hard work by his bandmates, Glen Buxton was responsible for the memorable opening riff and the lead fills that characterize 'School's Out'. 'Glen was a real rebel,' Dennis Dunaway says in the *School's Out* Box Set liner notes. 'He hated school and anyone who told him or anybody else how to live their life.' Buxton was also a rebel within the band, and his increasingly unreliable behavior would hasten the band's split in 1974.

Alice's lead vocal on 'School's Out' was equally 'bratty'. He was trying to sound like one of the Bowery Boys, who featured in several films from the 1930s and 1940s starring the comical slum kids, and he sings in that persona for much of the album. The band credits studio engineers, Roy Cicala and Shelly Yakus, who mixed the album and showed particular finesse on the title track so that Alice's distinctive voice would not be lost between the thrashing guitars, synthesizers and the band's hard-working rhythm section.

The song is built around a couple of easy puns: 'We got no class / We got no principals …' and a line that still makes me smile almost fifty years later, 'We got no innocence / We can't even think up a word that rhymes'. With references to the playground taunt, 'No more pencils / No more books / No more teacher's dirty looks...', an undeniably hooky chorus ('School's out forever / School's been blown to pieces'), and children's voices added by Ezrin, the song has become a summer perennial for ensuing generations. The novel ending, which gives the impression that the record has lost its power supply, is also unique.

There is also an air of deliberate cynicism around the second song, 'Luney Tune'. The original Warner Bros. studio was the home of Looney Tunes cartoons and, having grown up watching them on black-and-white TV in the 1960s, I understood the reference straight away. Written by Cooper and Dunaway (but with a lot of help from Mike Bruce) this is one of the best tracks on the album; the song has an ethereal quality, with a great orchestral score on the bridge ('I can't find the exit / I quit lookin' for doors ...'). The song contains some great imagery too ('I took a spit at the moon / It's all in this luney tune....', 'I stole a razor from the commissary / I just couldn't take it no more ...' and 'I'm swimmin' in blood / Like a rat on a sewer floor').

I remember thinking at the time that I had heard nothing like 'Luney Tune' before. Who would add strings on a garage band song and then have the whole thing grind to a halt as if the band just gives up? I learned that Bob Ezrin would, and it was Ezrin who added the reference to the band's favorite movie, *West Side Story*, at the end of the next track.

The opening to 'Gutter Cat vs. the Jets' is built around a clever bass run from Dunaway that opens up to a 'street fight' spoken narrative ('Some bad cats from 4th Street / Come down to our alley / Well, we say that's cool / But just stay away from me and my boys

…'), again in Alice's best Bowery Boy vocal delivery. Continuing the theater of the mind after the wonderful *West Side Story* coda ('When you're a jet …' etc.), the band conducts a street fight, with garbage cans flying, a police siren wailing and the echo of a cat's meow. Wonderful, wonderful stuff.

The final track on Side One, 'Blue Turk', features New York jazz trombonist Wayne Andre trading licks with Buxton and Bruce and sounds like something the Doors might have recorded (except there is no organ). Jim Morrison would have been proud to have written lines like, 'I'm lazy, you know it / I'm ready for the second show …' and 'Tastes like roses on your lips but graveyards on your soul …' According to Michael Bruce, the title is a favorite saying the band bandied around when they thought something they did was 'cool', as in, 'Yeah daddy-o! At the Blue Turk Café.'

If Side One of the album is full of teenage rebellion, madness, punk aggression and detached coolness, side two is a grab-bag of styles rescued by one forgotten gem of a song. I liked the first side of the album so much I played it over and over, rarely giving the second side a thought until some months after I bought it. Ezrin and Alice wrote 'My Stars', the longest track on the album, and the song features Bob Ezrin's ascending piano arpeggios, Dennis Dunaway's melodic bassline and guest guitarist Dick Wagner's sweeping guitar. As the track fades, someone in the band mumbles 'Klaatu barada nikto' (4:50), a phrase from the cult 1951 film *The Day The Earth Stood Still*.

'Public Animal #9' is the only other Cooper-Bruce composition on *School's Out*. It took me years to realize that 'G.B.' refers to Glenn Buxton in the opening line ('Me and G.B. we ain't never gonna confess / We cheated at the math test …'). 'I'd give a month of cigarettes for just a couple of lousy beers ...' is a great lyric (again, in the spirit of Jim Morrison) and the song descends into a John Lennon-like primal growl at the end. Number 9 might be a comically random number (why not Public Animal #7?), but the production company Ezrin worked with was called Nimbus 9 Productions and it's a cool reference to Ezrin's influence on the album.

There is a great video on YouTube of the Alice Cooper band playing the song live on *Beat-Club* in 1972, including the extended, warm-up introduction they used for various songs in their live performances. The band is dressed in their best glam outfits (courtesy of Cindy Smith – the sister of drummer Neal – who married Dennis Dunaway). Watching the clip, Neal and Dennis are a great rhythm section, Michael is all 'rock star' and it's great to see Glen Buxton in his prime. Alice, as always, looks resplendent in Morrison-like leather jacket and with can of beer in hand.

Which brings us to Neal Smith's 'Alma Mater'. With its Beatle-esque opening, a beautiful mixture of minor and flat chords, it has one of the best opening lines of any pop song: 'Rain is falling down my cheek searching for the sea / Tomorrow like the rain I'll be back home again ...' Alice saves his best vocal of the album for this fond farewell to Cortez High School (Camelback, Neal's alma mater, is also namechecked, along with various teachers and schoolyard events). 'I finally grew up, they finally let me out of school ...' Alice sings, and I particularly love the 'tumbling tumbleweed' ending and the poignant sign-off, 'Remember the Coop ... don't forget me or nuthin".

The grande finale on *School's Out* is called, not so surprisingly, 'Grande Finale'; a heavily synthesized instrumental that ends with a reprise of the Jets theme from *West Side Story*. At best it can be described as a filler, as if the band were a song short and producer Bob Ezrin cobbled this together. If the idea was to record a neat sign-off to 'tie whole album together,' as Michael Bruce suggests, the execution falls flat. The album would have been much better served if they had finished with 'Alma Mater' but that would have left them a song short (as it is, *School's Out* comes in at just under 37 minutes). Perhaps the band could have added 'Elected' to this set – the song was a reworking of 'Reflected' on the *Pretties for You* album in 1969 and was rushed into release in August 1972 to take advantage of the coming presidential elections. It appeared on the *Billion Dollar Babies* album the following February.

The group had enough clout at the time to demand an album cover from Warner's that was as colorful and theatrical as their live performances. Concept Packaging's Craig Braun, the creator of the Rolling Stones' *Sticky Fingers* zipper cover, came up with the concept of a semi-functional school desk that actually opens up. The final product was brought to life by Ernie Cefalu's spec sketches and Braun's then partner, Tom Wilkes (the designer of George Harrison's *All Things Must Pass* and Neil Young's *Harvest* among many others).

The sleeve opens out the wooden school desk depicted on the cover, the work of New York photographer and Greenwich Village documentary maker, Robert Otter. Each of the five members of the band actually scratched their names into an old school desk – Alice in a swirling 'A.C' logo; 'MICHAEL B', 'G.B.', 'N. SMITH' and an interlocking 'D.D.' – along with the *School's Out* title inside a dagger-pierced heart and the band name across it on a banner.

Lift the desktop flap and you find a report card, marbles, gum, a slingshot, a switchblade and a Liberace comic (a lovely touch). On the original pressing, the inside record was wrapped in a pair of paper panties. Unfortunately, the original panties made were seized by customs because they had no fire retardant in them, but it was a typically provocative move from the band and their media-savvy manager Shep Gordon. 'If you were 14 years old and on Monday morning you could sit at your desk and produce a pair of panties, you were the man,' Cooper later remarked. Those paper panties are now collector's items.

The image of the band on the inside of the cover, standing around a trashcan like alley cats, was shot by fashion photographer Roger Prigent (I had to look closely to work out who was who in this shot; Dennis Dunaway is actually crouching inside the garbage can). The details on the packaging were mind-blowing, right down to a picture of chewing gum stuck to the underside of the desk where the fold out legs were perforated.

Alice and the band took advantage of their growing popularity by launching a UK and European Tour that summer. The single 'School's Out' topped the UK charts in August 1972, largely on the back of Shep Gordon's marketing and the band's outrageous antics on stage. The celebrated *Rolling Stone* cover of a naked Alice draped only in his pet boa constrictor, taken by the then unknown photographer Annie Leibovitz, was put on the side of a huge truck and literally stopped traffic in Piccadilly Circus as it drove around the city on the eve of the band's only concert at Wembley. It was pure genius, and it worked. The Brits were smitten.

But perhaps Alice Cooper were a little too calculated for their own good. 'Not all of *School's Out* is, however, rock,' Ben Gerson opined in *Rolling Stone*. 'A good half is Broadway or movie soundtrack music, which is consistent with Alice's vaunted theatricalism.' Robert Christgau agreed: 'With its all-time ugly vocal, kiddie chorus turned synthesizer, and crazy, dropped-out thrust, the title hit is as raw and clever as it gets, but this album is soundtrack.' Today, not only is the song 'School's Out' a radio staple and the acknowledged peak of the career of the original band, but the album has stood the test of time as a pop culture masterpiece.

With the release of the even more cynical, more commercial and more successful *Billion Dollar Babies* album in 1973, Alice Cooper hit the rock stratosphere. With arguably a better list of songs ('Hello Hooray', 'Elected', 'No More Mr. Nice Guy', 'Generation Landslide' and 'I Love the Dead', each a Cooper classic) *Billion Dollar Babies* was brilliantly packaged pop-rock with '$' signs literally written all over it. The only problem was that Glen Buxton was only used sparingly on guitar because his demons were getting the better of him.

The Alice Cooper band was falling apart under the strain of constant touring and recording. In March 1974, they performed to a record 120,000 people in São Paulo, Brazil; the largest indoor audience to ever watch a rock and roll show. A hastily recorded documentary, *Good to See You, Alice Cooper*, sank without a trace (I saw it in early 1975 and there were three people in the theater ... me and a friend and the ticket collector).

The band's final album, 1974's *Muscle of Love*, was a huge letdown. Despite some stellar moments ('Hard Hearted Alice', 'Teenage Lament '74' and the title track are 'worthy') the album doesn't sound like classic 'Alice'. Moving away from Bob Ezrin as producer (Jack Douglas was the producer of this album), *Muscle of Love* lacked Alice Cooper's raw, garage rock sound and the band's individuality was brought undone when they were photographed wearing the sailor suits (the Rolling Stones had already done this better on the film clip for 'It's Only Rock and Roll'). The distinct feeling was that Alice had 'gone Hollywood' on his fans. The release of the band's Greatest Hits collection that Christmas, with a wonderfully realized album package by artist Drew Struzan featuring the band mingling with past Hollywood stars, tended to confirm it. Alice now was a star in his own right.

As a huge fan of the original band, I was dismayed when I learned that Alice was bringing out a solo album in 1975. The rift occurred when Alice wanted to push further into what was being described as 'theater-rock' and the band members wanted to return to their rock and roll roots. Alice's solo album, *Welcome to My Nightmare,* was a megahit, although I stayed true to the band and refused to buy it until the 40th anniversary CD in 2015. Alice was busy partying with Salvador Dalí, Groucho Marx and John Lennon in LA, and his resulting '70s solo output would bring increasingly diminishing returns.

Not that his bandmates fared much better. Bruce, Smith and Dunaway formed the short-lived Billion Dollar Babies but their 1977 album *Battle Axe,* sans Alice's sharp cynicism and razor voice, sank without a trace. That same year, Alice Cooper toured Australia for the first time on his 'Welcome to My Nightmare Tour', with Dick Wagner and Steve Hunters on guitars, Prakash John on bass, and drummer Whitey Glan.

Incredibly, Alice was initially banned from touring Australia. 'I am not going to allow a degenerate who could powerfully influence the young and weak-minded to enter this country and stage this sort of exhibition here,' declared Australian Labor and Immigration Minister Clyde Cameron, proving just what a backwater Australia was in the 1970s (Neil Diamond never had such problems). 'Isn't that crazy?' said Alice at the time. 'People still think I kill chickens onstage.'

No-one was happier than me when Alice survived his 1980s addictions and emerged clean and sober as a heavy metal icon at the end of the decade. 'Poison' was a Top 10 hit in 1989, and Cooper's cameo in *Wayne's World* (1992) introduced him to a whole new generation, including my young son. In the late '90s, I was a Year 6 teacher who took great delight in playing *School's Out* to my students on their last day of school before going off to high school. And they all knew the words to the song too.

In 2000, I caught Alice on tour as a guest performer on the British Rock Symphony Tour. Although the concert highlighted the best of British rock – the Who, the Stones, the Beatles, Led Zeppelin and Procol Harum – Alice was added to the tour schedule along with local stars Jimmy Barnes and Billy Thorpe to give the stage a little star power. Alice stole the overblown, orchestrated show, with his version of 'School's Out' segueing into Pink Floyd's 'Another Brick in the Wall, Part 2'. Both songs were produced by Bob Ezrin and feature children singing the chorus, with an obvious thematic link ('We don't need no education / We don't need no thought control …'). Alice was quick to take credit for Pink Floyd borrowing the idea from him. 'The two songs fit together like a glove,' he said.

Alice sang the two songs again when I saw him in concert in the mid-2000s, backed by a white-hot younger band featuring Chuck Garric (bass), Tommy Clufetos (drums) and Kerri Kelli and Jason Hook on guitars. I was close enough to the stage this time to see the sweat on Alice's brow (and get a bad case of tinnitus from standing too close to the speakers). The highlight of the night for me was when the band launched into a killer version of 'Public Animal #9' from *School's Out*. It sounded as good as the first time I heard it as a teenager in 1972.

Belatedly, in 2011, the original Alice Cooper band were inducted into the Rock and Roll Hall of Fame. Eligible for inclusion some years before, the band were forced to wait a little longer while critics and music snobs got over 'the Coop's' theatrics and finally focused on the great albums the band produced in the early 1970s. Alice Cooper, Michael Bruce, Neal Smith and Dennis Dunaway reconciled on stage (Glen Buxton passed away in 1997) and have since performed together again at selected events. All that remained was for the band to record again, which they did for some tracks on Alice's 2011 release, *Welcome 2 to My Nightmare*. A Hall of Fame gong for Alice as a solo artist is also now long overdue.

School's Out may not be Alice Cooper's best album, but like millions of other kids I found it at a time of my life when it really mattered.

School's Out / **Alice Cooper** (June 1972)   36:56

SIDE ONE		LENGTH
1.	School's Out (Alice Cooper, Glen Buxton, Michael Bruce, Dennis Dunaway, Neal Smith)	3:30
2.	Luney Tune (Cooper, Dunaway)	3:44
3.	Gutter Cat vs. the Jets (Buxton, Dunaway, Leonard Bernstein, Stephen Sondheim)	4:40
4.	Street Fight (Cooper, Buxton, Bruce, Dunaway, Smith)	0:55
5.	Blue Turk (Cooper, Bruce)	5:34
SIDE TWO		
1.	My Stars (Cooper, Bob Ezrin)	5:49
2.	Public Animal #9 (Cooper, Bruce)	3:55
3.	Alma Mater (Smith)	4:27
4.	Grande Finale (Cooper, Buxton, Bruce, Dunaway, Smith, Bob Ezrin, Mack David, Leonard Bernstein)	4:26

CHAPTER 12

Goodbye Yellow Brick Road

Elton John 1973

'Back to the howling old owl in the woods, hunting the horny back toad ...'

In the early 1970s, there was no harder working musician/composer/ rock star than Elton John. After joining forces with young lyricist Bernie Taupin, changing his name from Reggie Dwight and signing a record deal with Beatles publisher Dick James in 1969, the former Bluesology pianist released six albums leading up to what would be his career highpoint, *Goodbye Yellow Brick Road* in 1973. Having already released the top-charting *Don't Shoot Me I'm Only the Piano Player* album earlier in the year, the prolific songwriting team followed up with a double LP – 'our White Album' as Elton later described it – featuring 18 masterful songs, each a story on its own.

Goodbye Yellow Brick Road cemented the John-Taupin partnership as the songwriting heirs to Lennon-McCartney and was a No.1 hit around the world, selling 30 million copies. After that, there was no going back 'to the howling old owl in the woods' for John or Taupin. Superstardom awaited them both.

Reginald Kenneth Dwight, born in Pinner, Middlesex, in 1947, always wanted be a star. In the mid-1960s he played piano with

Long John Baldry's band, Bluesology, before branching out to forge his own identity. As the famous story now goes, Dwight answered an ad placed by Liberty Records A&R man Ray Williams in the *New Music Express* in 1967, looking to sign new talent. Williams gave Dwight, who wrote music, an envelope of lyrics that had been written by Lincolnshire teenager Bernie Taupin. Perhaps the pair could meet and work together?

And so started one of the most successful songwriting teams in popular music. The pair did not work in the same room, workshopping and shaping songs to fit each other's particular vision. Taupin merely gave his partner copies of his lyric sheets and the newly renamed Elton John – Elton after Elton Dean, the saxophonist for Bluesology (Reg just liked the name) and John, in honor of Long John Baldry – would assign a suitable melody on piano to the lyrics, rarely changing a word.

In 1968, the songwriting team signed a deal with Dick James Music (DJM), writing songs for various artists, including Roger Cook and Lulu. John spent some time as a session musician (that's him playing piano on the Hollies hit 'He Ain't Heavy, He's My Brother' in 1970) and recording cover versions of current Top 10 hits for budget music labels (the type of knock-off albums your parents bought you for Christmas for $2 because they didn't want to pay full price). DJM music publisher Steve Brown encouraged the pair to write songs that Elton John could record as a solo artist.

The first Elton John song I heard on radio was the ballad 'Your Song', which was a huge hit in 1970. His standing with me improved considerably when John Lennon was quoted in *Rolling Stone* saying that, of the contemporary music, he liked John's song because it sounded like ordinary people talking. That was the beauty of John-Taupin's songs; they made it sound so effortless. The lyrics were poetic; often cinematic in scope but also deeply personal. And apart from being a great piano player with a wonderful ear for a melody, John also had a remarkable falsetto voice that made the songs immediately recognizable and uniquely his.

After his debut album *Empty Sky* (1969) failed to find an audience, Steve Brown put Elton John in contact with producer Gus Dudgeon and arranger Paul Buckmaster. Subsequent albums featured a rich, orchestral approach to the music; *Elton John* (1970), the country-inspired *Tumbleweed Connection* (1970), *Madman Across the Water* (1971) and *Honky Château* (1972). I rediscovered these albums after his worldwide success in 1973, and it was as if Elton was still looking for his voice in the early 1970s – an unmistakable rock or pop voice that would broaden his appeal. He was already a cult hit in Los Angeles after his six-date residency at the Troubadour in 1970 (check out the live album *17–11–70* for *early* Elton John) but his best showing on the singles chart since 'Your Song' was the 'Space Oddity'-inspired 'Rocket Man' in 1972.

It was also the formation of Elton's touring and recording band – Davey Johnstone on guitar, bassist Dee Murray and Nigel Olsson on drums – that galvanized John's sound. Johnstone had played on Bernie Taupin's 1971 solo album (mainly Bernie reading his poetry to backing music) and he contributed guitar to four songs on *Madman Across the Water* before being invited to join John's band full-time. Dee Murray and Nigel Olsson had recorded with the Spencer Davis Group in 1969 before signing with DJM and actually played on some of Elton's early demos for his debut album.

John didn't come up on my radar again until the single 'Crocodile Rock' in early 1973. Interestingly, the song was inspired by 'Eagle Rock', a huge hit for Daddy Cool in 1971 (John had toured Australia that year and had taken note of the burgeoning Australian rock scene). When *Don't Shoot Me I'm Only the Piano Player* was released early in the year, I was also drawn to that album because of the great cover art – a pastiche of 1950s rock and roll in the year that George Lucas' film *American Graffiti* was released – with the support show being the Marx Brothers *Go West*, still one of my favorite movies. It didn't hurt either that *Don't Shoot Me* produced another hit single, the sad-eyed ballad 'Daniel'.

Elton John and Bernie Taupin had come a long way in just over three short years and were clearly building to something big. In January 1973, as *Don't Shoot Me* was climbing the album charts, the band convened to record songs for their new album. The oppressive DJM contract the duo had signed in the late 1960s demanded two albums of new material a year and they were falling behind.

Having made the previous two albums at the Château d'Hérouville outside of Paris (thus the album name, *Honky Château*), it was decided to record the follow-up in Kingston, Jamaica. An ill-fated attempt to record at Kingston's Dynamic Studio, which was 'not technically sound' was further delayed when new recording equipment had to be flown in and installed. Elton John, never one of the most patient artists when told to wait, decided to relocate to France after some local unrest surrounding the upcoming Joe Frazier vs. George Foreman heavyweight boxing match there spooked the group, their wives and their management team.

They did, however, write a song about the experience. 'Jamaica Jerk-Off', a parody of their time in Jamaica, and easily the most dispensable of the songs on *Goodbye Yellow Brick Road*, somehow made the final cut. The number of songs they had accumulated resulted in the new album becoming a double LP. The album, which would be called *Goodbye Yellow Brick Road*, was finished in only 17 days, including mixing. Elton John would record his vocal over the backing tracks, which were performed live by the band, and by the time he entered the recording studio the following day, Johnstone, Murray and Olsson had recorded backing harmonies so that the songs could be faithfully performed by the band on stage. The Elton John Band was a solid musical unit.

The album opens with the instrumental 'Funeral for a Friend', obviously a song attributed solely to John and reflective at the time, he later observed with a dramatic flourish, of the music he would have liked played at his funeral. The haunting melody is enhanced by numerous synth overdubs performed by David Hentschel on ARP 2500 synthesizer, a keyboard-based analogue competitor to the Moog synthesizer at the time. Hentschel had played on 'Rocket Man' and created a swirling, tonal effect for this new song, which was augmented by some slashing guitar work from Davey Johnstone. The song enters into Jimmy Webb territory with its syncopated 'call and response' movement on piano, which is then rescued once again by soaring guitar from Johnstone.

The song then launches into the John-Taupin composition 'Love Lies Bleeding', an easy segue as 'Funeral for a Friend' finishes in 'A' and 'Love Lies Bleeding' begins in the same key. 'The roses in the window box have titled to one side / Everything about this house was born to grow and die ...' is one of the great opening lines to an album (albeit, more than five minutes after the record starts!) and again, features some of Johnstone's most underrated guitar work. Elton is in great voice here, as he is on the entire album. I love the line, 'I was playing rock and roll and you were just a fan / But my guitar couldn't hold you so I split the band …' as if the singer is talking about something more than being a rock and roll singer. Towards the end of the song, Hentschel's synthesizer mirrors Elton's fine playing before Johnstone chimes in and finishes the song with heavy guitar, a la Mick Ronson. 'Funeral for a Friend' may be a piano song, but 'Love Lies Bleeding' is all guitar.

'Candle in the Wind' was one of the first pop songs to recognize the growing interest in the life and early death of actress Marilyn Monroe. That the song was written a bare decade after Monroe's death from an overdose in her Hollywood flat shows how in tune Taupin was with the prevailing pop culture. Taupin later admitted that he was not really a Monroe fan, per se – in the early 1970s, there were a number of schools growing around fallen heroes such as Humphrey Bogart and James Dean – but that the song is a brilliantly realized lament about the perils of fame. The tragedy surrounding Monroe's suicide, at age 36, is poignantly portrayed by Taupin ('And they made you change your name', 'Hollywood created a superstar' and 'you lived your life like a candle in the wind …') and the song found a ready audience, especially in America.

'Bennie and the Jets' can be viewed as a wry commentary by Taupin about the glam rock in the early 1970s. It's easy to see David Bowie ('Ziggy and the Spiders from Mars') or Marc Bolan (of T.Rex fame) as inspirations for the fictitious 'Bennie' ('Say, Candy and Ronnie, have you seen them yet / Oh, but they're so spaced out …'). Generational wars abound ('We shall survive, let us take ourselves along / Where we fight our parents out in the streets to find who's right and who's wrong …') and the stuttering 'B-B-B-Bennie and the Jets …' is reminiscent of Roger Daltrey on the Who's 'My Generation'. Everyone involved in recording the track felt that it was 'missing something' and producer Gus Dudgeon came up with the idea of adding the audience effects, apparently from a Jimi Hendrix concert. It's hard to imagine what appeal the song had without the applause effects; the added reverb and stomping and whistling noises bring a 'live' energy to the recorded track.

The song was a surprise hit single in the US and Canada, where it reached No.1 in early 1974. John apparently fought 'tooth and nail' to stop the single 'Bennie and the Jets' from coming out, but it was already on heavy rotation on Detroit radio and had been adopted by the city's black audience – so much so that John was invited to sing the song on the TV dance show *Soul Train* (much to his pleasure). The song's success is hard to pin down – there's not that much to the song except verse and chorus – but it works because of Elton's great vocal and staccato piano playing. 'Bennie and the Jets' became a crowd favorite with fans too and is a highlight of Elton's live shows.

The title track 'Goodbye Yellow Brick Road' was chosen as the second single off the album (after 'Saturday Night's Alright for Fighting') and was a Top 10 hit in most countries without hitting the top spot (the B-side was 'Screw You', re-titled 'Young Man's Blues' in the US so as not to offend American sensibilities). The best praise I can give it is that it could easily have come from the Beatles if they were still together in 1973. Dig a little deeper and the descending piano chord progression in the song's opening (F / C / Dm / C / B♭/ C / F) is resonant of the bridge to Paul McCartney's 'You Never Give Me Your Money', which begins and ends in the key of C.

'Goodbye Yellow Brick Road' is a yearning for the past, and whenever I hear that song it has that uniquely magical quality of transporting me back to the early 1970s. Taupin later said that the song was a response to his disillusionment with the glitz of fame

('When are you gonna come down? / Where are you gonna land?') and of the desire to go back to a simpler time ('You can't plant me in your penthouse / I'm going back to my plough ...'). John's younger falsetto voice never sounded so good, but it's not hard to view the lyric as a mild rebuke of him too.

A recurring theme on the album is the perils of celebrity – the title song is an allusion to the film *The Wizard of Oz*, and the sad fate of its star Judy Garland; other songs such as 'Danny Bailey', 'Roy Rogers' and 'Candle in the Wind' reinforce that theme. Elton John admits that he too became 'lost' in fame after the success of *Goodbye Yellow Brick Road*, playing concerts in increasingly outlandish outfits (the nadir being the Donald Duck outfit he wore at his September 1980 concert in New York's Central Park) that, in Taupin's mind at least, trivialized their music. 'With the costumes,' John later told rock critic Alexis Petridis, 'I wasn't just living out my fantasies onstage, I was trying to be someone else.'

The album itself has been described as 'cinematic' in scope, and that is because each song is a mini-masterpiece of storytelling. 'This Song Has No Title', which opens Side Two, is almost hymn-like and has some clever lyrics ('If we're all going somewhere let's get there soon / Oh this song's got no title just words and a tune ...'). 'Grey Seal' is episodic, asking the listener the big questions of life ('On the big screen they showed us the sun / But not as bright in life as the real one ...'), with a great, wah wah funky guitar finish. 'I've Seen That Movie Too' stretches the movie allegory to almost breaking point but features exceptional orchestration from Del Newman and eerie, pentatonic guitar work from Davey Johnstone.

The cinematic theme continues on Side Three with 'Sweet Painted Lady', one of the best album tracks on the set, which tells a totally evolved story about a loveless sailor ('back on dry land once again …'). 'The Ballad of Danny Bailey (1909–34)' mirrors the fate of '30s gangsters Bonnie and Clyde ('Some punk with a shotgun killed young Danny Bailey …') and, once again, is greatly enhanced by Newman's strings arrangement in the fade out. 'Dirty Little Girl' is an underrated rocker with a great vocal from Elton (especially on the 'hiccups' before each chorus). Johnstone gets everything he can out of the song (check out his lead guitar in the final refrain) and although somewhat misogynistic by today's standards ('Someone grab that bitch by the ears …') it's another example of Taupin's ability to write in character.

The narrative of 'All the Girls Love Alice' is a straightforward story about gender bending, so when I first heard the song in 1973 I thought it was clearly inspired by Alice Cooper (the prolonged finale is also similar to the street fight at the end of 'Gutter Cat Vs. the Jets' from *School's Out*). The Alice Cooper band had taken England by storm in 1972, and Taupin and leader singer Alice Cooper would later collaborate on Alice's solo album *From the Inside* in 1978 (Davey Johnstone would also join Cooper's backing band and work with him on the *Flush the Fashion* album in 1980). The track also features Kiki Dee on background vocals, two years before she had the megahit 'Don't Go Breaking My Heart' with Elton, as well as his long-time collaborator, percussionist Ray Cooper. The song goes on for too long, however, perhaps to pad out the vinyl.

At the beginning of Side Four, 'Your Sister Can't Twist (But She Can Rock 'n Roll)' is a wonderful faux '50s, doo-wop piece with great harmonies. The organ in the middle of the song gives the song a 'carousel' feel (resembling 'Peppermint Twist' in part) and is the perfect introduction to 'Saturday Night's Alright for Fighting'.

With an opening riff the Who would have been proud to play, 'Saturday Night's Alright' is full of testosterone ('It's seven o'clock and I want to rock / Want to get a belly full of beer…'). Featuring a great singalong chorus ('Saturday, Saturday, Saturday, Saturday night's alright'), the band is once again in exceptional form in the fade out, especially John's frenetic hammering of the keyboards. Released as the precursor single in September 1972 before the album's release, 'Saturday Night's Alright' was a great entrée to the album, and an 'EJB' live classic, but it was the only single between 1972 and 1975 not to make the US Top 10.

'Roy Rogers' shows Taupin's affinity with the American Wild West. Like many of his generation, he was heavily influenced by black-and-white cowboy movies shown on TV in the 1950s and early 1960s (Jeff Lynne sings about a similar experience on ELO's 'Wild West Hero' from 1977). The self-described 'Brown Dirt Cowboy', Taupin gives us a paean to the sameness of suburban life, wonderfully realized, complete with Elton's faux American accent and a sweeping orchestral score ('Turn off the TV, close out the lights / Roy Rogers is riding tonight …').

When I first heard 'Social Disease' I thought something was wrong with my stereo, such is the long fade in on that track. Similar to the funky style of 'Honky Cat', Elton John's hit from *Honky Château*, 'Social Disease' also has a country banjo-feel, but is one of the lesser songs on the album. It does, however, lead into 'Harmony', one of the better, and underrated, Elton John songs. The single that never was (it was selected as the B-side to 'Benny and the Jets' when the record label pushed for that song to be released in the US), 'Harmony', as the title suggests, has an amazing arrangement of harmonies from the band. For me, the song is one of Elton's lost classics, along with 'I Feel Like a Bullet (In the Gun of Robert Ford')' from *Rock of the Westies* and 'Someone Saved My Life Tonight', from *Captain Fantastic and the Brown Dirt Cowboy* (both 1975), and is a remarkable vocal performance from the band to finish the album.

During the recording of the album, Elton John's management team set into motion the design of the album cover art that would bring John and Taupin's masterpiece to life visually. The credits on the back of *Goodbye Yellow Brick Road* tell the story of how one of the best of the genre came to be made:

> Outside cover Illustration by IAN BECK. Inside cover illustrations by DAVID LARKHAM & MICHAEL ROSS except "Harmony" & "Saturday Night" (sic). Illustrated by David Scutt. Art Direction by DAVID LARKHAM & MICHAEL ROSS with thanks to DAVID COSTA.

In 1973, Steve Brown and Gus Dudgeon, along with John and Taupin, founded the Rocket Record Company. Brown conscripted artists David Larkham and Mike Ross, who had collaborated with John on various album covers, including *Don't Shoot Me*, to illustrate the new album. There was no title for the album as yet, and therefore no cover concept.

Larkham flew to Jamaica in January 1973 to hear the new batch of songs for the first time. With the band idle while they waited for new recording equipment to be installed, Larkham was treated to a mini-concert from Elton John, one on one, who played all the new songs for him. Larkham left with copies of Taupin's hand-written lyrics and returned to LA to work with colleague Michael Ross to illustrate them. Fellow artist David Scutt was also conscripted.

Larkham decided that the new album would have a triple panel, double gate fold with the illustrated lyrics across the three internal panels. The illustrations by David Scutt for 'Harmony' and 'Saturday Night's Alright For Fighting' are both standouts; Scutt went on to create the front cover painting of the 'alethiometer' on the first edition of Philip Pullman's *Northern Lights*, the first volume in the *His Dark Materials* trilogy (known as *The Golden Compass* in the US). The images for 'Candle in the Wind', 'I've Seen That Movie Too' and 'Your Sister Can't Twist (But She Can Rock 'n Roll)' are beautifully drawn, though less effective are the pencil drawings for 'Grey Seal' (a sketch), 'Jamaica Jerk Off' (culturally insensitive?) and 'All the Girls Love Alice' (lacking reference). Photos of John and Taupin are also utilized; John for 'Social Disease' (in tartans, no less), and Taupin with his then wife Maxine Feibelman (his inspiration for 'Tiny Dancer') for 'Danny Bailey'.

At the end of the summer, Larkham was informed that the title of the new album would be *Goodbye Yellow Brick Road* but the fine-art portrait of Elton John commissioned from world-renowned painter Bryan Organ was considered 'inappropriate' for the album cover. That painting, of a bespectacled Elton John wearing a Marilyn Monroe pop T-shirt, is on display at the Redfern Gallery, London.

Instead, Elton had found an image that he liked – the cover for Irish singer John Kelly's 1972 LP *Wait Till They Change the Backdrop*, drawn by artist Ian Beck – and Larkham was summoned to London to coordinate the new artwork. Larkham went to the Rocket Records offices in Soho to discuss the issue with Steve Brown, David Costa (son of the well-known 1950s radio entertainer and DJ, Sam Costa) and artist Ian Beck, but buying that artwork and somehow conscripting it into becoming the cover of Elton's new album was deemed impractical. 'How can you have two albums out with the same artwork?' Ian Beck reasoned.

So the artist was asked to come up with an original artwork centered around the theme of 'leaving the city for the country'. Looking through Beck's portfolio, the team liked a magazine cover he had drawn for *Creem* magazine of David Bowie standing in front of a brick wall with a poster of Bowie in the background. Larkham had been inspired by an ad for a travel agency of the image of a man staring at a travel poster, and pushed for the concept of Elton 'stepping' into a poster of the famous 'yellow brick road'.

Beck was given the task of coming up with the three-panel outer cover, which would be made up of a front cover image, a panel featuring the main players and a credits panel that had been flat-planned by Larkham. Given some time to listen to the album so he could come up with art that 'fit the mood' of the music, Beck drew some quick concepts on tracing paper and was then given just ten days to finish the project. 'I had been briefed about certain things to include on the front cover to please "Elsie",' Beck remembers. 'These included a Teddy Bear, and a piano. "Elsie loves pianos", they said. At first, I thought Elsie was perhaps a beloved tea lady at the offices of DJM or Rocket Records, and they were including these things to amuse her. Finally, I realized that they were talking about Elton.'

Inspired by the resurgence of 1930s American design and graphics at that time, Beck's image captures a dreamlike, Hollywood quality. Conscripting fellow artist Leslie Chapman to stand in for Elton, Beck took a polaroid photo of Chapman/Elton stepping into what would become the 'yellow brick road' poster. Chapman was wearing an old-style basketball jacket at the time so Beck adapted that aspect into his artwork, even adding sequins. The only minor issue was that Chapman was quite tall; Elton's legs seem to go on forever in the finished product.

Beck delivered his three panels to Rocket Records, having completed the work using watercolor, pastels and colored crayons on illustration board. The final cover to *Goodbye Yellow Brick Road* is a work of art and, as such, there is a lot for the eye to take in and enjoy. In England, the work won *Music Week*'s 'Album Cover of The Year' award, the British equivalent of a Grammy. Created in the days before artists were guaranteed ownership of their artwork and the finished product would end up in art galleries (or on the walls of the nearest Hard Rock Café), not one of the original three panels survives today.

Look carefully and you can see that Ian Beck signs his artwork on the front cover, on the step in the bottom right corner. Part of the original conversation between Larkham and Beck included having a reference to the cover of *Don't Shoot Me I'm Only the Piano Player* somewhere, and the edge of the poster displaying Elton John's name can be seen on the top right side of the 'Yellow Brick Road' image. Beck references his own work too; the factory smoke on the left is similar to the original John Kelly album cover and the brick wall has the same color and texture as the Bowie cover in *Creem* magazine.

Over the years, I have spent countless hours poring over the artwork on this album: Elton wearing ruby red platform shoes, a reference to Judy Garland's ruby slippers in *The Wizard of Oz*; the toy piano and musical note on the front cover, with accompanying shadow; the bluebird flitting past on the front cover that reappears on each of other two panels. The Teddy Bear is there too, and the 'Elton' logo and signature on the back cover credits are particularly effective. The antique car bonnet, the palm tree shadow and the cracking wear and tear of the stucco on the walls are wonderful touches from Beck.

The name 'Elton John' on the internal portrait matches the front cover lettering, while the names of the other players share a common style that was very popular in the early 1970s. The photos of Elton, Bernie and the three major band members (Davey Johnstone, Dee Murray and Nigel Olsson) have a 1930s, hand-painted effect but I love the prominence all the band members were given; this was a *real* band, with Elton at the helm and Bernie in the wings.

Goodbye Yellow Brick Road was a huge success when released – only *Rolling Stone* questioned its ambitiousness, 'a big fruity pie that simply doesn't bake,' Stephen Davis wrote in 1973. 'But, oh lord, how it tries.' But forty years later, *RS* had changed its tune, naming it in the Top 100 albums of all time. 'Elton John compared this double album to the Beatles' White Album, and why not?' the magazine writes:

> By this point he was the most consistent hitmaker since the Fab Four … everything about Goodbye Yellow Brick Road is supersonically huge, from the Wagnerian-opera-like combo of "Funeral for a Friend" and "Love Lies Bleeding" to the electric boots and mohair suit of "Bennie and the Jets." "Saturday Night's Alright for Fighting" is strutting rock & roll, "Candle in the Wind" pays tribute to Marilyn Monroe, and the title track harnesses the fantastic imagery of glam to a Gershwin-sweet melody.

And this is probably part of the problem; Elton John had no time to rest on his laurels. Months later, he found himself back in the studio, recording the album *Caribou*, which even Gus Dudgeon called 'a piece of crap'. Murray and Olsson were sacked ahead of 1975's

Rock of the Westies before John achieved mega-stardom with that year's *Captain Fantastic and the Brown Dirt Cowboy*, which debuted in the US at No.1 but is today largely forgotten.

There would be heartaches for John and Taupin in the years ahead; drug and alcohol excess, broken marriages and ruined relationships, and a momentary end to their songwriting partnership. But, more than four decades after the success of *Goodbye Yellow Brick Road* – now seen as the high point of both of their careers – the pair are still producing great music and the album sounds just as fresh today as it did back in 1973.

Elton John / **Goodbye Yellow Brick Road** (October 1973)   76:20

All songs written by Elton John and Bernie Taupin, except* (Elton John).

SIDE ONE	LENGTH
1. Funeral for a Friend*/Love Lies Bleeding	11:09
2. Candle in the Wind	3:50
3. Bennie and the Jets	5:23

SIDE TWO	
4. Goodbye Yellow Brick Road	3:13
5. This Song Has No Title	2:23
6. Grey Seal	4:00
7. Jamaica Jerk-Off	3:39
8. I've Seen That Movie Too	5:59

SIDE THREE	
9. Sweet Painted Lady	3:54
10. The Ballad of Danny Bailey (1909–34)	4:23
11. Dirty Little Girl	5:00
12. All the Girls Love Alice	5:09

SIDE FOUR	
13. Your Sister Can't Twist (But She Can Rock 'n' Roll)	2:42
14. Saturday Night's Alright for Fighting	4:57
15. Roy Rogers	4:07
16. Social Disease	3:42
17. Harmony	2:46

Honorable Mentions

1967–1976

'You always responded when I needed your help
You gimme a map and a key to your door ...'

S o many favorite albums, so many choices. The following bands and artists played their part in my musical education and, for a time, these albums took pride of place on my record turntable. It would be remiss of me not to give each an honorable mention. Perhaps some are your favorites too.

Pisces, Aquarius, Capricorn & Jones Ltd.
The Monkees (1967)

Growing up in the 1960s, it was hard not to be a Monkees fan. A TV show based on a fictional band, a la the Beatles in *A Hard Day's Night* ('The pre-Fab Four?'), may have been a cynical ploy by studio executives at the time, but the result was breakthrough pop art TV and timeless music written by the best songwriters available.

What also can't be denied is that *The Monkees* TV show, and the group itself, benefited greatly from the four strong personalities chosen to play the roles – LA's Micky Dolenz and Manchester's Davy Jones (both former child actors), Texan Mike Nesmith and East Coast folkie Peter Tork (born Thorkelson), two non-actors with music backgrounds.

The Monkees were a hit before the show even premiered, with the Tommy Boyce-Bobby Hart written and produced 'Last Train to Clarksville' topping the charts in the US and Canada. Although the TV show would run for only two seasons, having a weekly audience in the millions (the younger brothers and sisters of Beatles fans, as Mickey Dolenz observed) propelled their singles and albums to the top of the charts. 'I'm a Believer', written by the then relatively unknown New Yorker Neil Diamond, went to No.1 around the world in Christmas 1966, with 'Daydream Believer', written by the Kingston Trio's John Stewart, repeating the feat the following year.

The Monkees' self-titled debut album in 1966 was a quickly cobbled together compilation of available material and it reached No.1 in the US, UK, Canada and Australia. The opportunistic release of *More of the Monkees* just three months later angered the band, who did not even know the album had been released, and this led to the sacking of their music coordinator, Don Kirshner. Mike Nesmith was especially vocal about the musical standoff at the time, lamenting that the group did not actually play on their own records. The backlash from the press was predictably harsh, and hypocritical as it would turn out – the Beach Boys did not play on their albums either, or the Turtles for that matter – but overnight sensations the Monkees were held to a different standard.

Headquarters, which went to No.1 in May 1967, was the band's first attempt at playing on their records, under new producer Chip Douglas. The album did not produce a hit single, although Mickey Dolenz's 'Randy Scouse Git' ('Alternate Title') was No.2 in the UK when the Monkees toured there during the Summer of Love. Artistically, and critically, they would hit their peak with the release of *Pisces, Aquarius, Capricorn & Jones Ltd.* in November of that year.

Highlights on the album include 'Love Is Only Sleeping', written by Barry Mann and Cynthia Weil and featuring a masterful vocal from Nesmith; Harry Nilsson's 'Cuddly Toy', a song with a double entendre that went straight over the kiddies' heads; 'Words', written by Boyce and Hart, and a showcase for Dolenz's underrated pop vocal; the Gerry Goffin and Carole King classic, 'Pleasant Valley Sunday'; and two songs featuring Moog synthesizer, Nesmith's 'Daily Nightly' and Goffin-King's 'Star Collector'. For me, Nesmith is the star of the album, offering a great country-rock vocal on 'What Am I Doing Hangin' Round?' and giving 'Don't Call on Me' an evocative, detached feel.

Try and find another album from the era (other than the Beatles, that is) that has so many great songs on one LP. I have long shrugged off any guilt about being a Monkees fan – the songs were well-written and produced, and that's why they still remain fresh today; the Emmy Award-winning TV series was great fun and extremely well put together; and their 1968 movie *Head*, written by a young actor-director named Jack Nicholson, is a cult classic. Fifty years later, Mike, Davy, Mickey and Peter still make me smile.

Cosmo's Factory
Creedence Clearwater Revival (1970)

Creedence Clearwater Revival were the ultimate garage band; there was nothing fancy or artful about the group. The songs they recorded had catchy, commercial hooks and were simple enough for other garage bands to play. As realized by lead singer and chief songwriter, John Fogerty, Creedence pioneered what became known as 'swamp rock', playing songs that could have come out of the deep South; 'Susie Q', 'Green River', 'Proud Mary' and 'Run Through the Jungle' to name but a few. This was despite the fact that Fogerty had grown up in Berkley, California, with older brother Tom (rhythm guitar) and school friends Stu Cook (bass) and Doug 'Cosmo' Clifford (drums).

Originally called the Golliwogs (!), the reimagined Creedence Clearwater Revival had a series of top selling albums and numerous Top 10 singles in the late 1960s (the band were fated never to have a US No.1 hit single during their career), before releasing their career best *Cosmo's Factory* in 1970. Named after the warehouse where the band rehearsed their songs, the happy band portraits on the front and back covers of the LP belie the tensions behind their facade of comradery and informality. As John Fogerty outlines in his often bitter 2015 autobiography, the band were under his direction; rehearsing the parts he assigned to them and perfecting each song before recording multiple takes. Most of the songs Creedence recorded are extremely basic – drums, bass and two guitars – with Fogerty overdubbing organ, piano, harmonica or saxophone, and his own multi-tracked backing vocals. Fogerty did everything.

But as a classic LP of the era, *Cosmo's Factory* works so well because there is such a wide range of great songs on the album, including three hit singles – 'Travelin' Band' (US No.2) and its B-side, 'Who'll Stop the Rain'; 'Up Around the Bend' (US No.4) backed by 'Run Through the Jungle'; and 'Lookin' Out My Backdoor' (US No.2) and its B-side, 'Long As I Can See the Light'. That six of the album's 11 tracks could be sourced on singles did not detract from the success of the album, which was the band's biggest seller and a No.1 hit in the US, UK, Canada and Australia.

The opening track, the psychedelic 'Ramble Tamble', proves that CCR were a more than competent rock and roll band. The covers of Arthur Crudup's 'My Baby Left Me', Bo Diddley's 'Before You Accuse Me', 'Ooby Dooby' (Roy Orbison) and 'I Heard It Through the Grapevine' (a Motown hit for Marvin Gaye the previous year) reflects their broad repertoire. For me, the highlight of the album is 'Who'll Stop the Rain'. With allusions to Creedence's appearance at the Woodstock Festival in August 1969 (Fogerty disliked the sound of their midnight performance so much that he refused to allow their set to be featured on the documentary or record), the song takes on almost a mythic quality, coming as it did at the end of the '60s ('Long as I remember the rain been coming down / Clouds of myst'ry pouring confusion on the ground …'). This song sums up the end of an era.

Creedence's contract with Fantasy Records was the source of much of the existing friction within the band and ultimately destroyed any good will between the four players. Tom Fogerty left the band after the release of *Pendulum* in 1971, the result of unresolved sibling rivalry, and the band continued on as a three-piece before disbanding in 1972, shortly after their tour of Australia. John Fogerty was embroiled in court battles with Fantasy Records' CEO,

Saul Zaentz, for the next three decades regarding copyright issues, in the process freezing out the remaining members of the band. Tom Fogerty died in 1991 without reconciling with his brother.

It took years for John Fogerty to reclaim his musical legacy, and when I saw him on stage in 2005 he appeared to have reconciled his past with Creedence Clearwater Revival, come to terms with his successful 1980s solo career after it was stopped in its tracks by Saul Zaentz, and was now living in the present.

Teaser and the Firecat
Cat Stevens (1971)

Having already had a taste of teen stardom in 1967 with the single 'Matthew and Son', Cat Stevens (born Steven Georgiou) bounced back from a bout of tuberculosis with a new sound and a new 'seventies' sensibility. Hit albums *Mona Bone Jakon* and *Tea for the Tillerman* quickly followed, with songs from both of these featured in the 1971 cult film *Harold and Maude*, a movie about a morose teenager (Bud Cort) who falls in love with a grandmother (Ruth Gordon). The release of the *Teaser and the Firecat* album in October 1971, just as the movie was taking off, sent Stevens' career to a new level.

The first album I brought with my own pocket money, *Teaser and the Firecat* reached No.2 in the US and the UK (and Canada) and was a huge hit in Australia. With its distinctive cover paintings of the fictional characters (by Stevens, no less) and ten songs of sweet acoustic simplicity, the album represents Stevens' high point as a recording artist. As well as the classics 'Tuesday's Dead', 'Bitterblue',

'Moonshadow', 'Peace Train' and a wonderful version of the Christian hymn 'Morning Has Broken' (with light as air piano runs by Rick Wakeman), the album also contains lesser known gems 'The Wind' (not a second wasted at a bare 1:42), 'Rubylove' (with the wonderful sound of the Greek bouzouki) and the gentle 'If I Laugh', with accompanying acoustic guitar from the ever-reliable Alun Davies.

Stevens finally topped the US charts with his next album, *Catch Bull at Four*, but the LP did not produce a hit single and each subsequent album (*Foreigner* in 1973 and *Buddha and the Chocolate Box* in 1974) moved him a little further from his folkie fanbase as the pop market shifted away from singer-songwriters in the mid-1970s. This led to Stevens' loss of self-confidence, a conversion to Islam and a 25-year sabbatical from music. His return to touring and recording, first as Yusuf Islam and later as Yusuf Cat Stevens, was like welcoming an old friend back to the stage.

The Yes Album
Yes (1971)

I liked prog-rock band Yes the moment I heard them. In the early 1970s, my local radio station was playing a band or act for each letter of the alphabet in a popular promotion. I can't recall who they played for 'X', so I may have nodded off as the countdown approached midnight, but as soon as I heard the choral burst, 'I've seen all good people …' I was wide awake. In just under seven minutes, the band delivers a perfect musical suite upon the same theme – 'I've Seen All Good People', 'Your Move' and the reprise 'All Good People' – inspired by Jon Anderson's heavenly voice. It was an epiphany for me.

Who knew? I was a prog rocker! Discovering Yes opened my eyes to fellow travelers like the Moody Blues, Procol Harum, Genesis (before Peter Gabriel departed), Wishbone Ash, Emerson Lake and Palmer, Jethro Tull and, belatedly, Pink Floyd.

The Yes Album (1971) quickly became a firm favorite, and although the band line-up at that time – Jon Anderson (vocals, percussion), Chris Squire (bass), Steve Howe (guitars), Tony Kaye (keyboards) and Bill Bruford (drums, percussion) – would undergo numerous personnel changes over the years (especially with additions of drummer Alan White, and pianist Rick Wakeman) they would sound no finer than the first night I heard them on crackling AM radio.

Although Yes clearly held classical-rock pretentions, songs such as 'Clap' – recorded live the previous July at the Lyceum Theatre, London, and a showcase for Howe's considerable acoustic guitar skills (he plays a Portuguese guitar on 'All Good People') – and the epic 'Starship Trooper' display their virtuosity as prog-rock pioneers.

Given my penchant for choosing albums on the strength of their cover art, it's ironic that the album *before* the band started a relationship with artist Roger Dean (whose style would brand most of their subsequent album covers) would become a personal favorite. The cover of *The Yes Album* is an exercise in minimalism: photographer Phil Franks shot a photo of the band in his flat under a fluorescent kitchen light, using a mannequin head strung from the ceiling as his only prop. Note keyboardist Tony Kaye with his leg in plaster, the result of a car accident the previous night when the band was driving in pouring rain from a gig in Basingstoke.

Hunky Dory
David Bowie (1971)

There was no hotter act in the world than David Bowie in 1973. Wearing his 'Ziggy Stardust' persona at the height of the UK 'glam rock' movement, Bowie parlayed his success with the best-selling *The Rise and Fall of Ziggy Stardust and the Spiders from Mars* (1972) and *Aladdin Sane* (1973) into a full-on assault on the American market. Never really a fan of Bowie's gender-bending, over-theatrical and lyrically obscure take on the rock and roll dream, I much preferred his spaced-out folkie period, which reached its peak with the release of *Hunky Dory* in 1971.

Bowie (born David Jones) could have easily been a one-hit wonder given his failure to top the charts with a follow-up to his 1969 success 'Space Oddity'. His 1970 album, *The Man Who Sold the World* (1970), was a step in the right direction, establishing his rep as a new-age singer-songwriter (the controversial album cover showed a photograph of the long-haired artist reclining on a couch in a floral silk dress!). *Hunky Dory*, released the following year on RCA, was the first indication of Bowie's immense talent, albeit accompanied by a penchant for self-parody, which the artist himself would refer to as his 'Anthony Newley' imitation.

But then, Bowie always had a soft spot for the melodramatic (on the back of *Hunky Dory* on the handwritten liner notes he refers to himself in the third person as 'the actor'). The front cover portrays Bowie as a blonde starlet from a 1930s Hollywood magazine, his eyes a perfect, hand-painted blue; the back cover shows him in a pantsuit with long, flowing hair. 'Changes', the opening song of the album, is prophetic in that it predicted what lay ahead for Bowie

('Turn and face the strange …'). 'Oh! You Pretty Things' is a fond look back at late '60s stardom, and a reference to psychedelic rockers the Pretty Things, and a particularly strange selection for former Herman's Hermits frontman Peter Noone to release as a single. The melodramatic 'Quicksand', 'Queen Bitch' – an early prototype for his transformation into Ziggy – and paeans to Andy Warhol and Bob Dylan, all work their magic.

For some, however, the unheralded star of *Hunky Dory* is master guitarist and sometimes musical arranger, Mick Ronson. The Hull guitarist infuses 'Life on Mars?' with razor-like guitar runs and a soaring orchestral arrangement to match Bowie's dramatic apostrophizing ('Is there life on Mars?'). It's by far my favorite Bowie track (Barbra Streisand liked it too, as her faithful, 1974 cover of the song proves) with 'Sailors, fighting in the dance hall / Oh man, look at those cavemen go …' a wonderfully random image.

But then *Hunky Dory* is full of great musical flourishes (it's also hard not to like the naïve charm of 'Kooks' and 'Fill Your Heart') and the final track, 'The Bewlay Brothers', is a masterful oddity. With its reverbed, distorted vocal at the close, this enigmatic song (perhaps a call out to his half-brother Tony, who suffered from schizophrenia) hints at Bowie's inventiveness, and his pain too, but the lyric is impenetrable.

And for me, this is the problem with Bowie; his lyrics are rarely revelatory. It's all a syntactic game for him, cutting up random phrases that took his fancy and gluing them together to create non-sequiturs. But he was incredibly influential in the 1970s, and after almost disappearing into a drug hell after moving to LA in 1975, there was no one happier than me when he made his first comeback with 1977's 'Heroes' – as himself, finally – and then resurrected his

'Space Oddity' character Major Tom to top the charts with 'Ashes to Ashes' at the start of the new decade. Bowie, forever changing, now sadly missed.

Nilsson Schmilsson
Harry Nilsson (1971)

Being both a Beatles and Monkees fan, it was inevitable that Harry Nilsson would come into my orbit. Nilsson penned 'Cuddly Toy' (1967) and 'Daddy's Song' (1968) for the Monkees and came to the notice of John Lennon and Paul McCartney with his version of 'You Can't Do That' (1967), which incorporated 18 other Beatles songs into the mix. He achieved worldwide acclaim with his version of Fred Neil's 'Everybody's Talkin'' on the soundtrack of the Academy Award-winning *Midnight Cowboy* in 1969, but he was something of a maverick when it came to his career. Numerous albums would be released (*Harry*, 1969; *Nilsson Sings Newman*, 1970; and the soundtrack to *The Point!* 1971) before Nilsson struck gold with *Nilsson Schmilsson* at the end of 1971.

With Richard Perry as his producer, Nilsson harnesses his considerable talent and makes his first consistent musical statement with this album. Supported by star session players Jim Gordon, Jim Keltner, Chris Spedding, Caleb Quaye, Herbie Flowers, Bobby Keys and Jim Price, Nilsson adds real star power on this album with Jimmy Webb (the writer of 'MacArthur Park' among countless others), Gary Wright (ex-Spooky Tooth and George Harrison alumni) and Klaus Voormann (ex-Manfred Mann and Plastic Ono Band bassist). The resulting album reached a career best No.3 on the US charts.

Nilsson Schmilsson opens with the Paul McCartney-like 'Gotta Get Up'. 'The Moonbeam Song' is typically wistful, and 'Down' is clever, pop-orientated white soul. 'Coconut', on Side Two, is a reggae-style novelty song, its success assisted by a promotional film clip, years before MTV, of band members in ape suits pounding primitive instruments. In 'Jump into the Fire', Nilsson builds a rock song around a single chord (Cmaj) with band members displaying considerable skill in keeping the vibe from breaking down (bassist Herbie Flowers detunes his instrument towards the end of the song, believing at the time that it would be part of the fade out: in fact, it's the highlight of the song).

The major achievement on the album, however, is Nilsson's soaring, multi-tracked vocal on 'Without You'. One of three covers on the album (the others being 'Early in the Morning' and 'Let the Good Times Roll'), the song was written by Badfinger's Pete Ham and Tom Evans and was a worldwide No.1. That Nilsson had his greatest success with covers, rather than his own material, would certainly grate on him, and the fact that he never appeared in concert would diminish him in the eyes of some rock critics. But as Richard Perry pointed out in the wonderful documentary, *Who Is Harry Nilsson (And Why is Everyone Talkin' About Him)?* in 2010, for a time in the early 1970s Nilsson was the greatest white singer in popular music.

I'm such a huge fan of his work, but it frustrates me that Nilsson destroyed his career and ultimately smoked and drank himself to death at the relatively young age of 53, in 1994. The 1980 death of his close friend John Lennon also rocked him to his core. He did find some peace in his later years after marrying for a third time and raising a young family following his fortune being embezzled. His songs were once again in favor with a new generation of filmmakers who had grown up with his music (especially his album of standards, *A Little Touch of Schmilsson In The Night*, in 1973) and his reputation was restored.

Sail Away
Randy Newman (1972)

I first heard Randy Newman when watching the 1971 Norman Lear film, *Cold Turkey*. The story of a small American community that descends into chaos after accepting a financial inducement to give up smoking *en masse*, Newman's gentle piano ballad 'He Gives Us All His Love' plays over the credits. I immediately sourced the album *Sail Away* (1972) and read as much as I could about Newman. The singer-songwriter, and future arranger and film composer, is the nephew of Hollywood heavyweights Alfred, Lionel and Emil Newman, who composed the scores to many of my favorite films (*The Diary of Anne Frank*, *Compulsion*, *How the West Was Won*, *The Boston Strangler* and *Airport*, among countless others).

Newman's songs are sophisticated, almost cinematic and full of pathos. A quirky songwriter with a nasal, Southern quality to his voice (Newman was raised in New Orleans), his songs so enamoured Harry Nilsson that he recorded a whole album of Newman songs on *Nilsson Sings Newman* in 1970. Newman found early success as the writer of 'Simon Smith and the Amazing Dancing Bear', a hit for Alan Price in 1967, which he covered five years later on *Sail Away*. 'Mama Told Me Not to Come' was a hit for Three Dog Night, and appears on the Newman album *12 Songs* (1970), and

'You Can Leave Your Hat On' was a hit for Joe Cocker in the 1980s.

The title song on *Sail Away* is perhaps typical of Newman's writing style and, for me, is one of the most provocative pop songs of the 1970s. It's also resonant of the same ironic humor Newman would infuse into 'Short People' in 1977, which would become his biggest selling single. But *Sail Away*, in which a slave trader coerces a young African boy to sail with him to America ('Everybody is as happy as a man can be / Climb aboard little wog sail away with me …') is a minor 'work of genius', as Stephen Holden described it his contemporaneous review; centuries of human injustice laid bare in Newman's three-minute piano melody.

Harry Nilsson also covers the track, with full orchestration, on his 1976 album *… That's the Way It Is*. Both versions are great for different reasons; Nilsson's vocal is beyond peer, and the orchestration takes the song soaring to new heights, but Newman's original take is understated, and the pathos more effective.

Since 1980, Newman has concentrated on the 'family' business, writing film scores for some of the most popular movies to come out of Hollywood: *Ragtime* (1981), *The Natural* (1984), *Parenthood* (1989), *Toy Story* (1995), *A Bug's Life* (1998) and *Cars* (2006). Nominated for 15 Oscars for his movie scores or original songs, Newman won in 2002 for 'If I Didn't Have You' from the film *Monsters, Inc.* and for 'We Belong Together' from *Toy Story 3,* in 2011. I told my kids at the time, I knew Newman way back when …

Tubular Bells
Mike Oldfield (1973)

Mike Oldfield's *Tubular Bells* (1973) is that rare album; an artistic tour de force, a worldwide financial success and a pop culture phenomenon. Not that all the critics loved this multi-instrumental vision (Oldfield plays more than half of the 40 instruments on the album); American music critic Dave Marsh described the album as 'a fluke ... monotonous and far too long.' The debut album from an unheralded, 20-year-old musician went on to sell 15 million copies worldwide and spent 259 weeks on the UK album charts. It also secured the financial future of Virgin Records, and young entrepreneur Richard Branson.

'Tubular Bells Part 1' is more than 25 minutes long and takes up all of Side One of the album. Played in the peculiar 15/8-time measure, the song opens with its main theme played on piano (Oldfield composed much of the song on that instrument). This motif would be used in the film *The Exorcist* in 1973, introducing the tune to an even wider audience. I love the theme just after 9 minutes, interrupted by the high guitar two minutes later, and the edgy guitar at 13:30, followed by the gentle humming of the male choir, accompanied by piano. More edgy guitar interrupts; power chords that descend into the bass run that forms the formal part of the song.

The gradual introduction of various instruments by Viv Stanshall (of Bonzo Dog Doo-Dah Band fame) begins just after the 17-minute mark. Grand piano plays, followed by reed and pipe organ, glockenspiel and various guitars, before tubular bells play the main melody that finishes in a grand crescendo, female choral voices and a beautiful repose on Spanish guitar, which completes the track with a little rush. Perfection.

I don't know how many times I listened to this record over the years. Hundreds? I felt for my friends who refused to invest in the album and went and bought the single. Rather than getting the radio edit of the last seven minutes of the song, they got the sound of an obviously pissed Viv Stanshall calling 'the sailor's turnpike!' for their $2. The album was well worth the investment, even if Side Two was underutilized. Rather than putting the unknown Oldfield on the cover, Virgin opted for an iconic stainless-steel sculpture, resonant of the tubular bells title, superimposed over the sea and sky.

Was Oldfield a one-hit wonder? Hardly. His follow up album *Hergest Ridge* (1974) entered the UK charts at No.1, only to be toppled by a resurgent *Tubular Bells* on the back of the release of the Academy Award-winning film *The Exorcist*. He had a minor hit in 1981 with 'Moonlight Shadow' with Maggie Reilly, although that song had words on it. The measure of the esteem Oldfield is held in, if not for his accomplishment then for his enormous ambition, can be measured by his selection to perform his opus at the 2012 London Olympics. I, for one, saluted him.

Wish You Were Here
Pink Floyd (1975)

I resisted the temptation to jump on board the *Dark Side of the Moon* bandwagon when it was released in early 1973, having had a friend in high school who used to enjoy bringing early Pink Floyd albums, especially *Ummagumma* (1969) and *Atom Heart Mother* (1970), to parties and quickly clearing the room. I liked the single 'Us and Them' but I resisted investing in the album, with 'Time' and 'Money' played ad infinitum on the radio of the day. In America, the album stayed in the Billboard Top 200 charts for a record 917 weeks – until 1988 – so the LP never really went away. I probably bought the album around about then too, but on CD.

It wasn't until *Wish You Were Here* (1975) was released, however, that I really appreciated the genius of Pink Floyd. 'Shine on You Crazy Diamond', an ode to founding member Syd Barrett, who slipped away into drug-induced psychosis in the late 1960s, is at the heart of the album. 'Wish You Were Here' is a bittersweet lament for what had been lost along the way, with some of the best pop culture observations of life in general ('Did you exchange a walk on part in the war / For a lead role in a cage?'). 'Have A Cigar' is a wry observation on the traps of the record industry ('... which one's Pink?'). Then there was the album art; a beautifully integrated concept by Storm Thorgerson, with the image of a burning man shaking hands with a businessman, and its mechanical counterpart as a corporate logo. Simply brilliant.

Pink Floyd was subjected to one of the most ferocious band split ups in rock (tougher than the Beatles? Possibly). Bassist Roger Waters left the band after 1983's *The Final Cut* and then spent the next 25 years in a battle of wills with remaining band members, especially guitarist Dave Gilmour. I saw Waters perform *Dark Side of the Moon* in its entirety on his 2006–2007 world tour and was swept along by the musicianship, the visuals and the enormous scope of the band's reach. As I walked out of the stadium with a couple of friends, our ears and eyes still ringing, I couldn't help but observe that Waters had achieved what he may have always wanted: ownership of the band's musical legacy, even the songs he didn't write, and the role of leading new generations in discovering the band's music.

Desire
Bob Dylan (1976)

The relative charms of Bob Dylan largely escaped me in the early 1970s. By the time I became musically and socially aware as a teenager, Dylan was bringing out low key, country-inspired albums (*John Wesley Harding*, 1967; *Nashville Skyline*, 1969; and *New Morning*, 1970) as well as his disastrous double album *Self Portrait* (1970). The release of 'Knockin' on Heaven's Door' (1973) as the main theme of the *Pat Garrett and Billy the Kid* soundtrack put Dylan back in the mainstream, but even with the success of *Planet Waves* (1974) and *Blood on the Tracks* (1975), I still resisted Dylan until the release of *Desire* in 1976, my final year of high school.

Desire is dominated by the eight and a half minute epic 'Hurricane', about jailed boxer Rubin Carter. The budding middleweight champion, along with a man named John Artis, had been convicted of a triple murder during the course of a robbery in 1966, but the conviction was racially motivated and the witnesses to the crime less than believable. 'Hurricane', along with six other songs on the album, was co-written by playwright Jacques Levy, who solved the problem of how to tell the story of 'Hurricane' Carter by structuring the song as an unfolding narrative ('Here comes the story of the Hurricane / The man the authorities came to blame / For something that he never done …') with a vast cast of characters and injustices, driven by a flowing violin line. In an era before social media, the release of this protest song shone a light on Carter's case.

Desire was recorded in just four days using the core band of violinist Scarlet Rivera, guitarist Steven Soles, bassist Rob Rothstein (who played on Don McLean's *American Pie*), drummer Howie Wyeth and percussionist Luther Rix (congas); the same group he took on the Rolling Thunder Tour under the direction of Jacques Levy. Legal concerns about some of the lyrics forced Dylan to record a slightly faster version of 'Hurricane' that October, which was the version that appeared on the album. The single was only a Top 10 hit in one territory, Australia, but Carter received significant press coverage because of the song, although, incredibly, it would be another decade before he was exonerated.

There are other delights on the album, however, which was a No.1 hit in the US, Australia and Canada (No.3 in the UK). 'Isis' is the perfect antidote to the heaviness of 'Hurricane', although its message of loyalty and love is no less important; 'Mozambique' is a joyous showcase for Rivera on violin; 'One More Cup of Coffee' is a charming duet with Emmylou Harris; and the marathon 'Joey', about the dead gangster Joey Gallo, is well worth the effort despite its 11-minute length. But the most personal track on the album is the last song, 'Sara'; a love song of sorts to Dylan's wife, Sara Lownds, from whom he had separated ('Writin' "Sad-Eyed Lady of the Lowlands" for you …'). It's Dylan at his most vulnerable.

Desire at last gave me a pathway to explore and appreciate Dylan's extensive back catalogue. I have seen him in concert twice, first in 2007, and again with my son a decade later, and he never disappoints (even if he refuses to speak on stage between songs).

I was a latecomer to the broad church of Bob Dylan, but better late than never.

REFERENCES

The Beatles 'White Album' / The Beatles

Carr, Roy and Tyler, Tony *The Beatles: An Illustrated Record* (New English Library, London, 1975)

Davies, Hunter *The Beatles: The Authorised Biography* (Heineman, London, 1968)

Doggett, Peter *You Never Give Me Your Money: The Battle for the Soul of the Beatles* (Vintage Books, London 2010)

Lewisohn, Mark *The Complete Beatles Chronicle* (Pyramid Books, 1992)

Lewisohn, Mark *The Complete Beatles Recording Sessions* (Hamlyn, 1988)

Mansfield, Ken *The White Book: The Beatles, the Bands and the Biz* (Thomas Nelson, 2007)

Miles, *The Beatles In Their Own Words* (Omnibus, London 1978)

Skinner Sawyers, June *Read the Beatles: Classic and New Writings on The Beatles, Their Legacy, and Why They Still Matter* (Penguin, New York 2006)

Southall, Brian with Rupert Perry *Northern Songs: The True Story of The Beatles Song Publishing Empire* (Omnibus Press, London 2006)

The Beatles Anthology: By the Beatles (Chronicle Books, San Francisco 2000)

Turner, Steve *The Beatles: The Stories Behind Every Beatles Song, 1962–1970* (Five Mile press, 1994)

Tommy / The Who

A Decade of the Who: An Authorised History in Music, Paintings, Words and Photographs (Fabulous Music, London, 1977)

Barnes, Richard and Townshend, Pete *The Story of Tommy* (Eel Pie Publishing, London 1977)

Cawthorne, Nigel *The Who and the Making of Tommy* (United Ltd, London 2005).

Charlesworth, Chris *The Illustrated Biography of the Who* (Omnibus Press, 1982)

Clarke, Steve *The Who In Their Own Words* (Omnibus, London 1979)

Marsh, Dave *Before I Get Old: The Story of the Who* (Plexus, London 1983)

Led Zeppelin III / Led Zeppelin

Davis, Stephen *Hammer of the Gods: The Led Zeppelin Saga* (Harper Collins, London 2008)

Kendall, Paul *Led Zeppelin: A Visual Document* (Omnibus Press, London 1982)

Wall, Mick *A Biography of Led Zeppelin: When Gods Walked the Earth* (Orion Publishing, 2009)

All Things Must Pass / George Harrison

Clapton, Eric *Eric Clapton: The Autobiography* (Penguin, London 2007)

Clayson, Alan *George Harrison* (Sanctuary Publishing, London 2001)

Harrison, George *I Me Mine* (Simon and Shuster, New York, 1980)

Harrison, Olivia *George Harrison: Living in the Material World* (Abrams, London 2011)

Thomson, Graeme *George Harrison: Behind The Locked Door* (Omnibus Press, London, 2013)

L.A. Woman / The Doors

Densmore, John *Riders on the Storm: My Life with Jim Morrison and the Doors* (Penguin, New York 1991)

Holzman, Jac and Dawes, Gavin *Follow the Music* (Jawbone Press, New York 2000)

Hopkins, Jerry, and Sugerman, Danny *No One Here Gets Out Alive* (Grand Central Publishing, New York 1980)

Wall, Mick *Love Becomes A Funeral Pyre* (Orion, London 2014)

Weidman, Rich *The Doors FAQ* (Backbeat Books, Milwaukee 2011)

Ram / Paul and Linda McCartney

Doyle, Tom *Man on the Run: Paul McCartney in the 1970s* (Polygon, London 2012)

Du Noyer, Paul *Conversations with McCartney* (Hodder and Staunton, 2013)

Sounes, Howard *Fab: An Intimate Life of Paul McCartney* (Harper Collins, London 2010)

Sticky Fingers / The Rolling Stones

Dalton, David *Rolling Stones In Their Own Words* (Omnibus, London 1980)

Richards, Keith *Life* (Weidenfeld and Nicolson, London 2010)

Faithfull, Marianne with Dalton, David *Faithful: An Autobiography* (Cooper Square, New York 2000)

Imagine / John Lennon

Miles, *John Lennon In His Own Words* (Omnibus, London 1981)

Norman, Philip *John Lennon: The Life* (Harper Collins, 2009)

Ono, Yoko *Grapefruit: A Book of Instructions and Drawings* (Simon and Shuster, New York 2000)

The John Lennon Letters (Weidenfeld and Nicolson, London 2012)

Wenner, Jann S *Lennon Remembers* (Rolling Stones Press, New York, 1971)

American Pie / **Don McLean**

The Songs of Don McLean (Mayday Music Inc, New York, 1972)

Harvest / **Neil Young**

Inglis, Sam *Harvest* (Bloomsbury, 2003)

Durchholz, Daniel and Graff, Gary *Neil Young: Long May You Run* (Voyageur Press, London, 2010).

McDonough, Jimmy *Shakey: Neil Young's Biography* (Vintage, London 2003)

Williamson, Nigel *Journey Through The Past. The Stories Behind the Classic Songs of Neil Young* (Carlton Books, London 2002).

Young, Neil *Waging Heavy Peace* (Blue Rider Press, New York 2012)

School's Out / **Alice Cooper**

Bruce, Michael with James, Billy *No More Mr Nice Guy: The Inside Story of the Alice Cooper Group* (SAF Publishing, London 2000)

Cooper, Alice, with Zimmerman, Keith and Kent *Golf Monster: How A Rock 'n' Roll Life Led To A Serious Golf Addiction* (Aurum Press, 2007)

Dunaway, Dennis, and Hodenfield, Chris *Snakes! Guillotines! Electric Chairs! My Adventures in the Alice Cooper Group* (Thomas Dunne Books / St Martin's Press, 2015)

Goodbye Yellow Brick Road / **Elton John**

Humphreys, Patrick, *A Little Bit Funny: The Elton John Story* (Aurum Press, London 1998)

Two Rooms: Elton John & Bernie Taupin In Their Own Words (Boxtree Ltd, London 1991)

Others

Author's correspondence with Ian Beck, June 2015.

Cohn, Nick *Rock: From the Beginning* (Stein and Day, New York, 1969)

Creswell, Toby *Rockwiz Decades: The Greatest Song of Our Time* (Hardie Grant, London 2015)

Errigo, Angie, and Leaning, Steve *The Illustrated History of the Rock Album Cover* (Octopus, London 1979).

Fogerty, John *Fortunate Son* (Little, Brown & Company, New York 2015)

Hepworth, David *1971: Never A Dull Moment* (Bantam Press, London, 2016)

New Musical Express: The Rock and Roll Years (Hamlyn, London 1992)

Ochs, Michael *1000 Record Covers* (Taschen, Germany, 2001)

Thorgerson, Storm, and Dean, Roger *Album Cover Album* (Dragon's World Ltd, Surrey 1977).

Whiticker, Alan *British Pop Invasion* (New Holland Publishers, London 2014)

Box Sets

Goodbye Yellow Brick Road / Elton John (2014) Universal UMC – 375 348-0

Led Zeppelin III / Led Zeppelin (2014) Atlantic R2-536183

Old School / Alice Cooper (2011) Universal Music Group International 06025 276 893-4

Ram / Paul & Linda McCartney (2012) Apple PAS 10003

Sticky Fingers / The Rolling Stones (2009) Rolling Stones Records COC 59100

The White Album / The Beatles (2009) Apple 0094638246619

DVD

Alice Cooper Prime Cuts (1991)

Amazing Journey: The Story of the Who (2007)

Classic Albums: American Pie, Don McLean (2017)

Classic Albums: Goodbye Yellow Brick Road, Elton John (2001)

Classic Albums: Tommy, The Who (2013)

Don McLean: American Troubadour (2012)

George Harrison: Living in the Material World (2011)

Gimme Some Truth: The Making of John Lennon's Imagine (2000)

Goodbye Yellow Brick Road / Elton John (1973) Dick James Music DJLPD 1001

Hey Hey Its the Monkees (1999)

Mr Mojo Risin': The Story of L.A. Woman (2011)

Super Duper Alice Cooper (2004)

The Beatles Anthology (2003)

The Making of Harvest: Neil Young (2002)

The Who: The Kids Are Alright (2004)

Who Is Harry Nilsson? (And Why is Everyone Talkin' About Him) (2010)

On Record

American Pie / Don McLean (1971) United Artists UAS-5535

All Things Must Pass / George Harrison (1970) Apple STCH 63

Harvest / Neil Young (1972) Reprise MS 2032

Imagine / John Lennon (1971) Apple PAS 10004

L.A. Woman / The Doors (1971) Elektra EKS-75011

Led Zeppelin III / Led Zeppelin (1970) Atlantic 2401002

Ram / Paul and Linda McCartney (1971) Apple PAS 10003

Sticky Fingers / The Rolling Stones (1971) Rolling Stones Records COC 59100

School's Out / Alice Cooper (1972) Warner Bros. BS 2623

The Beatles 'White Album' / The Beatles (1968) Apple PMC 7067/8
Tommy / The Who (1969) Decca/MCA 914 624/5

Magazines

David Bowie: The Ultimate Music Guide (2017) Uncut
John Lennon: The Ultimate Music Guide (2009) Uncut
Led Zeppelin: The Ultimate Music Guide (2016) Uncut
Rolling Stone (Various) Wenner Media
Neil Young: The Ultimate Music Guide (2015) Uncut
Paul McCartney: The Ultimate Music Guide (2017) Uncut
The Beatles: The Ultimate Music Guide (2011) Uncut
The History of Rock (1968–1973) NME
The Rolling Stones: The Ultimate Music Guide (2016) Uncut
The Story of Pop (1974–75) Phoebus
The Who: The Ultimate Music Guide (2012) Uncut

Websites

All Music – www.allmusic.com
Classic Rock – www.loudersound.com
Consequence of Sound – consequenceofsound.com
Discogs – www.discogs.com
Genius – genius.com
George Harrison – www.georgeharrison.com
Google – books.google.com.au
Mick Taylor – www.micktaylor.net
Neil Young News – thrasherswheat.org
New Musical Express Music News – www.nme.com
Rolling Stone – www.rollingstone.com
Pitchfork – www.pitchfork.com

The Guardian – www.theguardian.com

Wikipedia – www.wikipedia.com

YouTube – www.youtube.com

Zacron – www.zacron.com

An interview with John Tout (1998)
 – jtl.us/nlightsweb/lib/reviews/tout98.htm

Buddy Holly Crash Documents – data.desmoinesregister.com

Don McLean's 'American Pie' (2005) – www.mixonline.com

Iceland Tour (22 June 1970 review) – www.ledzeppelin.com/show

Interview with David Larkham (2014)
 – albumcoverhalloffame.wordpress.com

Phil Franks, The Yes Album Sessions
 – www.ibiblio.org/mal/MO/philm/yes

Rolling Stones Tongue & Lips – rockpopgallery.typepad.com

The Day The Music Died – www.fiftiesweb.com

Tube Stop (2018) – samtimonious.com

You May Say He Was A Dreamer (2003) – www.telegraph.co.uk

What do American Pie's lyrics mean? (2015) – www.bbc.com

Album Cover Art

All albums shown in this book are owned by the author and are reproduced here for the purpose of fair comment and critique. The album art remains the property of the current copyright holders.

Lyrics

All lyrics quoted in this book are for the purpose of fair comment and critique, and remain the property of the current copyright holders.

UK AND US NUMBER 1 ALBUMS 1968–1973

DATE	ARTIST	TITLE	WKS

1968 UK CHARTS

DATE	ARTIST	TITLE	WKS
31 Dec 1967	Val Doonican	*Val Doonican Rocks, But Gently*	3
21 Jan 1968	Original soundtrack	*The Sound of Music*	2*
28 Jan 1968	The Beatles	*Sgt. Pepper's Lonely Hearts Club Band*	1
4 Feb 1968	The Four Tops	*The Four Tops Greatest Hits*	1
11 Feb 1968	Diana Ross & The Supremes	*Greatest Hits*	3
3 Mar 1968	Bob Dylan	*John Wesley Harding*	13*
12 May 1968	Scott Walker	*Scott 2*	1
9 June 1968	Andy Williams	*Love, Andy*	1
16 June 1968	Otis Redding	*The Dock of the Bay*	1
23 June 1968	The Small Faces	*Ogdens' Nut Gone Flake*	6
4 Aug 1968	Tom Jones	*Delilah*	2*
11 Aug 1968	Simon & Garfunkel	*Bookends*	7*
11 Aug 1968	The Hollies	*Hollies' Greatest*	7*
1 Dec 1968	The Beatles	**The Beatles** (White Album)	5

1968 US CHARTS

DATE	ARTIST	TITLE	WKS
6 Jan 1968	The Beatles	*Magical Mystery Tour*	8
2 Mar 1968	Paul Mauriat & His Orchestra	*Blooming Hits*	5
6 April 1968	Original Soundtrack	*The Graduate*	11*
25 May 1968	Simon & Garfunkel	*Bookends*	7*
27 July 1968	Herb Alpert & the Tijuana Brass	*The Beat of the Brass*	2
10 Aug 1968	Cream	*Wheels of Fire*	4
7 Sept 1968	The Doors	*Waiting for the Sun*	4*
28 Sept 1968	The Rascals	*Time Peace: The Rascals' Greatest Hits*	1
12 Oct 1968	Big Brother & the Holding Company	*Cheap Thrills*	7*
16 Nov 1968	Jim Hendrix Experience	*Electric Ladyland*	2
21 Dec 1968	Glen Campbell	*Wichita Lineman*	1
28 Dec 1968	The Beatles	**The Beatles** (White Album)	1

1969 UK CHARTS

DATE	ARTIST	TITLE	WKS
4 Jan 1969	The Beatles	**The Beatles** (White Album)	3*
19 Jan 1969	The Seekers	*The Best of The Seekers*	6*
9 Feb 1969	Diana Ross & The Supremes	*Join The Temptations*	4
9 Mar 1969	Cream	*Goodbye*	4*

* non-consecutive weeks at No.1

DATE	ARTIST	TITLE	WKS
4 May 1969	The Moody Blues	*On the Threshold of a Dream*	2
18 May 1969	Bob Dylan	*Nashville Skyline*	4
15 June 1969	Ray Conniff	*His Orchestra, His Chorus, His Singers, His Sound*	3
6 July 1969	Jim Reeves	*According to My Heart*	4
3 Aug 1969	Jethro Tull	*Stand Up*	5*
24 Aug 1969	Elvis Presley	*From Elvis in Memphis*	1
14 Sept 1969	Blind Faith	*Blind Faith*	2
28 Sept 1969	The Beatles	*Abbey Road*	12*
14 Dec 1969	The Rolling Stones	*Let It Bleed*	1

1969 US CHARTS

Date	Artist	Title	Wks
4 Jan 1969	The Beatles	***The Beatles*** *(White Album)*	8*
8 Feb 1969	Diana Ross & The Supremes	*Join The Temptations*	1
8 Mar 1969	Glen Campbell	*Wichita Lineman*	4*
29 Mar 1969	Blood Sweat & Tears	*Blood Sweat & Tears*	6*
26 April 1969	Original Cast	*Hair*	13
23 Aug 1969	Johnny Cash	*Johnny Cash at San Quentin*	4
20 Sept 1969	Blind Faith	*Blind Faith*	2
4 Oct 1969	Creedence Clearwater Revival	*Green River*	4
1 Nov 1969	The Beatles	*Abbey Road*	8
27 Dec 1969	Led Zeppelin	***Led Zeppelin III***	1

1970 UK CHARTS

Date	Artist	Title	Wks
27 Dec 1969	The Beatles	*Abbey Road*	6*
7 Feb 1970	Led Zeppelin	*Led Zeppelin II*	1
14 Feb 1970	Various artists	*Motown Chartbusters Vol. 3*	1
21 Feb 1970	Simon & Garfunkel	*Bridge Over Troubled Water*	24*
23 May 1970	The Beatles	*Let It Be*	3
11 July 1970	Bob Dylan	*Self Portrait*	1
22 Aug 1970	The Moody Blues	*A Question of Balance*	3
12 Sept 1970	Creedence Clearwater Revival	*Cosmo's Factory*	1
19 Sept 1970	The Rolling Stones	*Get Yer Ya-Ya's Out!*	2
10 Oct 1970	Black Sabbath	*Paranoid*	1
24 Oct 1970	Pink Floyd	*Atom Heart Mother*	1
31 Oct 1970	Various artists	*Motown Chartbusters Vol. 4*	1
7 Nov 1970	Led Zeppelin	***Led Zeppelin III***	4*
28 Nov 1970	Bob Dylan	*New Morning*	1
5 Dec 1970	Andy Williams	*Andy Williams' Greatest Hits*	5*

DATE	ARTIST	TITLE	WKS

1970 US CHARTS

3 Jan 1970	The Beatles	*Abbey Road*	3*
17 Jan 1970	Led Zeppelin	*Led Zeppelin II*	6*
7 Mar 1970	Simon & Garfunkel	*Bridge Over Troubled Water*	10
16 May 1970	Crosby Stills Nash & Young	*Déjà Vu*	1
23 May 1970	Paul McCartney	*McCartney*	3
13 June 1970	The Beatles	*Let It Be*	4
11 July 1970	Original Soundtrack	*Woodstock*	4
8 Aug 1970	Blood Sweat & Tears	*Blood Sweat & Tears 3*	2
22 Aug 1970	Creedence Clearwater Revival	*Cosmo's Factory*	9
24 Oct 1970	Santana	*Abraxas*	6*
31 Oct 1970	Led Zeppelin	***Led Zeppelin III***	4

1971 UK CHARTS

16 Jan 1971	Simon & Garfunkel	*Bridge Over Troubled Water*	3*
6 Feb 1971	George Harrison	***All Things Must Pass***	8
3 April 1971	Andy Williams	*Home Lovin' Man*	2
17 April 1971	Various artists	*Motown Chartbusters Vol. 5*	3
8 May 1971	The Rolling Stones	***Sticky Fingers***	5
5 June 1971	Paul & Linda McCartney	***Ram***	2
26 June 1971	Emerson, Lake & Palmer	*Tarkus*	1
3 July 1971	Simon & Garfunkel	*Bridge Over Troubled Water*	6
7 Aug 1971	Various artists	*Hot Hits 6*	1
14 Aug 1971	The Moody Blues	*Every Good Boy Deserves Favour*	1
21 Aug 1971	Various artists	*Top of the Pops, Vol. 18*	3
18 Sept 1971	The Who	*Who's Next*	1
25 Sept 1971	Deep Purple	*Fireball*	1
2 Oct 1971	Rod Stewart	*Every Picture Tells a Story*	6
30 Oct 1971	John Lennon	***Imagine***	2
27 Nov 1971	Various artists	*Top of the Pops, Vol. 20*	1
4 Dec 1971	Led Zeppelin	*Led Zeppelin IV*	2
18 Dec 1971	T.Rex	*Electric Warrior*	6

1971 US CHARTS

2 Jan 1971	George Harrison	***All Things Must Pass***	7
20 Feb 1971	Various Artists	*Jesus Christ Superstar*	3*
27 Feb 1971	Janis Joplin	*Pearl*	9
15 May 1971	Crosby, Stills, Nash & Young	*4 Way Street*	1
22 May 1971	The Rolling Stones	***Sticky Fingers***	4
19 June 1971	Carole King	*Tapestry*	15
2 Oct 1971	Rod Stewart	*Every Picture Tells A Story*	4
30 Oct 1971	John Lennon	***Imagine***	1

DATE	ARTIST	TITLE	WKS
6 Nov 1971	Isaac Hayes	*'Shaft' Soundtrack*	1
13 Nov 1971	Santana	*Santana III*	5
18 Dec 1971	Sly & the Family Stone	*There's A Riot Goin' On*	2

1972 UK CHARTS

1 Jan 1972	George Harrison & Friends	*The Concert for Bangladesh*	3
5 Feb 1972	T.Rex	*Electric Warrior*	8
19 Feb 1972	Neil Reid	*Neil Reid*	1
11 Mar 1972	Neil Young	***Harvest***	1
18 Mar 1972	Paul Simon	*Paul Simon*	4
25 Mar 1972	Lindisfarne	*Fog on the Tyne*	2
22 April 1972	Deep Purple	*Machine Head*	2
6 May 1972	T.Rex	*Prophets, Seers & Sages etc*	1
20 May 1972	T.Rex	*Bolan Boogie*	1
10 June 1972	The Rolling Stones	*Exile on Main St.*	8
17 June 1972	Various artists	*20 Dynamic Hits*	7
16 Sept 1972	Rod Stewart	*Never a Dull Moment*	1
30 Sept 1972	Various artists	*20 Fantastic Hits*	8
7 Oct 1972	Various artists	*20 All Time Hits of the 50s*	4
2 Dec 1972	Various artists	*25 Rockin' and Rollin' Greats*	3

1972 US CHARTS

1 Jan 1972	Carole King	*Music*	3
22 Jan 1972	Don McLean	***American Pie***	7
11 Mar 1972	Neil Young	***Harvest***	2
25 Mar 1972	America	*America*	5
29 April 1972	Roberta Flack	*First Take*	5
3 June 1972	Jethro Tull	*Thick as a Brick*	2
17 June 1972	The Rolling Stones	*Exile on Main Street*	4
15 July 1972	Elton John	*Honky Château*	5
19 Aug 1972	Chicago	*Chicago V*	9
21 Oct 1972	Curtis Mayfield	*Super Fly Soundtrack*	4
18 Nov 1972	Cat Stevens	*Catch Bull at Four*	3
9 Dec 1972	The Moody Blues	*Seventh Sojourn*	4

1973 UK CHARTS

13 Jan 1973	Slade	*Slayed?*	5
20 Jan 1973	Gilbert O'Sullivan	*Back to Front*	8
10 Feb 1973	Elton John	*Don't Shoot Me I'm Only the Piano Player*	3
24 Mar 1973	Alice Cooper	*Billion Dollar Babies*	4
31 Mar 1973	Various artists	*20 Flashback Greats of the Sixties*	2

DATE	ARTIST	TITLE	WKS
14 April 1973	Led Zeppelin	*Houses of the Holy*	1
28 April 1973	Faces	*Ooh La La*	1
5 May 1973	David Bowie	*Aladdin Sane*	5
9 June 1973	Various artists	*Pure Gold*	1
30 June 1973	Original soundtrack	*That'll Be the Day*	1
18 Aug 1973	Peters & Lee	*We Can Make It*	3
1 Sept 1973	Rod Stewart	*Sing It Again Rod*	1
22 Sept 1973	The Rolling Stones	*Goats Head Soup*	1
6 Oct 1973	Slade	*Sladest*	1
27 Oct 1973	Status Quo	*Hello!*	4
3 Nov 1973	David Bowie	*Pin Ups*	2
8 Dec 1973	Roxy Music	*Stranded*	2
15 Dec 1973	David Cassidy	*Dreams Are Nuthin' More Than Wishes*	1
22 Dec 1973	Elton John	***Goodbye Yellow Brick Road***	2

1973 US CHARTS

6 Jan 1973	The Moody Blues	*Seventh Sojourn*	1
13 Jan 1973	Carly Simon	*No Secrets*	5
17 Feb 1973	War	*The World Is A Ghetto*	2
3 Mar 1973	Elton John	*Don't Shoot Me I'm Only the Piano Player*	2
17 Mar 1973	Eric Weissberg & Steve Mandell	*Duelling Banjos*	2
7 April 1973	Diana Ross	*'Lady Sings the Blues' Soundtrack*	2
21 April 1973	Alice Cooper	*Billion Dollar Babies*	1
28 May 1973	Pink Floyd	*The Dark Side of the Moon*	1
5 May 1973	Elvis Presley	*Aloha from Hawaii: Via Satellite*	1
12 May 1973	Led Zeppelin	*Houses of the Holy*	2
26 May 1973	The Beatles	*1967–1970*	1
2 June 1973	Paul McCartney & Wings	*Red Rose Speedway*	3
23 June 1973	George Harrison	*Living in The Material World*	5
28 July 1973	Chicago	*Chicago VI*	5*
18 Aug 1973	Jethro Tull	*A Passion Play*	1
8 Sept 1973	The Allman Brothers Band	*Brothers and Sisters*	5
13 Oct 1973	Rolling Stones	*Goat's Head Soup*	4
10 Nov 1973	Elton John	***Goodbye Yellow Brick Road***	8

* non-consecutive weeks at No.1